Praise for *Sudden Deaths in St. Louis*

"This meticulously researched book uses nineteenth-century investigations of suspicious deaths as a window into the private circumstances and public meanings of the lives and deaths of St. Louisians. Lirley's exhaustive research into coroner's records is a treasure trove of information about the daily worlds of women, African Americans, and immigrants navigating work, domestic conflict, pregnancy, alcoholism, and depression."
—**Catherine E. Rymph**, author of *Republican Women: Feminism and Conservatism from Suffrage through the Rise of the New Right*

"Lirley provides a provocative look at the Gilded Age from a unique perspective that explores not just race and gender but also the seamy undersides of both cities in the period and the ways deaths were reported and treated."
—**Jeffrey Smith**, author of *The Rural Cemetery Movement: Places of Paradox in Nineteenth-Century America*

"In this captivating study of death, we learn a great deal about life, especially the lives of the marginalized in Gilded Age urban America. Lirley mines overlooked coroners' inquests in turn-of-the-century St. Louis, rich sources for historians of violence, medicine, family and labor, for the social meaning of death. In her gleaning of witness testimony, Lirley unearths obscured or hidden topics, affording historians a rare glimpse into the daily lives, and deaths, of poor and working-class Americans, including immigrants, prostitutes, the addicted and African Americans. This is a must-read book for anyone interested in the study of death."
—**Diane Miller Sommerville**, author of *Aberration of Mind: Suicide and Suffering in the Civil War-Era South*

"In the early Gilded Age, elected St. Louis coroners investigated unexpected death, such as those resulting from domestic violence, suicide, abortion, or traumatic accident. These coroners brought not only science and law to their work but social judgment. Similar deaths were often judged differently. They could spare a respected family embarrassment on the one hand, or effectively condemn those judged guilty of moral turpitude—prostitutes, the dissolute, the perpetrators of domestic violence, or the sin of poverty, on the other. Lirley's revealing study is the first to make systematic use of these now readily accessible records, reconstructing both the harshness and occasional charity that still resonate in our world of opioid and COVID-19 deaths."

—**Kenneth H. Winn**, editor of *Missouri Law and the American Conscience: Historical Rights and Wrongs*

SUDDEN DEATHS IN ST. LOUIS

Sudden Deaths in St. Louis

Coroner Bias in the Gilded Age

Sarah E. Lirley

SOUTHERN ILLINOIS UNIVERSITY PRESS

CARBONDALE

Southern Illinois University Press

www.siupress.com

Copyright © 2024 by the Board of Trustees,
Southern Illinois University

Printed in the United States of America

27 26 25 24   4 3 2 1

Publication of this book has been underwritten by
the Elmer H. Johnson and Carol Holmes Johnson criminology fund.

Cover illustration: City morgue, jail, and rear of the Four Courts Building,
much as it looked between 1875 and 1885. Courtesy of the
Missouri Historical Society, St. Louis, Missouri.

ISBN: 978-0-8093-3932-7 (paperback)
ISBN: 978-0-8093-3933-4 (ebook)

This book has been catalogued by the Library of Congress.

Printed on recycled paper ♻

SIU
Southern Illinois University System

To my grandmother, Hazel Hampton Lirley, who made higher education possible for me. Thank you for encouraging me and believing in my dreams. I would not have written this book without you and I wish that you were here to see it.

And to my beloved cats, Patches O'Houlihan, Burgundy, and Baxter, for their unconditional love and for adding so much joy to my life, including sitting by my side while I wrote this (or, sometimes, on my keyboard).

CONTENTS

Gallery of illustrations beginning on page 63

ACKNOWLEDGMENTS

I am thankful for the help and support of many people who helped me write this book and the dissertation that preceded it. Special thanks to my dissertation advisor, LeeAnn Whites, who oversaw this project in its very beginnings as a master's thesis and guided me in the research and writing process throughout graduate school and beyond. My advisor and my dissertation committee gave me many wonderful ideas to transform this project from a dissertation into a manuscript. Thank you, Keona Ervin, Mary Jo Neitz, Linda Reeder, and Catherine Rymph, for those ideas and support during and after graduate school.

Several friends and colleagues gave me ideas, research resources, mentorship, and feedback on my writing, all of which improved my work. Thanks to Megan Boccardi, Mary Beth Brown, Vicki Daniel, Jo Denzin, Autumn Dolan, Zach Dowdle, Signe Peterson Fourmy, Paula Hunt, David Karr, Caitlin Lawrence, Brad Lookingbill, Mindy McPherson, Heather Thornton McRae, Sean Rost, and Cassie Yacovazzi. The officers of the Collective for Radical Death Studies offered inspiration, community, and feedback on early stages of the work. Thank you, Michelle Acciavatti, Sarah Chavez, Kami Fletcher, Jennifer Tran, and Tamara Waraschinski.

Several scholars have given me excellent feedback on my work as well, especially on conference papers. Alison Clark Efford, Lorri Glover, Kris McCusker, Diane Miller Sommerville, Terri Snyder, and Jamie Warren—thank you.

Thank you to the anonymous readers for the manuscript proposal and first draft of the book. Your comments helped me improve the manuscript. And thanks to the staff at Southern Illinois University Press, especially editor Sylvia Frank Rodrigue, for making the manuscript stronger and offering professional guidance and support as I wrote and revised this book.

Finally, I would like to thank librarians, archivists, and editors for helping me access materials and improve my scholarship: the staff at the Missouri State Archives in Jefferson City, Mike Everman and the staff at the

Missouri State Archives in St. Louis, Kenneth Winn, the staff at the State Historical Society of Missouri, and the staff at Stafford Library at Columbia College. Not only did these individuals aid me in my research, but they showed enthusiasm for my project and gladly engaged in conversations with me about my work. Mike Everman even gave me a tour of St. Louis on one trip to the archives, including a visit to the Office of the Medical Examiner. Thank you, Baxter Leisure, Executive Assistant to the Chief Medical Examiner, for giving me an interview during that visit.

I also appreciate financial support from Columbia College to research and write my manuscript, specifically two Summer Research Grants from the Office of Academic Affairs. The funding provided me the time to focus on my research and writing as well as access to much-needed research materials. In addition, several organizations generously provided funding for the project in dissertation form: The Colonial Dames of America, The Center for Missouri Studies and its Women in Missouri Politics Fellowship, the William E. Foley Research Fellowship from the Missouri State Archives, and a Dissertation Fellowship from the Department of History at the University of Missouri. Thank you for making this project possible.

SUDDEN DEATHS IN ST. LOUIS

The Office of the Coroner in Late Nineteenth-Century St. Louis

J. W. MCELVAIN DECIDED to go fishing with some friends in Cahokia on July 11, 1881, an incredibly hot day. He and his friends fished for a while, but on the ferry ride back to St. Louis, McElvain complained that he was not feeling well. He felt well enough to walk ahead of his friends once they returned to the city, however, and his friends quickly lost sight of him. McElvain never made it home. He collapsed on the corner of Eleventh and Lafayette streets, likely because of the oppressive heat that day. A crowd gathered and one man gave McElvain some whiskey while he was lying on the ground—either because he requested it or because this stranger believed that it would help. McElvain died on that corner soon after collapsing there.[1]

Deputy Coroner Herman Praedicow investigated McElvain's death and quickly concluded that he died "from the effects of sunstroke," a verdict that he and Coroner John Frank rendered for dozens of people during a heat wave in July 1881. But Praedicow made no mention of alcohol use in his verdict, which differed from other men and women who died during the heat wave. Even when they had dozens of heat-related deaths to investigate, coroners distinguished between deaths that were caused by heatstroke alone and those in which illness or alcohol use were contributing factors. The fact that the coroners differentiated between heatstroke and heatstroke exacerbated by alcohol use during a time in which they were overwhelmed with cases illustrates that they based their death investigations and verdicts on factors beyond their own professional standards and medical training, including witness testimony and their own assumptions about race, class, gender, and reputation. In McElvain's case, a witness told the deputy coroner that the deceased was drinking, but he testified that a man was giving McElvain whiskey, not that he drank of his own accord. No other witness told the coroner that McElvain was a heavy or regular drinker. The witness testimony likely explains why the deputy coroner did not add "intemperance" to his verdict because in other aspects, McElvain was similar to other men and women who had received verdicts of heatstroke and intemperance. He was single, working class, and resided in a boardinghouse—not indicators of a bad reputation, but also not the hallmarks of a respectable, prominent one.[2]

J. W. McElvain's death is one of 120 coroners' inquests examined in this study of six types of coroners' verdicts: deaths from natural causes, alcoholism, suicide, abortion, homicide, and accidental deaths. By interrogating these different categories of coroners' verdicts to understand how and why coroners made their decisions, it is apparent that verdicts were not uniform but, rather, varied by coroner. Verdicts were not based solely on the characteristics of the investigation. St. Louis coroners based their investigations and verdicts on several factors: whether or not the deceased had family members to testify in a coroner's inquest, whether or not another person could be held legally liable for the death, and the reputation and social connections of the deceased. For example, verdicts of suicide reveal that coroners decided that some men and women were insane or temporarily insane when they died, but others were not. Women who were respected members of their communities, particularly mothers, frequently received such verdicts of suicide while suffering from insanity. Women with bad reputations and fewer social connections, notably those who worked as prostitutes, did not.

As the first book-length study of St. Louis coroners' inquests, this project examines valuable records for historians, which provide a glimpse into the daily life of ordinary men and women. These inquests are the remnants of the daily work of St. Louis coroners. Each day, they responded to various calls to investigate sudden or suspicious deaths. They interviewed witnesses, examined the body and its surroundings, and pieced together other clues, such as potential weapons near the body, letters, or suicide notes, to determine how and why a person came to a sudden death. Coroners' inquests create challenges for historians because they are sporadic—containing records of only a few years or perhaps decades at a time for a given city. Some of the records contain only demographic data, such as name, age, and place of birth, and the verdict, with no witness testimony. But other inquests are pages long with rich material—statements from family members, neighbors, coworkers, and, sometimes, police officers or treating physicians. They explain the routines of these men and women, their habits, their work patterns, and relationships, all of which were disrupted by an early and, often, unexpected death. Coroners' inquests also reveal the gritty details of life in an urban industrial center—the despair that some of the residents of St. Louis felt, the propensity that others had for violence, and the dangers of home and work.

Coroners' verdicts offer insight into the belief systems and practices of coroners as well as those of the witnesses they interviewed. Witnesses told coroners that men and women were "respectable" or "rough," whether they drank alcohol frequently, and whether they had threatened to die by suicide or to kill someone else. Members of a community contributed a great deal to coroners' investigations and verdicts. Testimony from a friend or relative could inform a verdict of "suicide while suffering from mental aberration," as well as provide evidence of domestic violence as a contributing factor for a suicide or homicide, or that a death was an accident, with no evidence of suicide or criminal negligence. In addition to witness testimony, the coroner's values and beliefs shaped verdicts. For instance, some coroners, such as John Frank, sought to find evidence to aid in the prosecution of physicians who performed criminal abortions more fervently than did other coroners. Other coroners, notably Hugo Auler, rendered more verdicts of suicide while suffering from insanity than did their counterparts.[3]

Coroners had to distinguish between various causes of death for accuracy and public records, including city statistics about natural and violent deaths. These records also had meanings for society, revealing whether violent crime increased, for instance, or if an epidemic or extreme temperatures threatened the health of the city's residents. A verdict also held meaning for families of the deceased. Coroners used a variety of verdicts both in their inquest records and in reports to the newly formed Health Department, often noting a specific ailment, weapon, or person who caused the death.[4] Coroners often framed verdicts in violent deaths with its type, such as "accident," "homicide," or "suicide," but not always. They seldom noted when a death came from natural causes but simply noted the illness—"pneumonia" or "congestion of the heart"—for instance. The evidence did not always clearly distinguish between the causes of death—a deadly fall could be an accident, a suicide, or a homicide, for instance, depending on the circumstances. Likewise, alcohol consumption could lead to a natural death from alcoholism or could have been a contributor to a suicide, a homicide, or an accident. These verdicts had—and have—social meaning. A death from suicide or alcoholism could be stigmatized, while a death from abortion, accident, or homicide could lead to a criminal investigation and charges.

Because over twenty thousand inquests exist for the city of St. Louis between 1845 and 1900, this study focuses on a narrow time frame of ten years: 1875 to 1885, a period that features many inquests with ample witness testimony. The city of St. Louis operated under a new charter in 1876 and reorganized the government over the following year, including the election of a new coroner. The new charter also mandated the formation of the Health Department, and the city began to compile mortality statistics from death certificates, the morgue, and the Office of the Coroner. The time frame also provides the opportunity to study families in greater depth by using the federal census, which is largely nonexistent for 1890.[5]

Even for a ten-year period, thousands of inquests exist, so the cases for this study were chosen by using a combination of random and selected sampling. The initial sample came from viewing every case for every fourth month of each year and changing that set of months each year to ensure that all months were covered. The sample included only records for men and women between the ages of twenty and fifty, in order to better study violent deaths, which are more likely to occur for that age range. The first sample yielded 868 coroners' inquests. Final selections to examine for this study were based on themes: prostitution, family violence, abortion, murder-suicides, verdicts of insanity, and investigations that required a coroner's jury to render the verdict. The final sample included 120 cases. An approximately equal number of cases involving men and women as well as a range of ages, dates, and races and ethnicities were selected for each chapter. Some of these verdicts allowed for a study of family violence, while others, such as jury inquests, gave information about suspected homicides and typically featured several pages of witness testimony. Accidental and natural deaths provided a contrast to suspected suicides or homicides, as they seldom led to verdicts that would have a social stigma or lead to criminal charges. However, research into these types of deaths soon revealed that they were not necessarily easy inquests to conduct, as coroners looked for criminal negligence, possible homicides, or suicides.

While coroners ultimately determined how and why a person died, their verdicts were informed by their interviews with witnesses and were subsequently reported on by the press. Witnesses in the inquest and newspaper accounts of the death investigation and any subsequent criminal trials are also crucial to understanding how these deaths were investigated and interpreted. As with other American cities in the late nineteenth century, St. Louis employed white, educated men who conducted death investigations to determine how and why someone came to an untimely or suspicious death. St. Louis coroners had a distinctive qualification, however, as licensed, practicing physicians—qualifications that surpassed the state requirements in Missouri and many other states. In addition to their professional training and guidelines from the Missouri statutes, these men were also informed by their assumptions about race, class, and gender. The social location of the coroner was not the only factor in their verdicts, however. Coroners gathered significant information from a variety of people. The witnesses whom the coroners interviewed were similar to the deceased—often poor to working class, immigrants, prostitutes, people with addictions, and others who were excluded from respectable parts of St. Louis society. African Americans, women, and immigrants who were not yet citizens could not serve as coroners, but their testimony contributed to a coroner's decision—that a loved one or neighbor died from a suicide, homicide, accident, or natural death. These witness statements offer a rare glimpse into the lives of people who often did not leave behind written records.

Coroners especially valued the testimony of family members, and at times, a tension existed between the evidence in an inquest and the interests of the family. Even when family members were not present at the time of death, such as workplace accidents, coroners often interviewed relatives first or put their testimony ahead of others in their records. When coroners rendered verdicts of alcoholism or suicide while experiencing insanity, it was not necessarily because of their medical training but because of the testimony of the loved ones of the deceased. Conversely, when men or women did not have family members or close friends to testify on their behalf, coroners were less likely to render sympathetic verdicts to soften the stigma of certain kinds of deaths, particularly suicides. Without family members to interview, coroners were also more likely to conduct shorter investigations—unless another party may have been legally responsible, such as potential homicides. Coroners did not always listen to relatives, however, especially when criminal charges, burial rites, or public scrutiny were unlikely consequences attached to the verdict, such as with natural deaths. A coroner might have ignored a wife's statement about stomach pains, for example, and determined that another illness caused her husband's death. Despite those anomalies, coroners relied heavily on witness testimony, particularly from relatives, to reconstruct the events that led to a sudden death. In the late nineteenth century, coroners had little else to rely on, as toxicology tests were rudimentary and autopsies rare.[6]

Coroners' verdicts have explanatory power, and their accuracy is important. Variations among the verdicts because of witness testimony or the coroner's own preferences impacted the data historically and in the present day. Determining that someone died from a criminal abortion, for instance, instead of an accident could lead to sensational press accounts of the death as well as criminal charges for the abortion provider—often a physician or midwife. Coroners' verdicts impacted public perceptions of a death and, in cases of homicide, abortion, or accidents caused by negligence, the criminal justice system. Coroners tended to conduct lengthier investigations into the deaths of men and women who were respected members of their communities, who had family members who testified about the causes of a loved one's death; deaths that could possibly lead to criminal charges; and deaths that occurred in public. Coroners also often, but not always, conducted more thorough inquests into the deaths of men and women whom they understood to be good wives, husbands, mothers, and fathers.

St. Louis coroners operated within a flawed system. Coroners were elected officials and often held their positions for only two to four years, meaning that a quick succession of coroners made it difficult to retain institutional knowledge. Every two years, voters elected one coroner to investigate suspicious and untimely deaths for the city of St. Louis. A new coroner took office in December and appointed one to two deputy coroners, a clerk for the Office of the Coroner, a superintendent of the morgue, and an assistant superintendent of the morgue. The city's mayor approved these positions. Because they were elected officials, coroners allied with either the Republican or Democratic Party and spent some of their time campaigning for office. Political campaigns do not seem to have consumed much of the coroners' time, however, and coroners seldom held more than two successive terms. The coroner's office also had a limited budget and one that was scrutinized by city officials and the public. Despite these limitations, as licensed, practicing physicians, St. Louis coroners possessed more education and training than many of their counterparts in Missouri and even the nation. Many served in the medical corps during the Civil War, with some coroners being veterans of the Confederacy and others having served for the Union. Most coroners practiced medicine when not holding office as the coroner for the City of

St. Louis. Some coroners, including Drs. Hugo Auler and Sylvester Nidelet, taught at local medical schools as well. They had the knowledge and experience to conduct thorough death investigations.[7]

Each coroner was assisted by at least one deputy coroner, but he often did not have the same training as his supervisor. Many deputy coroners had no medical or legal training before holding office. Still, deputy coroners investigated many cases on their own, usually those that the coroner's office believed would be simple to solve, such as deaths from natural causes. Coroners investigated more difficult cases, such as cases of suspected homicide or workplace accidents, sometimes with the assistance of deputy coroners. In instances of suspected homicide or other suspicious deaths in which someone else may have been responsible, the coroner convened a jury to render the verdict, as required by Missouri law. A jury of six white men heard witness testimony, viewed the corpse, and listened to autopsy results before rendering a verdict. In most cases, however, coroners and deputy coroners investigated and rendered verdicts without a jury. They spoke to friends, relatives, bystanders who literally witnessed these deaths, physicians, and police officers to determine how and why a man or woman died—by suicide, homicide, accident, or natural causes—with some variation among each kind of death. In some cases, the coroner would also order an autopsy to be performed by a local physician to determine the cause of death. Coroners depended on witness testimony and, in some cases, autopsy results and/or a jury's decision to render their verdicts.[8]

Missouri law was not the only factor that prevented coroners from investigating deaths objectively: their belief systems did as well. While coroners were trained officials, they were human beings who had assumptions about the men and women whose deaths they were investigating based on their experiences and the norms of their time. Coroners, such as Drs. Sylvester L. Nidelet, John Frank, Hugo Auler, and George Dudley, were highly educated, middle- to upper-class, able-bodied, white men—social locations that shaped their experiences and views of the world. They lived in a society in which white men held the most social and political power. They operated within a gender system in which men were supposed to be breadwinners, while women were supposed to be mothers and moral guardians of the home, although many African American and working-class women worked for wages and also ran their households. In part because of their assumptions, coroners were more likely to investigate the deaths of respected white men and women more thoroughly than those of people of color or disreputable men and women—those who worked as prostitutes, drank regularly, beat their wives, or lived in what were considered rough neighborhoods.

Like St. Louis coroners, reporters for the two most widely circulated newspapers in the city, the *St. Louis Post-Dispatch* and the *St. Louis Globe-Democrat*, were white men with some education. Because bylines did not become common until the twentieth century, it is impossible to know much else about these men. These reporters wrote sensationalistic stories about the coroners' investigations, particularly for violent deaths, with attention-grabbing titles such as "Sin and Death," "The Coroner's Temperance Lecture," or "Ruined by Rum." The Office of the Coroner may have been on these reporters' routine stops—or beats—because accounts of these inquests appeared regularly in the newspapers. Reporters for these two rival papers included statements from coroners as well as some of the witness testimony in their accounts of unexpected and suspicious deaths.[9]

Although the *Globe-Democrat* and *Post-Dispatch* had the widest readership, St. Louisans could also find information from smaller papers, such as the German-language *Westliche Post*, which also reported on untimely deaths, particularly from the German community. There were some African American newspapers, such as the *St. Louis Advance* and the *Negro World*. Unfortunately, while readers in the late nineteenth century could read these newspapers, they are not available in the present day. The *Post-Dispatch* and *Globe-Democrat* have the richest archival record. The local and national press also printed death or funeral notices in which they briefly listed the deceased, cause of death, and funeral information. They did not print obituaries, but these notices provided some details about the deceased and their families. Local reporters also often wrote articles about the circumstances leading up to these sudden deaths—particularly violent deaths, like suicides, homicides, and accidents. These accounts often included graphic details of the deaths as well as views of the deceased—detailing faults if they were not respected members of their communities or offering sympathy and highlighting their virtues if their communities respected them. In some cases, newspapers in major cities across the country also reported on these deaths.[10]

Both the *St. Louis Globe-Democrat* and *St. Louis Post-Dispatch* had origins as small newspapers with opposing political affiliations, but the two newspapers offered similar coverage of death investigations in the late nineteenth century. The newspaper industry as a whole was focused more on

objective reporting by this time, as well as national and local events, meaning that political alliances were far less pronounced than in earlier eras. The
Globe-Democrat tended to offer more sensationalistic coverage than its rival
for the deaths examined in this study, and at times, one paper may have had
more details or covered a story longer than the other. Otherwise, the two
papers offered similar reporting. Although both papers underwent name
and ownership changes in the 1870s, their coverage of untimely deaths and
coroners' inquests remained consistent during that time. The publications
competed for readers' attention with daily news, including stories of local
tragedies. And they both covered these deaths for several days or, sometimes,
weeks when the cause of death was uncertain or criminal trials were held,
particularly if murder was suspected.[11]

The local press reported on homicides most often, then suicides and accidents, often in sensationalistic articles with graphic details of these
deaths. Reporters seldom wrote about alcohol-related deaths, deaths caused
by abortions, or natural deaths. St. Louis reporters often wrote about the
reputation of the deceased when writing about their untimely deaths. Reporters tended to sympathize with prominent residents of St. Louis and
even ordinary men and women if they understood them to be respected
members of their communities. Their accounts were, in some cases, at odds
with people who knew the deceased well. Men and women who deviated
from white, middle-class gender conventions received little or no sympathy
from local reporters and, in some cases, were blamed for their deaths—even
when they were homicide victims. If these reporters understood the deceased to be respectable, they wrote about their every virtue: that they left
children behind, that they were good parents and spouses, hard workers,
and esteemed members of the community. For those who had questionable
reputations, however, the press offered mixed descriptions of them at best
and, more often, detailed every one of their supposed transgressions, such
as extramarital affairs, working as prostitutes, or abusing their wives and
children. In some cases, the St. Louis press offered nuanced accounts of various individuals, but more often, they oversimplified complex people and
their deaths.[12]

Reporters for the *Globe-Democrat* and *Post-Dispatch* almost always used
racist language to describe the deaths of African Americans, however, even
if they described their deaths with some sympathy. Just as coroners did in
inquest records, St. Louis reporters pointed out when their subjects were

Black, typically referring to them as "colored." In compassionate articles about the sudden deaths of Black women, the press used words like "dusky," "negress," or "female African." Reporters used harsh language when condemning Black men and women, however, particularly when they were accused of murder. One reporter used the phrase "brutal negro" to describe a Black man who killed his common-law wife and even claimed that he had "hooves." Similarly, a *Globe-Democrat* account referred to a Black woman as a "worthless colored Cyprian [prostitute]" after she shot and killed a white police officer. Newspaper accounts regarding disreputable white men and women, including those accused of homicide, did not reference their race.[13]

While political affiliations did not determine how the local press wrote about untimely deaths, politics impacted the Office of the Coroner. The positions of coroner and deputy coroner represented a political opportunity. These men were prominent citizens of St. Louis and members of professional organizations as well as the city's political organizations. Before and after serving as coroners and deputy coroners, they practiced in their fields and ran for a variety of offices: health commissioner, school board, superintendent of the morgue (a position appointed by the coroner), assistant circuit attorney, and members of the state legislature. One former coroner even ran for mayor, while a deputy coroner held a position in the federal government as inspector general for the Interior Department. The office may have been attractive for the possibility of leading to other political offices as well as good pay.[14]

Because the position of coroner was an elected one, critics accused the office of political corruption and called for reform of the coroner system. Throughout the nineteenth century, the Office of the Coroner was part of spoils and patronage systems of city governments across the country. St. Louis coroners participated in their share of political scandals, and critics even connected them with New York's infamous Tammany Hall political machine in the 1870s. Nationwide, it was not uncommon for coroners to accept bribes from local undertakers, a trend that may also have occurred in St. Louis. At least two deputy coroners faced accusations of running monopolies with local undertakers, although it is unknown whether those accusations were true.[15]

Even without scandals, partisan politics infused the St. Louis Office of the Coroner. Coroners ran on party tickets and participated in the city and state politics of their respective parties. Coroners generally appointed positions in their office along party lines, including deputy coroners, superintendent and assistant superintendent of the morgue, and clerk for the Office of the Coroner, although those appointments were subject to approval of the mayor. When one coroner dared to violate the rules of the spoils system and appointed a stenographer from the opposing party, it created a controversy. While white men held the positions of coroner and deputy coroner, at least one African American man worked as the assistant superintendent of the morgue and another washed bodies at the morgue. African Americans were not given positions of power, however, such as deputy coroner or coroner. Women did not work for the Office of the Coroner in the late nineteenth century.[16]

A reliance on the spoils system was not unique to St. Louis, and the city shared several other characteristics with other Gilded Age cities as well. In the 1870s and 1880s, the city experienced a growing economy and new industries but also social stratification, racism and segregation, and dangerous work environments. After the Civil War, urban areas across the country grew significantly. Increasingly, cities passed the population milestone of 100,000 residents, including St. Louis, which boasted a population of nearly 350,000 by 1880.[17] In the late nineteenth century, St. Louis featured the largest brewery and two of the largest tobacco factories in the world, as well as other factories and businesses. Industrialization and urbanization created opportunities but also social problems, such as poverty, dangerous workplaces, easy access to alcohol and drugs, and crime.[18]

The late nineteenth century was also a time when advocates for increased reliance on science sought to improve the process of death investigations by substantially reforming the coroner's office. These reformers hoped to eliminate political corruption in the coroner's office and ensure that death investigators possessed medical and legal expertise. Coroner's physicians, former coroners, medical examiners, and even attorneys criticized coroner's offices in Missouri and recommended reform between the 1870s and early 1900s. Some critics called for an end to the coroner's jury system, but most demanded more substantive reform: the abolition of the office altogether and its replacement with a new medical examiner system. In the 1870s, many cities and states created new medical examiner systems, with Massachusetts being the first to do so in 1877. The medical examiner movement spread to other cities, but it took a few decades. Several cities, including New York City, enacted a medical examiner system in the 1900s and 1910s. Unlike the coroner's office system, the medical examiner system required specialized training in the medical and legal aspects of death investigations. Medical examiners were typically physicians, often trained in pathology and experienced in performing autopsies in death investigations. While coroners were elected, medical examiners were appointed by the government that they served, usually the county. As science became more respected and influential, more local and state governments turned to medical examiners and also eliminated jury inquests. St. Louis coroners had substantial medical education and experience, but they did not necessarily have the medicolegal training that advocates for the medical examiner system demanded. In addition, Missouri law required them to rely on jury inquests in some cases, typically homicides. Despite calls for reform, St. Louis retained its coroner's system for another century, finally creating the Office of the Medical Examiner in 1977.[19]

Arguments for a medical examiner system were part of a larger shift toward the professionalization of medicine in the late nineteenth and early twentieth centuries. The requirements for the practice of medicine were changing in Missouri and nationwide. New organizations, notably the American Medical Association, argued that states should have education and licensing requirements for medical practitioners. Although coroners in St. Louis attended medical colleges and gained licenses to practice medicine, the state of Missouri did not require such qualifications to serve as coroner. In the 1870s and 1880s, medical practitioners increased their support for medical licensing nationwide, but licensed, practicing physicians did not dominate the profession until around 1930. Despite these national changes and some support for medical licensing in Missouri, lax enforcement of licensing laws meant that physicians in Missouri could practice without a college degree or state test until the twentieth century. In 1876, St. Louis mandated that physicians and midwives who practiced within the city provide their name and information about their medical degrees with the city's health commissioner. Still, across Missouri, many physicians practiced medicine with only a medical diploma, rather than a license as well. In addition, the education required for degrees from Missouri medical colleges varied widely, as their curriculum and requirements were not standardized. Diploma mills sprung up around the state and the State Board of Health had little power to require standardized exams before physicians could practice until 1901. Despite the inconsistency of education and state requirements, St. Louis coroners surpassed their peers in the state and nation with their education and professional experience.[20]

Although St. Louis coroners had considerable medical training and experience, relying on their medical expertise to help determine a cause of death was only part of their job. Criminal justice was the other important element of their work. Coroners had to be medicolegal experts, meaning that they had to understand the legal and criminal justice system in addition to possessing medical knowledge and experience. As such, St. Louis coroners worked closely with the Police Department, particularly in cases when criminal charges could be filed, such as homicide, criminal abortion, and some workplace accidents.[21]

The Police Department often worked closely with the Office of the Coroner not only to file criminal charges but also as part of their daily operations. They worked near each other geographically as well, as the morgue was near the jail, police department, and courthouses. A member of the Board of Police Commissioners also served on the Board of Health, which worked with the Office of the Coroner. In addition, several individuals worked for both the Police Department and the coroner's office. Dr. James C. Nidelet served as the Board of Police Commissioners' vice president and acting president. James Nidelet regularly performed postmortem exams for his brother, Coroner Sylvester L. Nidelet, and other coroners in the late nineteenth century. Deputy coroners also had various connections with the Police Department, such as assisting with police investigations or serving on the Police Court. However, the relationships with the police department were not always pleasant. While the coroner's office and the police department collaborated to prosecute cases, they did not always like each other. For instance, one police chief evidently pressured Coroner Auler to force one of his deputy coroners to resign. The fact that the chief of police believed that he should be able to influence the Office of the Coroner highlights how closely the two offices worked together as well as why critics claimed that the coroner system was corrupt in the 1870s and 1880s.[22]

While the Office of the Coroner was subject to criticism in the late nineteenth century, coroners nonetheless went about their work and recorded their findings. Coroners' inquests from St. Louis and elsewhere have been a rich source for historians. Only a few historians have studied coroners' inquests and violent deaths, however. In many cases, historians have used coroners' records to examine one specific type of violent death, such as suicide or homicide, or other phenomena, such as urbanization and its relationship to violence. Historians who have analyzed coroners' inquests, such as Roger

Lane, Jeffrey Adler, and Stephen Berry, have all noted that these records cannot provide infallible data about violence, in part because officials created new categories of violence that changed the data and because coroners' verdicts varied. In 1979, Roger Lane called coroners' inquests "largely unexplored records," and although they have proved to be a rich resource for historians of violence, death, and despair over the past forty-plus years, these records are still seldom studied. Stephen Berry's recent book, *Count the Dead: Coroners, Quants, and the Birth of Death as We Know It*, and his website, CSI: Dixie both strive to count and name the dead in order to give their deaths—and lives—meaning and to "write better history."[23]

Sudden Deaths in St. Louis builds on the work of Lane, Adler, Berry, and other historians of death and violence by closely examining death investigations, interrogating coroners' verdicts to see how and why they varied, and comparing and contrasting different kinds of violent or unexpected deaths. As a qualitative study, the project provides an opportunity to examine the ways in which ordinary men and women lived and died in a growing, industrial city in the late nineteenth century. Coroners' inquests provide insight into difficult-to-study topics, such as addiction, domestic violence, abortion, and everyday life among the urban poor and working class.

One purpose of this project is to respond to historian Stephen Berry's call for further research to understand death investigation in America in general and, more specifically, how and why the coroners' records were biased. He notes that coroners were "more likely to investigate the deaths of the friendless and the poor, and more likely to investigate deaths that occurred in public rather than private spaces." As this study reveals, coroners did, in fact, investigate deaths that occurred in public spaces more thoroughly than those that occurred in private ones, in part to determine if hospital or asylum attendants, carriage drivers, or employers were at fault for these deaths. Another reason that coroners' investigations were more thorough in bars, hotels, and hospitals than in homes and boardinghouses was because there were often more witnesses to interview in public than in private spaces.[24]

Coroners' inquests into early deaths in St. Louis also help explain why, overwhelmingly, the men and women whose deaths triggered a coroner's investigation were poor or working class, another trend that Berry observed. As he notes, "undoubtedly, elites could do much to deflect and resist the coroner's probe." One important reason for this is because wealthier residents of St. Louis could pay family physicians to falsify death certificates and were less likely to be surrounded by neighbors in tenements or boarding-houses who could notify the coroner of a sudden suicide or abortion that they were trying to conceal. Even in cases of natural deaths, a coroner investigated if there was no attending physician, which was more likely to be the case for the poor and working class than for the middle and upper classes. The few cases for affluent residents of St. Louis stand out because of their rarity, and the investigations into these deaths differ markedly from those of the poor and working class because of their length as well as the tendency of coroners to render more sympathetic verdicts, such as claiming that the deceased died by suicide during a bout of insanity.[25]

While poor and working-class white men and women are overwhelmingly represented in this study, African Americans of all classes are not well represented because of both the small population of African Americans as well as racism. Black residents of St. Louis comprised between 1 and 7 percent of the city's population between 1875 and 1885. Approximately 12 percent of the inquests in the original data sample used for this study were conducted into the deaths of African Americans, or about twice the Black population of St. Louis, indicating that African Americans frequently died sudden, early deaths. Health Department records also show low numbers for African American mortality, with an initial claim that the "colored population" showed remarkable "vitality," but later reports acknowledge that these deaths had been underreported. Coroners, the press, and white witnesses treated the deaths of Black men and women differently than they did those of whites, regardless of ethnicity or immigrant status. Each inquest into the death of an African American featured the abbreviation "col." next to it, for "colored," and this notation was made for Black witnesses as well. Newspapers were often more critical of the ways that African Americans lived and died than they were of whites.[26]

St. Louis had a diverse population, particularly a large immigrant population, and coroners' inquests reveal less bias toward immigrants than toward African Americans. African Americans were beginning to migrate to the city in the 1870s and 1880s but faced limited work opportunities and often lived in tenements in poor and working-class neighborhoods—some integrated, some not. Blacks comprised about 1 percent of the city's population in 1860, but that rose to about 7 percent by 1900. Many German immigrants lived and worked in St. Louis, often in their own German-speaking communities, but an immigrant status did not seem to prompt a negative bias in death investigations and newspaper coverage as it did with African Americans. Many Irish-born men and women appear in these records as well, and some negative stereotypes were evident, but not consistently.[27]

Coroners' inquests are especially useful for studying the white working class, who make up the majority of these cases. Each inquest offers a glimpse of an individual during a time of crisis. One may learn about the person's familial, workplace, and community relationships for years or months, but it is often a matter of only days or hours. Staff at the coroner's office recorded the testimony of witnesses verbatim, so these records provide a valuable source to study the lives of ordinary men and women who did not have the education or leisure time to write letters or diaries. Census records, used in conjunction with inquests, provide a way to trace the members of a family and their relationship to each other before and after the date of the inquest. Marriage, death, and other vital records provide these details as well.

St. Louis is a fascinating city to study because of its rich record source, expanding population, and location in between the North and South—a growing industrial center, but one in a former slaveholding state with a number of former Confederate residents, including some of its coroners. St. Louis had vice districts, saloons, immigrant neighborhoods, African American communities, affluent areas, and a variety of public institutions—the dynamics of which are apparent in coroners' inquests. Because of its large size and number of government institutions, there are a wealth of additional archival sources to supplement St. Louis coroners' inquests: criminal and civil court records, city guides, biographies, city newspapers, census records, and even some paper collections. St. Louis grew in the late nineteenth century and featured strong industries as well as river commerce, in addition to social institutions such as a large police force, facilities for the poor, several jails, schools, and benevolent organizations.

New St. Louis neighborhoods reflected the changing economy and growing class stratification of the late nineteenth century. Mansions adorned gated communities on the city's west side. The steadily growing middle class tended to live north and south of the city's center. To the east, near the river, were poor and working-class homes as well as places of business, including factories and warehouses. Many new city residents were Black men and women who hoped to find new employment opportunities and a better quality of life than in the rural areas they left behind. Over 32,000 Black men and women flocked to St. Louis between 1860 and 1900 and settled into neighborhoods in every section of the city. These neighborhoods became increasingly segregated over time. Although St. Louis provided new prospects for work and leisure for residents of all races and ethnicities, these opportunities were not equal.[28]

Coroners' inquests reveal not only how people died but also how they lived and worked in their homes, workplaces, and other public places, providing a foundation for a gender and social history. While men were expected to be (and often were) breadwinners and heads of household, some also went to saloons, fought with other men at work, visited prostitutes, and beat their wives. Women were supposed to (and often did) manage their households and raise children, but some also worked for wages, ran boardinghouses, worked as prostitutes, and drank regularly. These records reveal the details of daily life and, sometimes, conflicts between men and women, neighbors, and employers and employees.

To understand how coroners conducted their investigations and rendered their verdicts, this work is organized by cause of death. The first two chapters focus on deaths that coroners determined had no outside cause—natural deaths and deaths from alcoholism. The third chapter examines deaths caused by the deceased—deaths by suicide. The fourth chapter examines deaths from abortions, a category that falls between self-inflicted deaths and deaths caused by the actions of others, although, in some cases, coroners treated these deaths like homicides. The final two chapters examine verdicts in which the coroner could have determined that someone else took the life of the deceased—domestic homicides and workplace accidents. Each chapter focuses on one cause of death and compares and contrasts one atypical case with a case that is more typical of those kinds of inquests. No two cases are exactly alike, but themes emerge from the cases, and the selected inquests illustrate those themes. Similar cases are briefly discussed or footnoted throughout each chapter as well. Each chapter will also feature a brief biography of a coroner, deputy coroner, or, in one chapter, a physician who frequently conducted autopsies for the Office of the Coroner.

The assumptions that coroners made about race, class, and gender are evident in the kinds of investigations they conducted and the verdicts that they rendered. Chapter 1 examines natural deaths and argues that despite quick investigations and verdicts of illness or disease, some of the deaths of these men and women were more complicated than the verdicts suggest. Some cases feature verdicts that were not entirely accurate or feature times of death and other details that do not match witness testimony. In some cases, the verdicts of natural causes of death reflect a lack of thorough investigation rather than a truly easy-to-solve case, reflected in part by the fact that deputy coroners investigated over half of these deaths with no oversight from the supervising coroners. Coroners evidently assumed that these deaths would be easy to investigate because they were not looking for anyone else to potentially hold responsible for most of these deaths. As a result, they spent less time on these investigations than with other causes of death, even though most of these men and women had good reputations as well as close family members and friends to testify before the coroner. Chapter 1 examines the inquests into the deaths of Kate Williamson (a suspected homicide and atypical case) and Josephine Laddy, who died of an illness (and is a typical case). The chapter features a brief biography of Deputy Coroner William H. Renick, MD, because deputy coroners often investigated deaths from natural causes. Finally, the first chapter explains how the coroner's office operated on a daily basis.

Coroners treated deaths from alcoholism in much the same way that they did natural deaths, as did the press, the subject of chapter 2. Although men and women died by their own hand, in a way, by drinking to excess regularly or suffering accidents while under the influence, coroners treated these deaths differently from suicides. Unlike in many deaths by suicide, coroners did not consider alcoholism to be a form of insanity, either. One notable exception exists not just in this study but among the thousands of coroners' inquests that exist for St. Louis: Ann Donahoe, a respectable, working-class, Irish wife and mother who died from alcoholism and received a verdict of dipsomania from Coroner Sylvester Nidelet, a term meaning alcohol insanity. No other man or woman received such a verdict from a coroner. More often, they determined that men and women died from "alcoholism" with no qualifying statement, such as in the death of John Grady, whose inquest is more representative of investigations into deaths from alcohol use. Coroners typically investigated alcohol-related deaths quickly, interviewing just one to two witnesses before rendering a verdict, as they did with most deaths from natural causes. The press seldom wrote about alcohol-related deaths, likely because many occurred at home, rather than in public spaces. When St. Louis reporters did write about deaths from alcoholism, they often did so as a warning to others about the dangers of drinking. Although these men and women effectively drank themselves to death, because their deaths were unintentional, coroners treated them like natural deaths.

Chapter 3 examines deaths by suicide and argues that men and women who died by suicide were more likely to receive verdicts of insanity or temporary insanity if they had family members who told the coroners that their loved ones were insane. Claiming that a man or woman died by suicide while suffering from insanity was a way that coroners, such as Coroner Hugo Auler, mitigated the stigma of suicide, something important to family members for the sake of their reputations as well as for burial practices for some faiths, such as Catholicism. Coroners rendered verdicts of suicide "whilst suffering from mental derangement" or "while laboring under temporary insanity" based on several factors, most notably statements from relatives, as evidenced by the death of Estelle Johnson. Coroners relied on the testimony of family members to assess the deceased's state of mind more than their own medical knowledge or the testimony of other physicians. In addition, coroners only rendered verdicts of insanity for men and women with good reputations, which were based largely on their gender and family positions. Married mothers and fathers who were respected members of their communities were the most likely to receive these qualified verdicts, while unmarried men and women, particularly those isolated from relatives, were the least likely to receive these verdicts, including Franz Kurrus, whose case is contrasted in the chapter with Estelle Johnson's. Although many people who died by suicide experienced marital conflicts, alcohol and drug use, and mental and physical illnesses, these factors did not shape their death investigations and verdicts as much as did their reputations and testimony of relatives.

Chapter 4 examines deaths caused by complications from abortions and argues that although the practice was illegal, coroners and law enforcement officers tolerated the practice—except in cases of supposed malpractice, particularly when a woman died from an abortion performed by someone else. Coroners, some witnesses, and the press treated women, including Annie Roberts, whose death is discussed in this chapter, as helpless victims of so-called abortionists, disregarding the fact that women sought the services of these physicians and often tried to protect them from criminal charges. As with other causes of death, reputation and class mattered. The relatives and friends of women who could afford to hire physicians to perform abortions sometimes received falsified death certificates. In some cases, relatives, midwives, physicians who performed abortions, or other potentially culpable parties tried to conceal these unexpected deaths from coroners, as was the case with the death of Mrs. Kate McClure, whose inquest is contrasted with that of Annie Roberts. Some coroners, notably John Frank, worked hard to find evidence to prosecute abortionists. When the press reported on deaths caused by abortion, which they seldom did, they discreetly discussed the abortion-related deaths of married, respectable women, noting that they died from "operations." When physicians performed abortions that caused illness or death, the press often treated women as helpless victims of these alleged predators who sought profits and cared nothing about their patients.

Women's reputations also impacted how the press depicted them in cases of domestic homicide, that is, when they were killed by family members, most often, their husbands or romantic partners, the subject of chapter 5. Although these women were killed by husbands or lovers after enduring abusive relationships, the press did not treat all of these women as victims, only those whom they understood to be respectable, such as Nellie Lee. Just as in other causes of death, the press, coroner's court, and criminal court treated the men who committed domestic homicides differently based on race, class, and social standing. African American men, such as John Cordry, Lee's husband, faced stricter charges, longer sentences, and harsher criticism from the press than did their white counterparts. Conversely, the press exonerated some prominent white men of murder, such as Josiah Colcord, even if witnesses in the coroner's inquest did not. Even some women killed by their husbands or lovers were blamed for their own murders by the press—if they were believed to be disreputable. The press wrote scathing articles about Lillie Colcord, an alleged former prostitute who was killed by her husband, who had abused her throughout their relationship. The chapter focuses on two men who killed their wives after abusing them for years—a fact that witnesses told investigating coroners about, but the press and some friends and acquaintances of these men did not always recognize. The chapter also features a brief biography of Dr. James C. Nidelet, a physician who routinely performed autopsies for the Office of the Coroner.

Unlike domestic homicides, in cases of accidental deaths, the subject of chapter 6, coroners and their juries generally determined that no one was responsible for a person's death even though in some cases, employers, the deceased, or others took actions that caused these accidents. The chapter focuses on workplace accidents because many deadly accidents occurred at work and were highly scrutinized by investigating coroners. A coroner's jury held another individual accountable for a workplace death in only one case, the death of John Brennan. A coroner's jury found his supervisor, Nicholas Degendorf, to be liable for his death, but Degendorf faced no criminal charges. In addition, the coroner's jury did not hold the employer—the owners of the Collier White Lead and Oil Company—responsible for the deadly accident. In the late nineteenth century, workers and the public had fewer expectations of safety on the job, although many states, including Missouri, were gradually adding safety laws. Deputy coroners, such as Herman Praedicow, sometimes assisted coroners in investigating accidental deaths, indicating their high importance. Deputy Coroner Praedicow and Coroner John Frank investigated Henry Diekhoener's tragic death from an overloaded elevator, and this is more typical of an inquest into a workplace accident than Brennan's. Neither the Office of the Coroner nor law enforcement held anyone legally responsible for his death. Local newspapers covered Diekhoener's, Brennan's, and other deadly workplace accidents because they made for sensational stories, but reporters focused more on the companies' financial losses and insurance coverage than victims of accidents. Despite their sympathy for the deceased and their families, the press maintained that no one was to blame in these tragedies.

The men and women in this study all died unexpectedly and quite young, often in tragic circumstances, but investigations into their deaths and interpretations of their deaths varied based on their family relationships, reputations, and whether someone else caused or contributed to their deaths. Coroners did not investigate all deaths in the same way but rather based their investigations and verdicts on their own assumptions as well as their training and Missouri law. Family members offered critical testimony that shaped the verdicts of these coroners more than other factors, in many cases. Finally, the reputation of these men and women contributed to the length of their death investigations, their verdicts, and, especially, the interpretations of their deaths by the St. Louis press. The press offered sympathetic coverage for respected men and women, particularly for native-born white men and women, but often castigated those with questionable reputations, even blaming them for their own murders, in some cases. As these chapters will show by examining contrasting cases, two similar causes of death did not necessarily lead to the same verdict or the same kind of press coverage. A good reputation and strong family and community connections could not shield these men and women from tragic, early deaths, but it could garner compassion from neighbors, relatives, coroners, and even the local press. Coroners' verdicts were subjective, not objective.

CHAPTER ONE

Not as Simple as Disease

Coroners' Verdicts of Natural Deaths

J UST AFTER 6:00 A.M. on September 15, 1883, Mary Smith knocked on her neighbor's, Kate Williamson's, door. Smith hoped to return Williamson's dog to her, which she had rescued the night before during a fight between Williamson and her lover, Billy McCue. Hearing no answer to her knock, Smith called out, "Here's your dog," but was still met with silence. Smith knocked once more, then used her key to unlock Williamson's door. She found her neighbor lying on the floor, naked. She called to her again, then tried to wake Williamson, but the woman was dead. Smith found her face to be warm, but her toes and fingers were cold. She became excited, waking Williamson's nephew, who called out, "Mama? Mama?" to his aunt, the woman whom he considered his mother. Smith went downstairs and alerted another neighbor, Mrs. Casey, who returned to Williamson's rented rooms with Smith. Smith then called the St. Louis City Office of the Coroner, who sent Deputy Coroner George Peck to investigate the unusual and untimely death of Kate Williamson.[1]

Deputy Coroner George Peck arrived the following afternoon to determine if the thirty-eight-year-old had died from illness, alcoholism, homicide, or, less likely in Williamson's case, suicide. Peck soon learned from Smith and other neighbors that Williamson had fought with her lover the previous night and that Billy McCue had assaulted Williamson. Police arrested McCue and held him in jail until Peck could determine whether McCue had caused Williamson's death by having shoved, punched, and kicked her. Peck examined Williamson's body, interviewed witnesses, and even ordered an autopsy. Ultimately, he determined that McCue did not kill Williamson. Instead, he rendered a verdict of a natural cause of death: congestion of the heart and lungs. Williamson's death differed from most deaths from natural causes because of the possibility that she died by homicide. In most investigations into deaths from natural causes, coroners or, more often, deputy coroners, conducted quick, sometimes cursory, investigations before determining that illness or disease caused these deaths. Yet a close examination of these inquests reveals that even natural deaths were more complicated than they initially appeared.[2]

The lengthy investigation into the death of Kate Williamson, potential criminal charges, and autopsy were all unusual in investigations into natural deaths, that is, deaths caused by illnesses or disease. Williamson's is one of only three natural deaths in this study in which the coroner initially suspected that another person caused or contributed to it. More commonly, coroners investigated deaths from natural causes because no attending physician was present when the person died or the death occurred in a public place or institution. The inquest into the death of Josephine Laddy is more typical of investigations into deaths from natural causes. Laddy died of cancer with no physician present, and her case will be contrasted with the atypical inquest into Williamson's death. Because deputy coroners investigated many of these deaths, the chapter will feature a brief biography of Deputy Coroner William H. Renick, MD, who investigated Laddy's death, as well. The chapter will also explain Missouri statutes and the daily operations of the St. Louis Office of the Coroner.

In Laddy's case, as in most cases in this chapter, investigating coroners or deputy coroners quickly determined that neither the deceased nor any other person was responsible for these deaths. Instead, some kind of sickness caused them. Coroners investigated most of these deaths fairly quickly and, in some cases, overlooked details given by witnesses, such as ailments that their loved ones had. In some cases, the verdicts were inaccurate—reflecting causes of death that conflicted with witness testimony, for instance. Several cases, such as Laddy's, feature times of death and other details that do not match statements from relatives, neighbors, or other witnesses, suggesting that coroners and deputy coroners may have rushed their investigations. Williamson's case differed from typical inquests into natural deaths because there were two possibilities for her cause of death, in addition to heart and lung congestion: homicide or alcoholism.[3]

The reason for this apparent lack of attention to detail in the inquest records is likely because the investigating coroners did not believe that anyone else could have been legally responsible for most of these deaths and, therefore, did not expect the inquest to lead to criminal charges. Unlike homicides and some deaths caused by abortions and accidents, few natural deaths featured any evidence that anyone was to blame for them—the deceased themselves or someone else. In these cases, an inquest was not a first step in the criminal justice system. Natural deaths also differed from suicides because religious views, burial rites, and a stigma attached to the verdict were not at stake. In many cases, an inquest was simply a formality, rather than potential evidence for an indictment and criminal trial. As a result, investigating coroners placed less value on witness testimony, even from family members, who often contributed vital information for coroners' verdicts. Instead, coroners conducted their investigations and rendered verdicts as soon as they ruled out the possibility of homicide or suicide.

Newspaper coverage of natural deaths also differed from accounts of suicides, homicides, accidents, and some deaths from abortion. The local press offered little coverage of deaths from natural causes. In the few cases of potential homicides, reporters offered their typical sensationalistic accounts but lost interest once coroners determined that murder was not a possible cause of death. While reporters did comment on many of the deaths in this chapter, they often wrote brief accounts—sometimes just a single sentence. The details were often far less salacious than in cases of violent deaths. Deaths from illness often occurred at home and were not always unexpected, perhaps contributing to these brief newspaper accounts.

While coroners investigated about one-fifth of the cases in this chapter because they were possible homicides, they investigated most of them because they had unknown causes, occurred in public places, or were unattended by a physician. According to Missouri law, a person, institution, or business had to notify the coroner when a death appeared to be suspicious or when no physician was present at the time of death. Coroners also investigated unexpected deaths that occurred in public places, such as saloons, asylums, workplaces, or, in some cases, on the street. Coroners and deputy coroners worked to determine how and why the person died and if anyone else was responsible for the death. Coroners investigated four primary kinds of deaths: deaths that definitely occurred from violence (such as burns, stab wounds, or gunshot wounds); deaths that may have been caused by violence (such as poisoning, physical assault, or abortion); sudden, unexpected deaths that did not appear to be caused by violence but could have been (deaths in the street, unexpected deaths at home or work, or possible alcoholism); and deaths from unknown causes, especially those that occurred without witnesses.[4]

St. Louis coroners had several legal and medical duties, but one important task was to ascertain whether a death resulted from a criminal act. If a person died from a suspected suicide, homicide, or accident, St. Louis coroners had to determine the cause of death as well as if anyone else was legally responsible for the death. If the coroner determined that someone died from negligence, medical malpractice, or murder, then the person who caused the death could face criminal charges. The coroner sometimes aided with the arrest of the suspect, but most often, the police did so alone. The coroner investigated the death and sometimes ordered an autopsy or a toxicology analysis. If the inquest determined that the death was a homicide, the district attorney could press charges and try the accused. The coroner's inquest was a crucial first step in the criminal justice system, but the inquest alone did not determine a person's innocence or guilt.[5]

Coroners and their deputies often held inquests at the location of a person's death but sometimes held them in the Office of the Coroner. The investigating coroner called witnesses to interview, and by law, witnesses had to testify or face fines or even jail time. Coroners often called between two and four witnesses, although in some natural deaths, they only spoke to one. They spoke to anyone who found the body or saw the person die, physicians who treated the deceased, police officers who had recently encountered or arrested the deceased, and friends, relatives, and neighbors who could share information about how and why a person died. In cases of suspicious deaths, those close to the deceased could inform the coroner about recent fights, possible accidents resulting from negligence, or suicidal threats or actions. After hearing testimony, and perhaps after ordering an autopsy and/or toxicology analysis, the coroner or deputy coroner rendered his verdict.[6]

While death investigators in the twenty-first century determine a *manner* of death and have five options to choose from (suicide, homicide, accident, natural, or undetermined), St. Louis coroners in the late nineteenth century rendered a *cause* of death and had a wide range of choices. Coroners used a wide selection of verdicts in their inquest records. Verdicts ranged from the general "suicide," "homicide," or "accident" to the specific, such as "criminal abortion," "dipsomania," "congestive chill," or "burns caused by tar catching fire."[7] Verdicts varied by and among coroners and deputy coroners, however. Some coroners and deputy coroners offered details to explain how and why a person died, while others did not. For example, some determined that a person died from "cancer," while others added a more specific cause, such as "cancer of the foot" or "cancer in the throat and mouth." Deaths caused by sunstroke illustrate this point. Some coroners determined that men and women died from sunstroke as well as alcoholism, while some concluded that the sun alone killed these men and women. With regard to natural deaths, coroners sometimes noted that the deceased was not attended by a physician, hence the reason that they were called for an inquest, but more often, they did not. Coroners and deputy coroners seldom wrote "natural causes," instead offering specific causes of death, such as "consumption" or "heatstroke."[8]

If the coroner determined that a man or woman came to his or her death because of an accident, suicide, or natural causes, he simply recorded his verdict, and the district attorney did not file criminal charges. In cases of suspected homicide, however, Missouri law required the coroner to convene a coroner's jury to consider the evidence in the case and render a verdict. While deputy coroners often investigated deaths without supervision, they could not convene and supervise jury inquests; only coroners did. The coroner selected six white men to view the body of the deceased, listen to witness testimony, and render a verdict. Missouri law had several requirements for jurors in courts of law but had only a few mandates for selecting coroner's jurors. Missouri statutes only required the coroner to "summon a jury of six good and lawful men, householders of the same township."[9] While the regulations did not specifically state that these jurors had to be white, it was implied. The coroner's jury had four duties: to view the body of the deceased, listen to the evidence presented, consider how the death occurred and whether someone caused the death, and render a verdict. In jury inquests, the coroner often called more witnesses than they did in other investigations and questioned them in more detail. To conclude the inquest, the coroner's jury deliberated and rendered a verdict. Unlike in other inquests, the coroner did not render the verdict but essentially authorized it by signing the jury's verdict. While the manner in which coroner's jury inquests were conducted was similar to criminal court trials, the coroner's court did not have the legal status that a court of law did. If the coroner's jury found that the deceased died from homicide, malpractice, or criminal negligence, they did not have the authority to arrest a suspect, even if they named one in their verdict. The district attorney had to file charges and the verdict of the coroner's jury would be admitted as evidence in a criminal trial, if a trial occurred.[10]

Just as Missouri law had few requirements for coroner's juries, it also required little training for coroners, but St. Louis coroners were remarkable because they far exceeded the minimal state requirements. The only state guidelines were that a coroner be "a 'suitable person,'" a citizen of the United States, and a resident of Missouri for one year before taking office.[11] Missouri law did not require any medical or legal training for the position, but every St. Louis coroner who served between 1875 and 1885 was a licensed, practicing physician. St. Louis also differed because its coroners served the city, rather than county, beginning in 1876, when St. Louis City formally separated from St. Louis County. Like other areas in Missouri, coroners were elected officials and ran for office every two years.[12]

While voters elected coroners to office, they did not elect deputy coroners, who often had less training than did their supervisors. Of seven deputy coroners in this study, four had expertise in the medical or legal fields, with two working as licensed, practicing physicians and two working as attorneys when they did not hold office as a deputy coroner. Upon election, a coroner appointed one to two deputies. Coroners could appoint any deputy coroner of their choice and often based the decision on party politics. The position of deputy coroner was also more transient than that of coroner. As appointed officers, deputy coroners could be replaced by the coroners whom they served. Some deputy coroners served different coroners over the years, while others held only a two-year term or less.[13]

Deputy coroners regularly investigated deaths and rendered verdicts without direct supervision from coroners, particularly in cases that seemed to be easy to solve, such as natural deaths. Because they often anticipated that these deaths would not result in criminal charges of homicide, manslaughter, or criminal negligence, deputy coroners investigated over half of these deaths with no oversight from the overseeing coroners. Coroners were more likely to investigate suspicious deaths than were deputies, particularly potential homicides.

Deputy Coroner William H. Renick differed from most deputy coroners because he had as much medical training and experience as the coroner who appointed him: Dr. Sylvester Nidelet. The position of deputy coroner tended to be transient, but it was particularly short term under Coroner Nidelet. Nidelet appointed three deputy coroners between 1882 and 1886, including both of the deputy coroners discussed in this chapter: George W. Peck and William H. Renick, MD. Renick worked as a licensed, practicing physician when he did not serve as deputy coroner. Renick graduated from Bellevue Medical College in 1861 and earned his MD from St. Louis Medical College in 1865. He served as an acting assistant surgeon in the U.S. Army, a resident physician of the St. Louis Smallpox Hospital, and the physician to the City Dispensary—the position that he held when Coroner Nidelet appointed him as his deputy in 1882. When Renick resigned in 1883, Nidelet appointed Peck to replace him. Neither Peck nor the subsequent deputy coroner, Thomas Hennessy, had medical training or experience, although both had some experience with the law before or after their terms as deputy coroners. Their inexperience in the field of medical jurisprudence was common. Renick's career in medicine and public health stood out among deputy coroners. After serving for approximately one year as Sylvester Nidelet's deputy, Renick returned to medicine. Unlike some other coroners and deputy coroners, he did not hold other political offices but rather focused on treating patients until his death in 1889.[14]

When Deputy Coroner Renick arrived to investigate the death of Josephine Laddy on December 22, 1882, he had substantial medical knowledge to draw on, unlike some of the other deputy coroners in this study. The Black forty-three-year-old mother of two died without medical attendance overnight, prompting a coroner's inquest. Renick's medical training and experience notwithstanding, the inquest into the death of Josephine Laddy is typical of inquests into natural deaths for several reasons. First, a deputy coroner, rather than a coroner, investigated her death. Second, Renick investigated her death relatively quickly. He interviewed three witnesses, which was a moderate number of people to interview, but he spoke to them briefly. Renick did not order an autopsy, as he had no reason to; there was no evidence of foul play. All of the evidence pointed to cancer as Laddy's cause of death. Finally, Renick did not ensure that all aspects of his report were accurate, as happened regularly in cases of natural deaths. In Laddy's case, witness testimony contradicts the time of death that the deputy coroner recorded. While Laddy's time of death is a small detail, it illustrates the fact that in deaths from natural causes, coroners were more likely to close cases quickly, without being as thorough as they often were in investigations into violent deaths.[15]

While Laddy had been suffering from cancer for months, her children did not expect her to die just three days before Christmas. Her fourteen-year-old son, Joe Laddy, awoke at 4:00 A.M. on December 22, 1882, to find his mother "cold and dead" next to him.[16] When he had climbed into bed with his mother at 8:00 the night before, she had been alive, although not well, having been ill with cancer of the foot for about six months. Perhaps in denial that his mother was dead, or maybe not wanting to bother his sister, Joe waited until 7:00 A.M. before going to his sister's house to alert her about their mother's sudden death. Charity Moore rushed to her mother's home to care for her younger brother and report her mother's death to the coroner's office. Josephine Laddy's death was not unexpected or suspicious, so it is likely that her daughter informed the Office of the Coroner about her mother's death because she was not attended by a physician when she died.[17]

Deputy Coroner Renick arrived at 11:00 that morning to determine how and why Josephine Laddy came to her death. Renick interviewed three witnesses in his investigation: Laddy's two children and her treating physician, Joseph Whittaker, MD. All three told the deputy coroner that Dr. Whittaker had been treating Laddy for cancer. Moore told Renick that her mother worked as a cook, when she was able to work at all, which she had not been able to do since she had been bedridden for the past six months. Dr. Whittaker testified that it was a malignant tumor in her foot that ultimately caused Laddy's death, although he had not seen his patient for eight to nine weeks.[18]

Laddy's case was a simple one for Renick to solve, but not all of the details in his record match the testimony. Renick did not order an autopsy, in part because Laddy's treating physician testified as to her cause of death, but also because he had no evidence of homicide or medical malpractice. He had no reason to believe that Laddy may have died by suicide, either. While Laddy's death was sudden, it was not entirely unexpected, and there was no evidence of homicide. The deputy coroner determined that she died "from the effects of a cancer of the leg" at 4:00 on the morning of December 22, 1882.[19]

But Josephine Laddy did not die at 4:00 A.M. Her son testified that her body was cold at 4:00 A.M. and that he last saw her alive at 8:00 the night before, meaning that she died between 8:00 P.M. and 4:00 A.M. Coroners could—and often did—record an estimated time of death when they could not determine an exact time.[20] They also relied on witness testimony, especially from relatives, when rendering their verdicts and adding other details to the inquest record. But in Laddy's case, no one would be charged with homicide, manslaughter, or negligence. She simply died in her sleep, unattended by a physician, and the visit from the deputy coroner was little more than a formality. Her time of death did not matter.[21]

The press wrote two brief articles about Laddy's death, reporting only the minimal details, which reporters often did when discussing deaths from illness or disease. The *St. Louis Globe-Democrat* reported that an inquest was performed on Laddy and concluded that she died of cancer, with the reporter commenting on her race, calling the deceased "a negress." The press routinely noted when a deceased man or woman was not white, often using the word "colored," "negro," or, in some cases, "dusky." Surprisingly, the *St. Louis Post-Dispatch* did not further comment on Laddy's race and simply reported that she died "without medical attendance" at 4:00 that morning. Both articles were a single sentence long. Neither mentioned Laddy's family, even though she left behind two children, or her funeral. Her death was not sensationalistic, so the fact that it was even mentioned briefly is remarkable, but the widow and mother likely was a respected member of her community, which may account for the reports.[22]

While Deputy Coroner Renick had no reason to believe that someone else may have caused or contributed to Josephine Laddy's death, Deputy Coroner George Peck had ample reason to believe that Kate Williamson, whose death was discussed in the opening story, had died from homicide. In fact, Deputy Coroner Peck initially suspected that injuries caused by an assault from Williamson's lover, Billy McCue, caused her death between 3:00 and 6:00 A.M. on September 15, 1880. Williamson's death differs from most investigations into natural deaths because, at first, Peck believed that Williamson's death was a homicide and investigated it as such. Peck interviewed seven witnesses—several more than the two to four witnesses whom coroners typically interviewed in deaths that were not suspected homicides. Peck also ordered an autopsy in Williamson's case—another uncommon step in a death investigation. Peck examined Williamson's body, then interviewed witnesses to determine how Williamson came to her death. Meanwhile, Dr. James C. Nidelet performed a postmortem examination, or autopsy, on Williamson's body.[23]

Police also arrested William "Billy" McCue because they suspected that he had inflicted deadly injuries upon Williamson. Officers had no trouble finding McCue; he arrived at Williamson's home shortly after Officer Charles Landers arrived. Landers immediately arrested McCue while the deputy coroner investigated Williamson's death. Deputy Coroner Peck spoke with Williamson's nephew (who was, essentially, her adopted son), three of her neighbors, Landers (the investigating police officer), and Dr. James C. Nidelet, after he completed the autopsy. Peck had found no marks on Williamson's body when he examined it, but witness testimony alerted him to a potentially deadly assault. Emily Vincent, Sally Casey, and Mary Smith all told Deputy Coroner Peck that McCue had shoved and punched Williamson. At one point, McCue said that he wanted to give Williamson "a good licking" but "did not want to give her any marks," presumably because bruises or cuts would provide evidence that he had beaten her.[24] McCue even pulled an earring from Williamson's ear and broke it. Williamson's nephew called a police officer, but he would not arrest McCue unless she pressed charges, which she refused to do. Williamson's neighbors sat with her after the incident and made sure that she closed her windows and locked her door before they went to sleep. Casey asked Williamson to come home with her, but Williamson stayed in her own home. The neighbors reluctantly left Williamson after the incident, worrying that McCue would break into her rented rooms overnight. They did not, however, expect to find their friend dead the next morning.[25]

McCue's statement to Williamson's neighbors shows that he felt at least partially responsible for her death. When he arrived at Williamson's home the morning of the coroner's inquest, McCue asked Sally Casey if his lover was, in fact, dead. When she confirmed his suspicions, McCue cried, saying, "Oh My God what did I do?" McCue left, ostensibly to go to work, then returned a couple of hours later, this time wanting to see Williamson's body. He "threw himself on the table and cried" and said, "Oh my God Kate, what have I done to you, but you have no marks," as if he believed that a lack of visible bruises meant that he could not have beaten her to death. His tears were probably for himself, not Williamson, as he also expressed concern over facing execution by hanging for her death. He told Casey, "Well, I'll swing I guess-but they'll hang me innocent."[26]

While Williamson's neighbors seemed certain that McCue had killed Williamson, the evidence from the coroner's inquest proved to be less conclusive. Deputy Coroner Peck considered witness testimony along with the results from Dr. Nidelet's autopsy. Nidelet did not find evidence that McCue's attack had killed Williamson. Instead, he found that her heart and lungs were congested and concluded that these illnesses were "evidently the result of alcoholism."[27] In addition to Nidelet's autopsy results, Deputy Coroner Peck gathered witness testimony that Williamson may have had a habit of drinking to excess. Evidently, Peck asked witnesses about her drinking, because several neighbors testified about it, insisting that Williamson drank only beer, as opposed to hard liquor, and that they believed that she was not a heavy drinker. Sally Casey remarked that Williamson drank the same amount of beer that "all hard working women do." Williamson was rather young, at thirty-eight, but her sister-in-law testified that she had a history of a heart condition. Despite the autopsy results, Deputy Coroner Peck rendered her cause of death as "congestive heart and lung failure" with "fluid buildup, perhaps from heart disease." Peck's verdict made no mention of alcoholism or a physical assault. Once the inquest concluded, police released McCue from custody. He faced no criminal charges in Williamson's death.[28]

The St. Louis press initially covered Kate Williamson's inquest in detail because it was a suspected murder, but once it was clear that McCue would not face charges, their articles became much shorter. Reporters for the *Post-Dispatch* and *Globe-Democrat* both wrote about the suspicious circumstances surrounding Williamson's death, McCue's assault on her, and some details of McCue's reaction to the news of his lover's demise. A *Post-Dispatch* reporter commented on McCue's alleged poor character, commenting that "the police say that he has a bad reputation." The reporter also suggested that "Red" McCue was drunk at the time, remarking that he had to be "shaken out of an apparent stupor" by police who told him of his lover's death—and then arrested him. (In fact, the arresting officer testified in the inquest that Mc-Cue was sober, although he did examine the man to determine if he was intoxicated.) The *Globe-Democrat* also published a lengthy account detailing the couple's quarrels and noting McCue's arrest. Once the inquest concluded, both papers printed much shorter articles that noted the verdict and McCue's release from custody. The *Post-Dispatch* reported only the deputy coroner's verdict, while the *Globe-Democrat* added information from the autopsy—that the cause of death was alcoholism. With no murder charges forthcoming, the press lost interest in Williamson's case.[29]

Although the St. Louis press often relayed the gruesome details of sudden deaths, especially suicides and homicides, they wrote little about natural deaths, and their early attention to the death of Kate Williamson was unusual. The lengthy inquest into Kate Williamson's death and initial suspicion of homicide were also atypical for deaths caused by disease or illness. The initial possibility of different causes of death was not unusual, however. Despite brief investigations and verdicts that determined that the men and women in this chapter died from natural causes, not all of these cases were simple to solve. Coroners and, more often, deputy coroners may not have felt the need to determine an accurate time of death or pinpoint a specific illness with certainty because these men and women died from sicknesses, not suicide or homicide. Their verdicts would not implicate or exonerate anyone in most cases, nor would the verdict carry a social stigma. These death investigations, unlike those from violent deaths, were often a professional duty—a requirement of the position, rather than an effort to determine what caused a suspicious death. While it was the job of the coroner to determine an accurate cause of death, evidently, their duty was less pressing in these cases. Nonetheless, witness testimony reveals that these natural deaths were more complicated than their investigations and verdicts made them appear.

CHAPTER TWO

"She Was a Hard Drinker"

Gender, Deaths from Alcoholism, and Insanity

THE AFTERNOON OF FEBRUARY 29, 1884, proved to be no ordinary workday for sixteen-year-old Michael Donahoe. The young man returned to his family's rented rooms in a boardinghouse on 119 Howard Street around noon that day and checked on his mother, Ann Donahoe, when he arrived. She had been ill for a few days and had been asleep when his father left for work that morning. His mother was still lying in bed that afternoon, but when he looked in on her, he was shocked to find that she had died. His father was not yet home, so Michael ran to get his neighbor, William Ryan, who confirmed that fifty-year-old Ann Donahoe had, in fact, passed away. She lay "on the bed her arms crossed . . . & head bent upon her chest. She was cold & stiff."[1]

The family called the Office of the Coroner, and Dr. Sylvester L. Nidelet arrived the next day to conduct an inquest into the unexpected, early death of Ann Donahoe. Following standard procedure, Coroner Nidelet examined her body and its surroundings to determine if there was evidence of an illness or, potentially, a suicide or homicide. He also interviewed witnesses to learn about Donahoe's health and recent behavior. He did not order an autopsy or interview a treating physician, likely because his examination and witness testimony sufficed for him to render his verdict. Coroner Nidelet learned from Ann Donahoe's husband, also named Michael, and neighbor, William Ryan, that Donahoe had been ill shortly before her death because of a problem that she had experienced for a few years since two of her children had died: she had "indulged in liquor to excess."[2] Her body was also weakened from a recent bout of scarlet fever. Coroner Nidelet determined that Ann Donahoe had succumbed to dipsomania, or alcohol insanity.[3]

The death of Ann Donahoe is a remarkable inquest into a death from alcoholism because it is the *only* verdict of dipsomania among the tens of thousands of inquests that exist for the city of St. Louis between 1845 and 1900.[4] Coroners rendered verdicts of "intoxication," "alcoholism," or "intemperance" when they believed that alcohol caused or contributed to a death, but Coroner Nidelet believed that Donahoe suffered from a special form of alcoholism—a "madness" for alcohol. Physicians who specialized in alcohol treatment understood dipsomania to have several distinctive characteristics that differed from other forms of habitual drunkenness, including intemperance or alcoholism. Dipsomaniacs, like other alcoholics, drank to excess regularly, but because they suffered from insanity. The term emphasized that its sufferers were not committing a sin or lacked willpower but, rather, had a medical or mental health problem that they could not control. Specialists understood women to be particularly susceptible to dipsomania, primarily because of their biology and supposedly delicate reproductive systems. Ann Donahoe's grief, gender, age, and status as a mother contributed to Coroner Nidelet's understanding of her as someone who suffered from dipsomania and, therefore, deserved sympathy.[5]

Ann Donahoe's verdict distinguishes it from other deaths from alcoholism as well as from deaths from natural causes. In the late nineteenth century and even to the present day, coroners typically treated deaths from alcoholism like deaths from illness or disease. Interestingly, in the late nineteenth century, many people, including most physicians, did not consider alcoholism a disease. Still, coroners investigated deaths from alcoholism in a similar manner to illnesses, rather than violent deaths. As discussed in chapter 1, coroners tended to investigate deaths from natural causes quickly and did not always take witness testimony into account when rendering their verdicts or documenting the details of the death in their inquest records. Most investigations into alcohol-related deaths followed this pattern, as coroners interviewed one to two witnesses and quickly rendered a verdict of "alcoholism," "intemperance," "drink," or a similar word or phrase. They seldom sought a root cause for alcoholism, and if a witness offered a cause, such as grief, coroners rarely noted that in their verdicts. But in Ann Donahoe's case, Coroner Sylvester Nidelet took seriously the statements from her husband, notably that the loss of two of her children caused such grief that she developed a form of alcohol insanity. Her verdict carried a stigma, but one much less pronounced than the alternatives.[6]

The inquest into the death of Ann Donahoe is atypical for inquests into alcohol-related deaths. A verdict of dipsomania is more similar to some inquests into deaths by suicide, in which coroners sometimes determined that a person died while suffering from insanity. As will be discussed in chapter 3, coroners often sought a cause for deaths by suicide, such as ill health, a job loss, or grief. The inquest into Ann Donahoe's death shares those characteristics. Witnesses offered explanations for her excess drinking, including grief and a recent illness of scarlet fever. As a middle-aged woman and mother, Ann Donahoe differed from the stereotypical alcoholic of the late nineteenth century. As will be discussed in this chapter, physicians and the general public understood alcoholism to be a largely male affliction. Her working-class status and Irish ethnicity fit into period stereotypes of alcoholics, but her gender defied them. Ann Donahoe's case will be contrasted with a more typical inquest into a death from alcoholism, that of John Grady. Grady was an unmarried, thirty-four-year-old, native-born white man. As with inquests into natural deaths, a deputy coroner investigated Grady's demise and determined that he died from alcoholism. Witnesses did not search for a cause for Grady's drinking. The press wrote only a brief account of his death, which they commonly did for deaths from alcohol use as well as other natural causes. The chapter also features a brief biography of Coroner Sylvester L. Nidelet because he rendered the lone dipsomania verdict in this study.

Definitions of alcoholism were in flux in the late nineteenth century among physicians who treated inebriety and also among the coroners in this study, who used terms like "alcoholism," "intoxication," and "intemperance" interchangeably. But Coroner Nidelet did not simply render a verdict of dipsomania in the case of Ann Donahoe because he had several options available to him. Although verdicts in alcohol-related deaths varied somewhat by the investigating coroner, they tended to use fairly consistent language. When men and women died from alcohol use alone, St. Louis coroners typically determined that "alcoholism" caused the death. Coroners also added alcohol use to other causes of death when they believed that excessive drinking was at least partly responsible for those deaths, including other natural causes, accidents, or even some homicides. Coroners rendered verdicts such as "congestion of the brain, superinduced by intemperate use of alcoholic stimulants," "concussion caused by fall down stairs while intoxicated," or "sunstroke and intemperance."[7]

Although coroners added alcohol use to other verdicts, they almost never added words or phrases for insanity to verdicts of alcoholism. Coroners typically reserved those terms to deaths by suicide, and even then they seldom noted that the deceased ended his or her own life "while of unsound mind" or "suffering from temporary insanity." As with deaths from natural causes and alcoholism, verdicts of insanity in deaths by suicide varied by coroner, and Coroner Nidelet rendered as many of those verdicts as his counterparts. Burial rites were not at stake with a verdict of death by "drink" or "alcoholism," as they sometimes were in deaths by suicide, but this alone does not explain the difference. Few people believed that alcoholism was a mental illness, disease, or another form of sickness. While physicians often connected suicide with insanity by the late nineteenth century, they were just beginning to believe that drinking to excess was some kind of illness—a disease or a form of insanity. Physicians who specialized in treating what would today be understood as an addiction to alcohol were the most likely to understand habitual intoxication as some kind of a disease. Although St. Louis coroners, including Coroner Sylvester Nidelet, were licensed, practicing physicians, they did not specialize in treating alcoholism. It is remarkable that Nidelet was familiar enough with dipsomania to determine that it caused the untimely death of Ann Donahoe.[8]

Coroners' verdicts reveal that they believed that alcoholism could contribute to suicide, and insanity could lead to suicide, but alcoholism itself was not a form of suicide or a result of insanity. Although deaths from alcohol use resulted from injuries that were self-inflicted, they differed from suicides because coroners understood those injuries to be *unintentional*. Intent was (and is) a crucial determining factor in a cause of death. Many witnesses told the coroner that their friend, relative, or acquaintance had died because of their "intemperate" or "dissipated" habits, but they did not believe that these men and women sought to kill themselves. Even if someone died after a recent drinking spree, coroners distinguished these deaths from suicides. They did not seek to uncover a cause for the sudden onset of heavy drinking, as they often did when loved ones testified about recent bouts of melancholy or despondency that they believed led to a suicide. They seldom noted in their verdicts that a recent tragedy sparked a round of heavy drinking. Although coroners distinguished deaths from alcoholism from deaths by suicide, they did believe that alcohol use contributed to some deaths by suicide. They typically added the word "alcoholism" to verdicts of suicide in cases in which someone died by suicide while intoxicated or when coroners believed that longtime excessive drinking contributed to the suicide.[9]

While Coroner Nidelet determined that Ann Donahoe suffered from a form of alcohol insanity, in most cases, coroners rendered verdicts of "alcoholism." Deputy Coroner Thomas Hennessy rendered such a verdict in the death of John Grady, who died in the overnight hours between July 4 and 5, 1885. The inquest into the death of John Grady is representative of a typical inquest into an alcohol-related death. Deputy Coroner Thomas Hennessy pieced together the few clues he had as to how the thirty-four-year-old, native-born white man died in order to render a verdict. On July 6, 1885, Hennessy examined Grady's body in the city morgue. He did not conduct his inquest at the location of death, probably because it was not ideal for the procedure. Grady's body had been found outside, between the railroad track and river at the levee between Vine and Washington Avenue. Although Grady had been staying in a lodging house shortly before his death, he did not sleep there the night of his death. Hennessy spoke to two witnesses: the deceased's brother, Michael Grady, and a friend of over a decade, John Sullivan. Michael Grady told Hennessy that he had last seen his brother two weeks before his death and that the thirty-four-year-old had been a "hard drinker" for the past five to six years. He did not give a reason for the onset of heavy drinking, which was fairly common in these cases. Grady was unmarried, so Hennessy had no spouse to interview. Hennessy also interviewed John Sullivan, who was, evidently, the last person to see Grady alive. Sullivan told Hennessy that Grady had been working around the levee where his body was found as a "general laborer." Sullivan told the deputy coroner that Grady "was a hard drinker." He had last seen his friend around 9:30 P.M. on the night of his death and he was "under the influence of liquor" and "had a chill" the day before his death. The next time that he saw his friend, he was dead, "lying on the levee" where he had been working. There was no evidence of violence or foul play, but because the death was unexpected, Sullivan called the police, who then called Deputy Coroner Hennessy to investigate.[10]

Hennessy could not determine the cause of Grady's death from a physical examination and witness testimony alone, so he ordered an autopsy, a relatively uncommon procedure in any type of inquest, but particularly in deaths from alcohol use. In fact, Grady's inquest is one of only two deaths from alcoholism in which the coroner ordered a postmortem examination. Dr. James C. Nidelet, the brother of Coroner Sylvester L. Nidelet, performed the postmortem examination, as he routinely did for the Office of the Coroner, on July 5, 1885, the day before Hennessy conducted the formal inquest. Nidelet found that Grady had an "immensely enlarged," fatty liver and determined that John Grady died from alcoholism. The autopsy, combined with testimony from two witnesses that Grady had a history of heavy drinking, prompted Hennessy to render his verdict—that "the effects of alcoholism" caused Grady's death sometime between the hours of 10:00 P.M. on July 4, 1885, and 5:00 A.M. on July 5, 1885. His brother arranged for John Grady to be buried in Calvary Cemetery, a Catholic cemetery. A verdict of alcoholism did not preclude a Catholic burial, nor did faith seem to be a concern when it came to burial rites for men and women who died from alcoholism. As in most cases of death caused by alcohol use, Hennessy offered no qualifying statements to his verdict. He did not claim that Grady suffered from insanity, grief, or physical pain. Alcoholism alone killed Grady, he determined.[11]

Although the autopsy and public location of his death were unusual, the inquest into the death of John Grady was typical for deaths caused by alcoholism. He died alone, and the investigating coroner ultimately rendered a verdict of alcoholism, both of which were common. Most men and women who died from alcoholism died at home, however. People who died in public tended to receive longer, more thorough investigations, regardless of the cause of death, which is likely why Hennessy ordered an autopsy. Coroners seldom ordered autopsies in deaths from alcoholism or natural causes, but Grady's death was difficult to determine based on a physical examination and witness testimony alone. While the autopsy was unique, the brief testimony given by just two witnesses was common for alcohol-related deaths, which often featured one to two witnesses. Men were also more likely to die from alcoholism than women. Finally, like most other men and women who died from alcoholism, Grady had a history of hard drinking.[12]

Grady's death also garnered little press attention, as most deaths caused by alcoholism did. Homicides, suicides, and accidents covered the pages of the *St. Louis-Globe Democrat* and, to a lesser extent, the *St. Louis Post-Dispatch*, but they published very few articles about men and women who died from alcoholism. The reason for this could be because many of these men and women died at home, rather than in public places, so these deaths drew less attention than homicides, accidents, or suicides. When the press did publish stories, they were quite brief, sometimes only a sentence or two long, and the *St. Louis Globe-Democrat*'s account of Grady's death was no exception. The reporter did not even provide the correct details, referring to him as Charles, not John, and stating that he was found dead in the lodging house where he had been staying, rather than the levee. St. Louis reporters did not describe these men and women as insane or seek a root cause for their heavy drinking, as they sometimes did with suicides. They did not necessarily condemn the deceased either, however. The St. Louis press routinely spoke to coroners when reporting on untimely deaths but seldom did so in deaths from alcohol use or deaths from natural causes. The details of these unexpected deaths seem to have been of less interest to reporters.[13]

Although deaths from alcoholism were seldom fodder for sensationalistic reporting, sometimes the St. Louis press wrote stories about deaths from alcoholism as moralistic warnings about the dangers of alcohol. For example, the *St. Louis Globe-Democrat* wrote a piece on June 3, 1880, probably because the coroner investigated two deaths on the same day—those of John Nicely and James Hardy. The reporter conveyed a self-righteous tone with the title, "The Coroner's Temperance Lecture," but the article itself provided only brief discussions of the deaths of both Nicely, a former steamboat captain and insurance salesman at the time of his death, and Hardy, a steamboat cook. "Captain" John Nicely, the reporter observed, perished after a drinking "spree" while Hardy died in a saloon, the result of "congestion of the brain, superinduced by alcoholism." The reporter offered no explanation for the men's recent heavy drinking as they often did in deaths by suicide, blaming unemployment or other misfortunes. They also refrained from detailing the events leading up to these deaths, as they often did in violent deaths, particularly suicides and homicides. Although the attention to these deaths and dramatic title were unique, the little attention to the details of these alcohol-related deaths was typical, as it was with deaths from other natural causes.[14]

The reporter for the *St. Louis Globe-Democrat* was not alone in his condemnation of heavy drinking. Other social commentators, including Joseph A. Dacus and James W. Buel, authors of *A Tour of St. Louis: or, The Inside Life of a Great City*, carefully distinguished respectable and deviant drinking patterns in their city guide. Although St. Louis had over 2,500 beer halls and saloons in the late nineteenth century, Dacus and Buel distinguished between respectable, moderate drinking and the "worst scoundrels in America" who visited "dives" into the wee hours of the morning in working-class and poor neighborhoods.[15] In respectable areas, they noted, drinking was common among all ethnicities and among men and women. In these middle and upper-class areas, St. Louisans patronized respectable establishments and seldom became intoxicated. Respectable women could drink in public as long as they avoided hard liquor and visited the more genteel establishments, presumably with their husbands. According to these authors, the critical difference between social drinking and disreputable drinking was that respectable men and women did not become drunk and were not "addicted" to visiting saloons. The purpose of the guide was to cast a positive light on the city of St. Louis, and throughout the work, the authors distinguished between the city's positive attributes and its unsavory ones. While its details regarding the drinking establishments in the city may be inaccurate, the guide reveals that they expected their readers to agree that any kind of alcohol addiction was immoral, shameful, and even dangerous.[16]

In St. Louis, as in most cities, few resources existed for men or women who sought treatment. In the 1870s and 1880s, most alcoholics who received care for their addiction ended up in St. Vincent's Insane Asylum, which provided medical care for a variety of addictions and mental illnesses. Others served stints in the Work House if they committed a crime while drunk and received no care for their affliction there. Some St. Louisans argued for the need for a facility, but the request went unheeded in the late nineteenth century. The closest facility for alcohol addiction was the Willow Bark Institute in Jerseyville, Illinois, a private facility that many people could not afford. Willow Bark resembled many treatment centers at the time as it exclusively accepted men.[17]

Despite commonly held assumptions that alcoholism was a male problem, women like Ann Donahoe also drank heavily on a regular basis and, sometimes, were understood to suffer from dipsomania. Although Coroner Sylvester Nidelet rendered this distinctive cause of death, his training and professional experience resembled that of other coroners. The residents of St. Louis elected Nidelet to serve as coroner in 1882 and 1884, and he had decades of experience as a physician by that time. Like other St. Louis coroners in this study, he attended medical school, having graduated from St. Louis University School of Medicine in 1852. He had also attended St. Louis Medical College. Nidelet gained medical experience in the Civil War, where he served as an assistant surgeon, surgeon, and chief surgeon for the Confederate Army. Serving for the Confederacy was likely a natural choice for Nidelet, whose father was a "gentleman" and a slaveholder who had lived in San Domingo for some time. As many former Confederates did, Nidelet ran for political office as a member of the Democratic Party. Sylvester Nidelet was licensed to practice medicine in Missouri, Virginia, and Illinois. When he died in 1906, Sylvester L. Nidelet's family buried him in a Catholic ceme- tery, and his Catholic faith may have impacted some, but not many, of his verdicts. For instance, when he rendered verdicts of suicide, he did not rou- tinely qualify them by determining that the deceased was insane. As will be discussed in chapter 3, determining that someone was insane when they died by suicide mitigated the stigma of the verdict and may have made possi- ble some burials in Catholic cemeteries.[18]

Although Nidelet's professional experiences provides few clues as to why he sympathized with Ann Donahoe, his other investigations provide evidence that he showed compassion for other middle-aged women, at least those whom he understood to be good wives and mothers. For example, in 1885, one year after he investigated Ann Donahoe's death, Nidelet rejected the conclu- sion after an autopsy that forty-six-year-old Matilda Reynolds had died from alcoholism—even though his own brother conducted that postmortem exam. Reynolds had vomited frequently before she died and had recently experienced hallucinations—both symptoms of dipsomania. However, in Reynolds's case, Nidelet had reason to suspect a possible homicide, unlike in the death of Ann Donahoe. The coroner believed that Reynolds's much-younger husband had poisoned her to acquire her property. He ordered a toxicology analysis, which showed that Reynolds had, in fact, been poisoned with arsenic—either by her own hand or by her husband's. Nidelet tried to convince the coroner's jury that Reynolds had been murdered, in part, by challenging witnesses' characteriza- tions of her as a heavy drinker and "fighting woman." As he led the inquest, Coroner Nidelet described Matilda Reynolds as "very quiet" and "a good busi- nesswoman" before she met her husband (and likely murderer). Nidelet even tried to prove that Reynolds's husband prompted her to drink heavily. Despite Nidelet's efforts, he did not convince the coroner's jury that Reynolds had died by homicide. Instead, they ruled her death to be a suicide. Nidelet's assertions that Reynolds was a good woman who had been swindled by her husband throughout the inquest illustrate that he showed compassion for some women who experienced alcoholism, however.[19]

Coroner Nidelet did not display such empathy for women who deviated from the gender norms of the time, particularly women who worked as pros- titutes. He did not consider these women to be insane when they died from alcohol-related deaths, even when witnesses testified that they drank, in part, because of grief, as Ann Donahoe did. Coroner Nidelet determined that

Maggie Tyler died "from the effects of alcoholism" on May 18, 1883. Tyler was a native-born white, thirty-year-old widow but resided in a brothel with primarily African American prostitutes during the last ten days of her life. An acquaintance told the coroner that she began to use alcohol and drugs more heavily after the death of her sister. Other witnesses observed that she had asthma, was in general poor physical health, and died because of her "long dissipated habits." Like Donahoe, who died a year later, Tyler was grieving a death and, as a widow, might have garnered some understanding from the coroner. Unlike Donahoe, however, witnesses told Coroner Nidelet that her "dissipation and other bad habits," such as opium use, caused her death, not her asthma or other physical ailments. While her use of alcohol and opium increased after her sister died, it was a roughly two-week period and, unlike Donahoe, Tyler grieved for a sibling, not her children. She did not have a special status as a mother. In fact, Tyler defied expectations of respectable white womanhood by working as a prostitute, freely associating with Blacks, and using alcohol and drugs regularly. Despite her grief, Coroner Nidelet did not consider her a dipsomaniac.[20]

Although the verdict that Coroner Sylvester Nidelet gave in the death of Ann Donahoe differed from other alcohol-related deaths, the other characteristics of the inquest were similar. When Coroner Sylvester Nidelet arrived at Donahoe's home in the late afternoon of February 29, 1884, he spoke to just two witnesses, an average number for an investigation into a death caused by alcohol use. Nidelet first interviewed Michael Donahoe, Ann's husband, who told the coroner that his wife had been physically ill for the previous two months, having severe stomach troubles, including vomiting and diarrhea. He told Nidelet that his wife "was in the habit of drinking stimulants and sometimes to excess" for the previous five years. Michael Donahoe testified that his wife "was a person of good constitution and health until she lost a couple of children some years ago and since that time has indulged in liquor to excess." He connected her recent ill health and death with her drinking and also provided a cause for her drinking: grief over the loss of her children. He told the coroner that a cup of coffee that morning set off "violent retching and vomiting" and that when he returned home, he thought that she was asleep and left her undisturbed. When the couple's son came home from work later that day, he discovered that his mother was dead.[21]

Additional witness testimony adds another possible contributor to Ann Donahoe's death: scarlet fever. After concluding his interview with Michael

Donahoe, Coroner Nidelet also interviewed a neighbor, likely to gather more evidence to render an accurate verdict. The inquest does not state why he did not interview Ann Donahoe's son, also named Michael Donahoe, although he discovered his mother's body, but it is possible that he gained enough information from her husband or that her son felt too distraught to talk to the coroner. The neighbor, William Ryan, provided his own negative opinion of Ann Donahoe's character as well as the facts of the case. He told Coroner Nidelet that he had known Ann Donahoe for two years, since the family had moved into rented rooms next to his. As had Michael Donahoe, Ryan noted that Ann Donahoe had fragile health, which the neighbor attributed to scarlet fever the previous October, "which left her in a weak condition." He added that Donahoe did not work for wages and was instead financially supported by her son. He stated that Donahoe "was in the habit of stimulating to excess but never interfered with anybody. I have frequently spoken to her upon this subject but she merely laughed at me and continued in the same way."[22]

William Ryan's testimony provided important information for Nidelet to render his verdict and illustrates that to her family and neighbors, Ann Donahoe had a reputation as a heavy drinker. First, his statements suggest that he believed that Donahoe was lazy and a drunk. He pointed out to the coroner that Ann Donahoe did not work for wages and "was supported almost altogether by her son," although it is unknown whether she engaged in paid labor. Most women, including working-class women, cared for their homes and families without working for wages in St. Louis in the 1880s, but most of her women neighbors did have paying jobs. Some working-class women who kept house also engaged in paid labor within the home, such as sewing or laundry, to supplement the male breadwinners' income, but Ann Donahoe evidently did not. Coroner Nidelet recorded her occupation as "housewife," and the inquest and census records suggest that both Ann Donahoe's son and husband financially supported the household. Second, the neighbor did not simply relay the facts of Ann Donahoe's last days but pointed out that he believed that she drank too much and had even warned her about the ill effects of her drinking, but to no avail. Finally, he offered a specific illness that may have, in fact, contributed to or caused her death: scarlet fever.[23]

Coroner Nidelet chose from several options when he rendered his verdict. The evidence presented made alcoholism the likeliest verdict, especially given Ann Donahoe's social location as a working-class woman with a history of heavy drinking, as well as an Irish immigrant an ethnicity that Americans often stereotyped as alcoholic. Nidelet also could have determined, based on the testimony of these two witnesses, that Ann Donahoe died from scarlet fever and excessive drinking or, less likely given the evidence presented at the inquest, simply scarlet fever. Typically, testimony from family members had more influence on a verdict than that of other witnesses, although as discussed in chapter 1, that was not always the case with natural deaths. In Donahoe's case, the two witnesses both attested to her regular drinking as well as digestive issues, both of which were hallmarks of dipsomania. In addition, Ann Donahoe's age of fifty was characteristic of dipsomania. Perhaps most important, her husband described her as a good, loving mother. Donahoe's age, gender, and social position as a mother likely prompted Coroner Nidelet to render this verdict, all information that her family provided in the inquest.[24]

The verdict of dipsomania mitigated some of the stigma attached to a death from alcoholism but did not eliminate it. Determining that Ann Donahoe died from a form of alcohol insanity was not the same as deciding that someone who died by suicide suffered from insanity, which absolved them of the intent to take their own life. Coroners already considered alcohol-related deaths to be unintentional. If Coroner Nidelet rendered his verdict out of sympathy or to eliminate the stigma attached to alcoholism, he could have determined that Ann Donahoe died from scarlet fever (or another physical illness) without mentioning alcohol at all. A more likely and accurate verdict, however, would have been similar to other verdicts in this study—an illness in addition to alcohol, such as "pneumonia and drink," or for several deaths during a heat wave, "heat and liquor." The St. Louis newspaper accounts offer no additional insight into this verdict. They did not even print an obituary, an omission common for men and, especially, women who died from alcoholism.[25]

The coroner's inquest into Ann Donahoe's death made public a struggle that many physicians and some historians have understood to be private: alcoholism among women. In the late nineteenth century, physicians who specialized in alcoholism believed that women often hid their drinking and even lied to their family doctors about it. Some historians have also argued that women's drinking was largely secretive, but this view has been challenged more recently by historians such as Patricia Prestwich, who points out that their drinking only appeared to be private, or even hidden, because many women drank at home, which was their workplace. Historian Michelle

McClellan has also emphasized the importance of understanding gender differences with regard to alcohol consumption and treatments for alcoholism. Experts perceived alcoholism as a male problem, McClellan argues, in the late nineteenth century and well into the twentieth, but women were not immune to an inability to resist strong desires to drink, despite repeated negative consequences and efforts to stop.[26]

Because of the assumption that alcoholism was a male affliction, however, there was a double standard for men and women who suffered from alcoholism. Many Americans, including specialists in treating addiction, believed that women who drank to excess were more dangerous than men because they threatened not only their own health and their families' well-being but their communities as well. According to this view, as mothers or future mothers, women needed to care for their children and provide an appropriate moral example for them. These ideas about motherhood stemmed from the notion of separate spheres of home and work, which were idealized by many Americans in the late nineteenth century, despite the growing number of women who attended college, worked for wages, and engaged in public activities like club work. Despite their compassion for their patients, physicians who specialized in treating alcoholism expressed concerns about women in particular because their drinking threatened their families as well as society as a whole. A mother who did not care for her children, husband, and home because of frequent drunkenness failed to prepare her children to contribute to society as adults. They also neglected their homes as well as their husbands and children, depriving their families of the moral center that guided them away from the vices of the public sphere. When women did receive treatment for alcoholism, specialists focused on returning women to their roles as wives and mothers.[27]

Another reason for the belief that women alcoholics posed a special threat to their families and communities came from prevalent beliefs about alcoholism as both a moral and medical problem. Many physicians who treated active and "reformed" alcoholics saw heavy drinking as a disease caused by insatiable cravings for alcohol. The view of alcoholism as disease-like contradicted the more prevalent, coexisting belief that it was a moral problem. Despite the dominant understanding among physicians who studied alcoholism as a disease, or at least disease-like, most Americans still saw individuals who regularly drank heavily as lacking morality and self-discipline. Ann Donahoe's neighbor, William Ryan, shared those views, as his remarks to the coroner about her drinking, refusal to work for wages, and dismissal of his warnings illustrate. Many St. Louis coroners likely shared these views as well, despite their medical education and practice. Coroners were not alcohol specialists and probably did not learn about alcoholism as a disease or addiction in medical school, so they were likely unable to understand these deaths in those terms.[28]

Although specialists believed that women alcoholics were more dangerous than men, they also believed that they were more vulnerable to dipsomania than their male counterparts. Dipsomania, as a form of insanity, absolved its sufferers of moral responsibility for excessive drinking; they could not control their urge to drink. Physicians who treated alcoholism argued that women were particularly susceptible to dipsomania because of their reproductive systems. Period medical journals described numerous cases of women with dipsomania who attempted to hide their drinking until they became so ill, often vomiting, having other digestive issues, and/ or hallucinating, that the family called a doctor who uncovered their secret drinking. Ann Donahoe exhibited these symptoms, although whether they were from alcohol alone or a recent bout with scarlet fever as well is unknown. Her husband's explanation for her drinking was not uncommon; many other relatives of women and physicians who treated them made similar claims, demonstrating that there was, in fact, a stigma toward alcoholics, and women alcoholics in particular, that they felt the need to mitigate. Ann Donahoe was fifty, and while her inquest did not indicate that she had recently experienced "the change of life" (as some inquests did), menopause could be one reason why Coroner Nidelet believed that she had this form of alcohol insanity.[29]

The temperance movement reinforced these stereotypes about men and women alcoholics, although the movement itself was small in St. Louis. Temperance advocates argued that women were the victims, not perpetrators, of alcoholism and its related problems, notably neglect and abuse of the family and failure to provide financially. Many middle-class, native-born women participated in the movement and also held to gender stereotypes about drunkenness, often believing that only Irish women drank. St. Louis lacked a large temperance movement. Even though the Women's Christian Temperance Union (WCTU) held its national conference in St. Louis in 1882, the movement was not active in the city. Most WCTU members lived in small towns outside of the city or even the state.[30]

Despite concern for alcohol addiction among physicians who specialized in its treatment, many Americans and residents of St. Louis blamed those who died from alcohol use for their deaths. While views were shifting toward a disease model of alcoholism in the late nineteenth century, that position existed alongside the long-held understanding of regular, heavy drinking as a moral failing. The compassion that some witnesses showed in their testimony before St. Louis coroners when friends, relatives, and neighbors died was rare. These witnesses either did not understand alcohol as an addiction or wanted to distance themselves from behavior that they understood as immoral. Like deaths from natural causes, many deaths from alcoholism occurred quietly at home and did not attract the attention of the press. When St. Louis newspapers did write rare accounts of these deaths, they tended to be brief and, often, laden with judgment of the deceased.

Although Coroner Sylvester Nidelet understood Ann Donahoe as someone who suffered from a disease, his view and her verdict were rare. No St. Louis newspaper reporter eulogized Ann Donahoe, who, probably like John Grady, fell asleep drunk and never woke up. While the coroner's ruling of dipsomania in the death of Ann Donahoe was unusual, the circumstances leading to her death were all too typical. Both Donahoe and Grady drank to the point of drunkenness on a regular basis. Donahoe's drinking interfered with her ability to care for herself and her children, and it is possible that Grady also struggled to care for himself—by keeping a job, for instance. She drank at home, perhaps more when her husband and son were at work, as other women did. Neither Donahoe nor Grady had many—if any—resources for help if they sought it out. The St. Louis press ignored both of their deaths and coroner's inquests, as they often did in deaths caused by alcohol use.[31]

But Ann Donahoe differed from the other men and women in my larger study. She was older than most, was perhaps menopausal, and had begun drinking after the death of two of her children, all factors that, for Coroner Nidelet, overcame her Irish ethnicity and working-class status to make her a somewhat sympathetic figure. He evidently saw her primarily as a good wife and mother, one whose love for her children drove her to drink when she lost them. He was familiar with the concept of dipsomania and decided that Donahoe was a special kind of alcoholic, one who was, in fact, insane. The verdict rendered Donahoe an object of pity rather than scorn, distinguishing her from most men and women who died from alcoholism.

CHAPTER THREE

"Whilst Laboring under Mental Derangement"

Coroners' Verdicts of Insanity, Suicide, and the Family

CHARLES P. JOHNSON RUSHED HOME from his law office at 4:00 P.M. on September 2, 1879, to attend to his wife, Estelle, whom he had just learned was very ill. She was being treated by Drs. Smith and Ware when he arrived. The physicians told Charles the reason for his wife's sickness: an intentional overdose of arsenic. Panicked, Charles asked, "Great God! Ese? Why did you do this?" and she replied, "Oh pet, I could not help it." His panic subsided when Estelle seemed to get better. Charles probably hoped that she would recover and finally overcome the melancholy from which she had suffered for months, since the death of their two-week-old daughter, who had been born prematurely. Charles returned to his office, confident of his wife's recovery, and came home that evening. Unfortunately, his hopes were soon dashed. Estelle grew worse and passed away at 10:00 that night, leaving behind her husband and four children. Charles attributed his wife's suicide to a "mania" due to the loss of their two-week-old child. He claimed that her mental illness became especially severe because of her devotion to her family, adding that "there was no nobler, and truer little wife, or a more kinder and affectionate mother."[1]

The next day, Coroner Hugo Auler arrived at the Johnsons' home to investigate her death. He examined Johnson's body and spoke to Charles, her mother-in-law, one of her daughters, a household servant, and Drs. Smith and Ware, the two physicians who treated her. These witnesses told the coroner about Johnson's grief over the loss of her daughter as well as a longer history of her mental health. Auler learned that she had attempted suicide before and had become addicted to opiates, which she initially took to treat insomnia. Her family members told Auler that Johnson had developed "signs of temporary aberration" two to three months before her suicide. Dr. Smith had cared for Johnson for some time, but her condition had not improved. She simply could not get over her grief of the loss of her baby or her addiction to opiates. Her relatives told Coroner Auler that Estelle Johnson was a religious woman who loved her family very much, but she was overcome by an "impulse" to die by suicide. Coroner Auler determined that Johnson died "from the effect of Poisoning by arsenic, administered by her own hands, result of mental aberration, caused by grief, at the death of her child."[2]

The suicide of Estelle Johnson is just one inquest that shows that St. Louis coroners rendered verdicts of suicide while suffering from insanity based on several factors, most notably the reputation of the deceased, the testimony of family members, and the investigating coroner. Instead of simply determining that men and women died by suicide, in a few cases, coroners added phrases such as "whilst suffering from mental derangement" or "while laboring under temporary insanity." The investigation into the death of Estelle Johnson, which resulted in an atypical verdict for a death by suicide, will be contrasted with that of Franz Kurrus, whose inquest is representative of a typical inquest into a death by suicide. Although Kurrus's family provided testimony that suggested that he may have experienced some kind of mental illness, the investigating coroner did not render a verdict of suicide because of insanity. The chapter will also feature a brief biography of Coroner Hugo Auler because he rendered most of these verdicts of suicide with an explanation of insanity. As this chapter will illustrate, coroners relied on the testimony of spouses, children, siblings, and parents to understand the mental state of the deceased at the time of their suicide. Coroners were more likely to render verdicts of insanity if these relatives used phrases such as "mental aberration" or "insanity" in their testimony, likely out of respect for the families and to mitigate the stigma of a suicide verdict.[3]

The reasons why coroners rendered verdicts of suicide attributed to insanity have seldom been studied by historians. An exception is Roger Lane, who observed that an insanity verdict provided a way for coroners to address a family's feelings when a loved one died by suicide in his study of violent deaths in late nineteenth-century Philadelphia. More often, historians have examined medical discourse surrounding suicide and insanity in the late nineteenth century. Historians such as Howard I. Kushner have pointed out that psychologists and psychiatrists often understood suicide as the result of mental illness, while sociologists blamed urbanization and the vague concepts of "civilization" or "modernity." Coroners, however, were not psychologists, nor were the friends, relatives, and neighbors whom they interviewed to determine how and why a person came to his or her death. Coroners sometimes determined that men and women died by suicide because of insanity, but they did so because of the testimony of family and friends, not because of medical diagnoses. In many cases, including that of Estelle Johnson, the deceased had no psychiatric care or a formal diagnosis of insanity. Although St. Louis coroners were medical and legal professionals, they were not trained as psychiatrists or psychologists, nor did they interview these specialists, unless a person died in an insane asylum, which happened rarely. Instead, interviews with witnesses—often family members—constituted the basis of their verdicts, including those believed to be caused by insanity.[4]

Coroner Hugo Auler and his colleagues had several options when they investigated sudden, violent, or unexpected deaths, including suspected suicides. Just as they did in cases of natural deaths and deaths from alcoholism, St. Louis coroners and deputy coroners examined the body and its surroundings to determine how and why a person died. If a cause of death was not apparent upon a physical examination or if they suspected poisoning, coroners could order an autopsy, which was performed by a local physician. They ordered autopsies and toxicology analyses more often in suspected suicides and other violent deaths than in cases of alcohol-related deaths or illness. In cases of suspected suicide, coroners interviewed friends, relatives, neighbors, and, on occasion, family physicians to determine if the deceased intentionally inflicted fatal injuries upon himself or herself. Coroners asked witnesses if the deceased had a history of threatening or attempting suicide and sometimes worked to understand the immediate cause of the suicide, such as grief or disappointment in love. Once death investigators had evidence that the deceased had, in fact, intentionally taken his or her own life, they rendered a verdict of suicide. In some instances, they rendered a verdict of suicide caused by insanity, physical illness, or another cause but, most often, simply wrote "suicide" or referred to an injury caused "by his/her own hands with the intention of taking his/her own life."[5]

Auler and other coroners relied on the statements of family members more than their own medical knowledge or the advice of other physicians to render verdicts of mental illness, which are what may be defined as a "qualified verdict." A qualified verdict refers to a verdict of suicide with an explanation of mental or physical illness—insanity, temporary insanity, grief, sickness, or a similar explanation for the suicide. Coroners did not have a clear definition of insanity or specific criteria to determine that someone was insane or temporarily insane. Coroners may have also rendered qualified verdicts to lessen the stigma of a suicide ruling, which could tarnish a family's reputation or prevent burial in a Catholic cemetery.[6]

Coroners rendered these qualified verdicts for a few reasons. First, most of these men and women had family members to explain to the coroner why they died by suicide—grief, melancholy, or, for men, a loss of employment. Second, relatives, neighbors, and friends told Coroner Auler and his colleagues that these men and women were respected members of their communities—they represented the ideals of manhood and womanhood at the time. It is noteworthy that every wife and mother and most husbands and fathers in this study received a qualified verdict from the investigating coroner. Family members, friends, and newspaper reporters described these women and men as loving and devoted to their families. Finally, in each case, family members told investigating coroners that their loved ones suffered from what they understood to be insanity. Family members and coroners searched for a root cause for deaths by suicide, something they did not always do in other death investigations, particularly deaths caused by alcohol use or deaths from natural causes.[7]

Women were less likely to die by suicide than were men because men tended to use more lethal means, such as firearms. In the nineteenth century, social scientists and medical experts often claimed that women died by suicide less often than men because they were protected from the harsh effects of civilization and modernity within the home. However, historians have shown that, in fact, women attempted and contemplated suicide as often as men.[8]

While understandings of insanity and suicide varied by gender, it is difficult to determine whether they also varied by race because few African Americans appear in coroners' inquests with verdicts of suicide. One possible reason is that African Americans were a small part of the St. Louis population in the nineteenth century and appear less often in all inquests than do native-born and immigrant white men and women. But there is also evidence that part of the reason that there are fewer suicide verdicts for African Americans is because coroners did not expect them to die by suicide. One deputy coroner, Herman Praedicow, told the *St. Louis Post-Dispatch* in 1882 that he knew of no Black men and women to die by suicide in his twenty years in the St. Louis Office of the Coroner. Coroner's office statistics also show that

African Americans received fewer suicide verdicts than did their white counterparts. In an annual report issued by Coroner Sylvester Nidelet in 1883, 121 African Americans appear among 670 inquests for the year, but zero were listed among the sixty-nine suicides. The following year, two African Americans were counted among a total of eighty-one suicides. Whether or not these statistics are accurate is unknown, and there is some evidence that coroners ruled some suicides as accidental deaths.[9]

While race may have been a factor that contributed to qualified verdicts, one factor that certainly did was that of the investigating coroner. Some coroners rendered more qualified verdicts than others. Coroner Hugo V. Auler rendered more verdicts of suicide while suffering from insanity than any other coroner in this study. Auler was an experienced coroner, having been elected to the position three times. He was also a knowledgeable physician, working in private practice and also as a professor when he did not hold political office as coroner. He earned a degree in medicine from St. Louis Medical College in 1865, after serving in the medical corps for the Union during the Civil War. While he studied medicine, it is unlikely that he also studied psychiatry. In the mid-nineteenth century, physicians served as residents in psychiatric facilities if they pursued psychiatry as a specialty; few colleges and universities offered courses in the field. Auler was similar to other coroners in that he was an experienced, well-trained physician, meaning it is unlikely that his medical training alone is the reason why he determined that so many men and women suffered from insanity when they took their own lives, when contrasted with other coroners at the time.[10]

Auler's faith and background may have contributed to his decision to render more verdicts of suicide while experiencing insanity than other coroners. Both of his parents were German immigrants, and he was of the Catholic faith. His faith may have been one reason that he was especially concerned about burial rites and the perceived sin of suicide. His German heritage may have been another reason, as several men and women who received verdicts of insanity were buried in German Lutheran or Evangelical cemeteries. It is impossible to determine exactly why Coroner Auler believed that more men and women suffered from insanity than his colleagues, but the fact that he did illustrates that verdicts of insanity were somewhat arbitrary and varied by coroner.[11]

Coroner Auler was similar to other coroners and deputy coroners in that he distinguished between men and women whom he understood to be insane and those whom he did not. These understandings were largely based on family relationships, including marital status, especially for women. Unmarried men and women were less likely receive qualified verdicts from investigating coroners than their married counterparts, as were married men who abused their wives or children. These men and women violated family norms and were also less likely to have sympathetic relatives to testify on their behalf. Even in cases in which there was evidence that their suicides were impulsive decisions and/or that they had a history of mental illness, coroners seldom determined that these men and women suffered from insanity or temporary insanity.

Interestingly, coroners almost never granted qualified verdicts to women who worked as prostitutes, again because their reputations mattered as much as—if not more than—the circumstances surrounding their deaths. Auler is no exception to this trend. Even though he rendered far more verdicts of suicide caused by insanity or temporary insanity, the only explanation that he gave for the suicide of a prostitute was "intoxication."[12]

Verdicts of insanity were likely also out of respect for the faith of the deceased and their families. St. Louis was a predominantly Catholic city, and while only a few coroners were Catholic, including Hugo Auler and Sylvester Nidelet, who was discussed in chapter 2, they likely respected the beliefs of the families of the men and women whose deaths they investigated. Most Judeo-Christian sects stigmatized suicide in the nineteenth century and some, such as the Catholic faith, had doctrines that deemed it to be a sin. However, suicide was considered a sin only if one was sane when they committed the act. If one was understood to be insane, then that person did not commit a sin because a rational, conscious decision was not made to take his or her own life. Until recently, Catholic churches did not allow the burial of those who died by suicide in Church cemeteries, although there were often exceptions made for those who were determined by officials—including coroners—to be insane. Religious proscriptions against suicide changed over time. By the late nineteenth century, there was an increased sympathy for people who died by suicide, and burials in sanctified grounds were common, although practices varied.[13]

Qualified verdicts were not simply given to ensure a church burial, however. Three people who received verdicts of insanity were buried in the Potter's Field, and several people were buried in church cemeteries who did not receive a qualified verdict. While church burial or a family's social position was one reason for these verdicts of insanity, they were not the only reasons. Most of the men and women who died by suicide in this study whose faith could be determined were Protestant, but most Protestant sects had stigmas against suicide, even if they permitted burials in church cemeteries. Only one person in this study received burial in a Catholic cemetery, and he received a verdict of suicide caused by insanity. Regardless of the verdict they received, most of these men and women were buried in church cemeteries, with others being interred in Bellefontaine or other nondenominational cemeteries.[14]

A verdict of suicide without qualification did not prevent Franz Kurrus's family from laying him to rest in Old St. Markus Cemetery, a German Evangelical Cemetery, in 1884. Kurrus, unlike men and women who received verdicts of insanity, did not garner the sympathy of Coroner Sylvester Nidelet, who investigated his suicide. Kurrus deviated from the ideal male breadwinner and protector of his family by abusing his wife and failing to provide for his family. Witnesses considered Kurrus's decision to shoot himself in the head on October 28, 1884, to be impulsive, but Coroner Sylvester Nidelet did not render a verdict of temporary insanity. Like Auler, Nidelet was of the Catholic faith and did determine that some men and women were insane when they died, although not nearly as many as Coroner Auler. But he did not believe that Kurrus was insane, although there was some evidence in the witness testimony that would have supported such a verdict.

Franz Kurrus is one of a few men and women who left a suicide note, and he claimed that he took his own life because he had been wronged by his wife. The forty-six-year-old left for work on the morning of October 28, 1884, but returned home to ask his wife for money, which he evidently spent on alcohol. When he came home that afternoon, ostensibly for lunch with his family, he was agitated and drunk. Ignoring his meal, Kurrus sat down at the dining room table and wrote a letter to his brothers, August and Constant. He wrote, "This is my last will. Take care of my children as well as you can so far as it reaches. I was badly swindled and wronged by my present wife and by her company George Hekel." He referred to Fredericka Kurrus as his "present wife" because he had been widowed seven years earlier. He told his brothers that he had $2,000 in life insurance and carefully listed the details for them. He told them that the money belonged to his children from his first and second marriages. He closed by saying, "God help you all." Kurrus evidently did not trust his wife, as he asked his brothers to care for his six living children—three from his first marriage and three from his second. He wrote a second note to his children, saying, "Children think of me and bring me to my beloved wife and mother. Forgive the step that I take. Your father."[15]

After writing the letters, Kurrus stood up and left the table, telling his wife that he wanted no more to eat. He walked into the bedroom and grabbed his revolver. His wife, terrified that he would finally follow through on his threats to shoot himself, begged him "to do nothing rash."[16] He then threatened to shoot her. Kurrus returned to the dining room, kissed his children and told them goodbye, then went into the front room and shot himself in the head. He lived for only about ten minutes, his wife told Coroner Nidelet, when he conducted his investigation the following day at the city morgue. Coroner Nidelet determined that Kurrus had died "from the effects of a gunshot wound of the brain inflicted by a ball fired from a pistol in his own hands with the intent of taking his own life." Nidelet made no remarks about Kurrus's mental health or any other cause for his suicide in his verdict.[17]

Coroner Nidelet learned a great deal about Franz Kurrus while investigating his death, but nothing that convinced him that the man suffered from insanity. Nidelet learned that the Kurruses had been fighting a great deal in the weeks before his death, particularly after he lost his business as a cooper who made and sold beer kegs and barrels. He had found another job working for someone else but complained to his wife that it was "very hard and laborious work." Not only did Kurrus increase his drinking after he lost his business, but he verbally and physically abused his wife. He was also forced to move his family to different rented homes, and he often could not pay the rent. Kurrus felt desperate. The family was about to be evicted from their latest home when Kurrus died by suicide.[18]

Kurrus's act was evidently committed on impulse and, perhaps, under the influence of alcohol. His suicide could have been considered an act of temporary insanity or one caused by intoxication, but Coroner Nidelet rendered a suicide verdict without a qualifying statement for a few probable reasons. First, Kurrus strayed from the ideal male role as a breadwinner and protector. His wife told Nidelet that the couple "lived pleasantly and happily together" when the couple had money, but such had not been the case for the past four years. He took $575 of his wife's money that had been sent from Germany four years before his death and quickly spent it. Since then, "he has used me very badly and last fall hit me until the blood came out of my mouth and nose." Instead of providing for his family, Kurrus complained that his wife cost him money and told her to "go out washing and try to get bread in the house and help support the family," although it is unclear if Fredericka earned wages. Second, the family did not have a notable reputation in the community. Nor does it appear as though burial rites were at stake. The Kurrus family was poor, relatively new to St. Louis, and of a German Evangelical faith.[19] Perhaps Coroner Nidelet did not believe that he needed to mitigate the stigma of a suicide verdict. Finally, the two witnesses in the death investigation—Kurrus's wife and oldest son—made no claims that Kurrus was insane.[20]

And yet, their statements to the coroner suggested a mental illness of some kind. Kurrus had previously threatened to die by suicide, "when he was out of work and money and under the influence of liquor," his wife testified. If previous suicide threats were not enough, Franz Kurrus also evidently believed that he had spoken with his deceased wife just days before his death. He visited his late wife's grave and asked her what he should do, since he believed that his current wife was unfaithful. Evidently, his deceased wife replied that he was unhappy in his marriage and confirmed his suspicions that his current wife had "swindled him." He had his revolver with him and immediately concluded that he should shoot himself, although it does not seem as though he believed his deceased wife advised him to do so. However, he changed his mind, deciding to talk to his current wife, Fredericka, before he died by suicide. Fredericka Kurrus told Coroner Nidelet, "I could not tell whether he was drunk or of unsound mind. I told him it was impossible to talk to the dead and he answered he thought so too until he found it to be otherwise." Kurrus's fourteen-year-old son, William, corroborated his stepmother's statements regarding Kurrus's conversation with his deceased wife, intoxication, verbal and physical abuse of his wife, and recent threats of suicide. Nidelet may have concluded that Franz Kurrus was, in fact, intoxicated when he believed that he spoke to his deceased wife because he rendered a verdict of suicide without any mention of insanity.[21]

Newspaper reporters offered Franz Kurrus none of the sympathy that they gave to respectable men and women who died by suicide, writing brief, unsympathetic accounts of his death. They did offer some details of his death and explanations for his suicide, however. A reporter for the *St. Louis Globe-Democrat* attributed his suicide to his loss of work, writing that losing his job was "more than he could endure." The *St. Louis Post-Dispatch* wrote only three sentences in an article titled, "Why He Killed Himself," and concluded that he did so "because he had been swindled by relations," meaning his wife, presumably. The reporter did note that he was a member of two fraternal organizations in Quincy, Illinois, but said nothing about loved ones he left behind, being central to his community, or any of the other kind phrases that the press offered other men and women, including Estelle Johnson.[22]

Kurrus's case and a verdict of suicide with no qualification is more typical of the suicide verdicts in this study than are those with qualified verdicts. He was a German immigrant, although he became a naturalized citizen in 1866, just a few years after arriving to the United States. He had lived in the St. Louis area for over twenty years but did not come from a prominent, well-known Missouri family. Perhaps most important, he did not provide for and protect his family as was expected of a man in the late nineteenth century. Kurrus, unlike many immigrants whose deaths appear in coroners' inquests, had relatives to testify before the coroner. But those relatives described an angry, drunken man, not one who suffered from insanity—temporary or otherwise. Kurrus's relatives, unlike men who received qualified verdicts, did not describe him as "kind" and hardworking.[23]

The inquest into the death of Estelle Johnson differed dramatically from that of Franz Kurrus, as she received a qualified verdict as well as the compassion of her family and community. Johnson was not of the Catholic faith, but she was a respected, prominent member of her community and active in her church, all reasons why she received a verdict of suicide caused by insanity. Estelle Johnson's case was especially unusual when compared to the suicides of other women and men because she was the wife of the former lieutenant governor of Missouri and received a lengthy coroner's inquest. Charles Johnson was also a well-known defense attorney in St. Louis. Estelle Johnson came from a wealthy political family from Washington, D.C. Her husband left behind a paper collection that includes diaries—offering a rare glimpse into the family's lives before and after Johnson's death. Like the suicides of other men and women, relatives, friends, and newspaper reporters looked to find a cause that drove her to take her own life, and her race, class, and gender shaped their interpretation. She was a respectable, upper-middle-class, native-born white woman and a mother who was grieving for a deceased child, so it was easy for her husband, family members, and reporters to conclude that her grief must be what drove her to take a lethal dose of arsenic.[24]

Relatives, reporters, and Coroner Hugo Auler believed that Johnson was insane when she died by suicide, in part because she was a mother. In

Johnson's case and in other cases of mothers who died by suicide, witnesses, reporters, and even coroners blamed grief, insanity, illness, or, in some cases, bad husbands for the suicides of these women. The causes of suicide are multiple and complex and cannot be reduced to a single factor, although friends, relatives, coroners, and newspaper reporters often sought to find one reason or at least a "triggering event" that drove a person to take his or her own life. White, middle- and upper-class mothers were supposed to love their children and husbands and care for them; the gender system in the late nineteenth century depended on that. Men were supposed to provide for and protect their wives and children—sometimes even from themselves. When mothers did not fulfill this idealized role by killing themselves, friends, relatives, coroners, and newspaper reporters often described them as suffering from insanity. This differs markedly from the suicides of fathers, whom people often believed killed themselves because they were out of work and thus unable to provide for their families. In Estelle Johnson's case, she may well have experienced postpartum depression—a phenomenon that was not yet understood by the new field of psychiatry and is still little understood. In the late nineteenth century, relatives and her treating physicians considered her sadness to be "melancholy."[25]

Johnson was one of several men and women whose relatives described her as having a long history of what they understood to be "insanity," "melancholy," "despondency," or "mania." Coroners relied on this witness testimony to determine that a man or a woman died by suicide while suffering from insanity or temporary insanity. In the months leading up to Johnson's suicide, there is some evidence that she suffered from what would be understood today to be mental illness, although her husband did not use that language. He documented in his diary that she was frequently sick and sometimes had what he called "the blues." She raised four children—two daughters and two sons—although she had given birth to nine children. The couple lost five of those children. According to her husband, Estelle Johnson maintained a warm, comfortable home, frequently shared long talks with her husband, traveled regularly, and managed household servants. Newspaper reporters described her as "open," "loving," and "the domestic wife and the best of mothers." Her husband called her his "darling little wife" who contributed to the fact that "in domestic surroundings no man was Ever more happily situated."[26]

Charles Johnson felt devastated when his "Essie" died on the night of September 2, 1879. Although she had been treated by a physician before she died, her death was unexpected and a probable suicide, which is likely why the St. Louis Coroner's Office sent Hugo Auler to investigate. Auler interviewed six witnesses to determine how and why Johnson died. Six was a fairly large number of witnesses for a coroner to interview. They often spoke to two to four people when working to determine how and why a person died, often a combination of relatives, neighbors, treating physicians, and, of course, anyone who was a literal witness to the death.

When Estelle Johnson poisoned herself on September 2, 1879, her family immediately attributed it to a form of temporary insanity caused by the death of her two-week-old daughter, even though she had been suicidal for months—ever since her baby's death. Even before her daughter died, she was distressed because she feared that the baby would not live because she was born prematurely. In most cases, "temporary" insanity referred to a seemingly hasty decision to take one's life, not someone who had been contemplating it for months, but the family described her suicide as a sudden, impulsive decision, and the coroner noted that. Johnson's husband, mother-in-law, and household servants struggled during the months before her death to prevent her from taking her own life. They took turns watching her in hopes of ensuring that she did not die by suicide.[27]

Estelle Johnson had a loving husband and a team of relatives and servants to care for her and watch for suicide attempts, but they could not prevent her suicide. After the Johnsons' prematurely delivered daughter died at only two weeks old, Charles recognized that his wife was under great distress. He became alarmed when she attempted to die by suicide by taking laudanum two months before her death. In an effort to prevent future suicide attempts, he tried to encourage his wife's recovery by traveling to visit her parents and siblings in her hometown of Washington, D.C., and to travel to New York and other areas on the East Coast. The trip helped her immensely, and Johnson was "greatly improved," yet every time she saw a baby, she became despondent again. Charles Johnson's efforts to cheer his wife through travel were common to treat melancholy in the late nineteenth century. After their return to St. Louis, Johnson still felt "miserable" and, in late August, drank morphine. She claimed that it was to ease her misery and not a suicide attempt, but Charles was understandably concerned that she was lying.[28]

The entire family and servants kept a close watch on Estelle Johnson to make sure that she did not make another suicide attempt. On the Sunday before her death, Charles believed that his wife was feeling much better. Her improved mood did not last, however, or was perhaps a result of her decision to take a fatal dose of arsenic. She had obtained arsenic before their trip east and on September 2, 1879, managed to hide it in the folds of her dress and slip it into her tea without her family's knowledge. Her family did not know that she had poisoned herself until she began to show symptoms. They immediately summoned Drs. Ware and Smith, who did everything they could to save Estelle but could not. Despite their efforts to treat her, Estelle Johnson died that night.[29]

Johnson's family immediately explained her suicide as an impulsive act caused by grief, even though her numerous suicide attempts that year suggested that she had long been planning to take her own life. Her mother-in-law told Coroner Auler that Johnson had taken arsenic on impulse and immediately regretted it because she told her, "'Ma, I am afraid I'll die this time'" and "afterwards prayed fervently, and asked to be forgiven." She said that she believed that her act was "under the impulse of the moment." Johnson's daughter, Elvira, added that the previous Sunday that her mother had asked her to pray for her because "she was anxious to get over her feeling of misery." She struggled with her love for her family and her faith, but also her overwhelming sadness. Despite these attachments and possible religious proscriptions against suicide, Johnson felt that her only choice was to take her own life.[30]

Her family probably told Coroner Hugo Auler that Estelle Johnson was a good wife and mother, a religious woman, and one who was temporarily insane not only because they believed it to be true but also because they likely hoped to reduce the stigma of her suicide. Coroner Auler listened. He determined that Estelle Johnson died "from the effect of Poisoning by arsenic, administered by her own hands, result of mental aberration, caused by grief, at the death of her child."[31]

There was no medical basis for Auler's verdict of suicide while suffering from insanity. Drs. Ware and Smith, the physicians who had been treating Johnson for some time, discussed only her symptoms, evidence of arsenic poisoning, their efforts to treat her, and her death in their testimony before the coroner. They mentioned nothing about insanity. Johnson's family, however, told the coroner about a history of despondency since her last child died. Coroner Auler took her family's testimony seriously.[32]

The local newspapers wrote sympathetic accounts, but considering her family's prominence, they likely would have even if she had not received a verdict of insanity. Even though several men and women who died by suicide, especially mothers, gained sympathy, there was still a stigma attached to suicide during the late nineteenth century, one that seems to have been softened if these men and women were understood to be insane. In an article titled, "A Sad Death," the *St. Louis Post-Dispatch* attributed Estelle Johnson's death to "melancholia consequent on the Death of a Child." The reporter described Johnson as a "lady" who had a "large circle of friends, who were drawn towards her by her cheerful happy nature and her amiable life." The reporter added that "her husband was envied as much then [when she was alive] as he is sympathized with now in his bereavement." The reporter concluded by noting that Charles Johnson did not wish to discuss the "very painful subject," instead preferring to provide details about his wife's death via the coroner's inquest. The St. Louis press was not known for its sensitivity in times of crisis in the late nineteenth century, illustrating the respect that the reporter had for the family of the former lieutenant governor of Missouri.[33]

Although the Johnson family had more community, political, and financial resources than most residents of St. Louis, tragedy nonetheless struck the family. A respectful newspaper article and coroner's verdict of insanity helped reduce the stigma of her suicide and honor the family, however. Estelle Johnson was understood by her family and community to be the epitome of a good mother and wife. In contrast, the relatives of Franz Kurrus provided testimony that depicted him as a failure as a husband and father.[34]

The reputations of Johnson and Kurrus are just one reason why one of them was understood to be insane and the other was not. Coroners did not render verdicts of insanity with consistency; they each had their own set of criteria. One common factor, however, was the statements of family members that their loved ones had suffered from some kind of "melancholy," "mental aberration," or "insanity." While Kurrus's wife and son gave statements that indicated he may have suffered from some kind of mental illness, Johnson's family explicitly told the coroner that she suffered from a "mania" and "despondency." While insanity was a medical term, albeit a nebulous one, these cases show that when coroners determined that men and women suffered from insanity, it was because of testimony from their family members, not physicians. But even testimony from relatives was not enough to overcome perceived shortcomings in one's character. Estelle Johnson was a grieving mother who deserved sympathy. Franz Kurrus was a neglectful, abusive husband who, apparently, did not.

This map shows the city boundaries of St. Louis in 1876. Courtesy of the Missouri History Museum, St. Louis, Missouri.

The city jail as it looked in 1870. Courtesy of the Missouri History Museum, St. Louis, Missouri.

Dr. James Nidelet, a physician who routinely performed autopsies for the Office of the Coroner. He served in leadership roles for the Board of Police Commissioner and was the brother of Dr. Sylvester Nidelet, coroner from 1882 to 1886. Courtesy of the Missouri History Museum, St. Louis, Missouri.

Charles P. Johnson, lieutenant governor of Missouri from 1873 to 1875. He was the husband of Estelle Johnson, who died by suicide in 1879, after the sudden death of their prematurely born daughter. Courtesy of the Library of Congress, Washington, D.C.

A SAD DEATH.

Suicide of Mrs. Charles P. Johnson Last Night.

The Lady, Suffering from Melancholia Consequent on the Death of a Child,

Takes a Fatal Dose of Arsenic, and Passes Away.

The *St. Louis Post-Dispatch* wrote a sympathetic article about Estelle Johnson's death in 1879. "A Sad Death." *St. Louis-Post Dispatch*, September 3, 1879, 1.

An ad for Pennyroyal Pills, a commonly used abortifacient, from *The Washington Post* in 1884. Ads such as these discreetly advertised their product nationwide. "Display Ad 4—No Title." *The Washington Post*, October 14, 1884, 4.

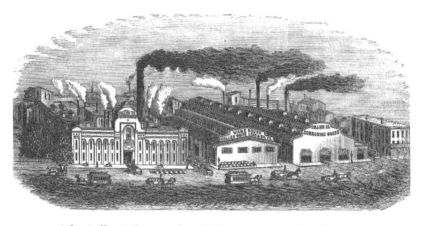

The Collier White Lead and Oil Company in 1878. Courtesy of the Missouri History Museum, St. Louis, Missouri.

BLOWN UP.

Terrible Explosion at the Collier White Lead Works.

Exciting Scenes—Hunting for the Buried Workmen.

The *St. Louis Post-Dispatch* wrote an article about the explosion at the Collier White Lead Works. John Brennan was still alive, but seriously injured, at the time of this report. "Blown Up." *The St. Louis Post-Dispatch*, June 5, 1876, 4.

This lead bar from the St. Louis Shot Tower Company is similar to the one that Henry Diekhoener would have worked with in 1881. Courtesy of the Missouri History Museum, St. Louis, Missouri.

CHAPTER FOUR

"With the Intention of Producing an Abortion"

Coroners as Enforcers of Abortion Laws in St. Louis, Missouri

ANNIE ROBERTS LAY IN BED suffering from "pains all over" on the night of December 3, 1878, while her fiancé, Reuben Underwood, waited at her side. He had come to her room in a St. Louis boardinghouse perhaps still hoping that Annie, just twenty-five years old, would recover.[1] But she no longer held out hope. Realizing the time remaining to them was short, she spoke her last words to Underwood and then she died from the surgery that she had wanted to keep hidden from him.[2]

Roberts had requested help from two physicians—Stephen Metcalf and William Stapp—but neither attended her that night as she grew increasingly ill. While both men had helped her earlier when she sought their care, they chose not to be present when she died. The reason was simple: they had helped her procure an illegal abortion. Roberts had asked Metcalf to perform the procedure days before her death, on November 26, and he referred her to Stapp, who frequently performed abortions. Roberts feared that her fiancé would leave her if he learned that she was pregnant with another man's child, prompting her to seek an abortion. While her reasons for having an abortion were unique to her life and circumstances, Roberts's decision was a common one in the late nineteenth century, particularly among married women who already had children.[3]

A gap existed between abortion practice and policy in late nineteenth-century Missouri. Much earlier, in 1825, the state's lawmakers had criminalized the use of abortifacients. The law was supported, in fact advocated, by physicians concerned for the well-being of their patients. Missouri and other states subsequently expanded their laws to include more types of abortion, yet women continued to perform abortions upon themselves as well as

to seek them from medical practitioners. Statutes intended to prevent malpractice targeted physicians and midwives who performed abortions, while
treating the women who sought abortions as their victims. But the laws often went unenforced, and even in fatal cases such as Roberts's, criminal
abortion was difficult to prosecute. Coroners, police officers, and prosecutors had to collect substantial evidence that a physician or midwife performed an abortion and that the abortion caused a woman's death. And
although that evidence might clearly demonstrate that a practitioner was
guilty of malpractice, it was still difficult to secure a conviction in a court of
law. These circumstances surrounding the policies and legal processes regu-
lating abortion both shaped and were shaped by the experiences and choices
of women like Annie Roberts.

Although Missouri law in the 1870s made drug-induced, instrumental,
and surgical abortions illegal at all stages of pregnancy, the general public,
physicians, and law enforcement often tolerated the practice of abortion—
except in cases of supposed malpractice. This was true not only in Missouri
but also in most states. After all, most women remained healthy following
abortions they had obtained or performed on themselves. The term "abortion" is used in this essay as historians James C. Mohr and Leslie Reagan de-
fine it: "the purposeful ending of pregnancy at every stage."[4] Although many
antiabortion physicians claimed that abortionists specialized in the practice,
many abortion providers were in fact practicing obstetricians and gynecologists who performed abortions along with other services. Officials worked to
prosecute physicians for abortions, however, if their patients were injured or
died. Coroners investigated some of these deaths, leaving behind a record of a
largely hidden practice that was nevertheless fairly commonplace.[5]

Physicians across the country joined the effort to criminalize abortion in
the nineteenth century. Medical and legal experts held various views on why
women sought abortions: some passionately argued that so-called evil women
were to blame, while others advocated contraception or sex education to prevent unwanted pregnancies or, failing that, education about fetal development
to dissuade women from seeking abortions. But they agreed on a few key
points. First, criminal abortion was a social problem that had to be solved.
Second, despite stereotypes and sensationalistic stories about unmarried
pregnant women, they believed, and used evidence to support their claim,
that married women who already had children and did not want another

accounted for most abortions. In addition, most of the experts believed that abortions had become more prevalent in the late nineteenth century.[6]

As the historian James C. Mohr argues, physicians lobbied for state laws against abortion for a variety of reasons. Many of them wanted to protect women from dangerous procedures, but they also sought to avoid losing patients to other doctors who were willing to perform abortions. They worked to create a professional niche for themselves as obstetricians and gynecologists and to eliminate competition from so-called irregular physicians and midwives, particularly after the formation of the American Medical Association in 1847. As physicians began to create professional standards and organizations, they turned to the law to regulate each other. New research about pregnancy created a general belief among many physicians that life began at conception and the law should protect fetal life at all stages. These doctors dismissed the traditional "quickening doctrine," which held that abortion was moral as long as it was before "quickening"—the moment when a mother could feel the fetus move, around the fourth month of a pregnancy. In this way, the beliefs of many physicians overshadowed the experiences of women that had been respected for centuries.[7]

But the concerns of physicians who opposed abortion were not simply driven by professional motives and moral concerns. Some also worried about "race suicide"—that the birth rate was declining among married middle- and upper-class white, Protestant women while it increased among African American and immigrant women, particularly Catholics. Many also feared the destabilization of gender conventions and believed that abortion made it possible for women to avoid motherhood.[8]

As the historian Leslie Reagan observes, however, while many physicians advocated for laws against abortion and joined the American Medical Association and other organizations that supported these efforts, doctors also were performing abortions in response to women's needs, their own consciences, and their fear of losing paying patients. In addition, physicians could legally perform therapeutic abortions—those to save the life of the mother—an exception added to Missouri abortion laws in the 1840s. Physicians had the sole discretion as to what constituted a therapeutic abortion.[9] Yet when it came to malpractice, St. Louis coroners and district attorneys did not tolerate any motives for performing abortions but sought to convict abortionists of violating Missouri law.

Missouri was a national leader in creating and strengthening laws against abortion. The 1825 law made it the second state to criminalize abortion, following Connecticut. This initial Missouri law targeted poisonous abortifacients because they harmed and even killed women. Lawmakers revised the statute in 1835, adding the criminalization of abortions performed with surgical instruments, but only after quickening. A decade later, lawmakers specified that physicians, midwives, or anyone else who performed an abortion was committing a crime, whether they used drugs or an instrument. But legislators also relaxed the law by adding that physicians could perform therapeutic abortions to save a woman's life. Later revisions to the statute altered the prescribed punishments, making them harsher if a doctor or midwife performed an abortion after quickening. The Missouri statutes in 1872, 1879, and 1889 all declared that if an abortion provider harmed a woman after quickening, he or she would be charged with first-degree manslaughter; only misdemeanor charges were brought for harm caused by an abortion performed before quickening. The physician or midwife could face murder charges if the mother died as a result of the procedure, however, and the statutes did not specify whether quickening mattered in that case. Lawmakers probably expected charges to be filed soon after the procedure when they could connect an abortion to a specific person, most likely a midwife or physician. While these later laws established more specific punishments, their substance changed little. Missouri abortion laws always targeted physicians and midwives, not the women who sought abortions.[10]

Although lawmakers sought to prevent such deaths, it was uncommon for women to die from abortions. Coroners in St. Louis investigated far fewer abortions than suicides, accidents, homicides, or other causes of death. Only four deaths from abortion appeared in the original sample of 868 cases for this study, and all four were analyzed for this chapter. In fact, of the tens of thousands of inquests into the deaths of men and women in St. Louis conducted by coroners between 1845 and 1900, only 180 verdicts mention "abortion" in the cause of death. Because abortion was a medical term, these numbers include "spontaneous" or "accidental" abortions, which would today be called miscarriages. Of these 180 inquests, coroners only investigated the deaths of 40 women; the other 140 were conducted on fetuses and infants, some of whose identities were unknown. As with other causes of death, the verdicts are inconsistent and vary by coroner; some list the cause of death as "homicide, self-induced abortion" or "criminal abortion," while others simply say "abortion." Coroners, rather than deputy coroners, often investigated deaths from abortion. When a midwife or physician could have been liable for the death, they convened a coroner's jury, just as they did with homicides. Because there are few records for the illegal procedure, it is impossible to determine how many women terminated their pregnancies or died as a result, but historians estimate that abortion was about as safe as childbirth. Women were also more likely to die from self-induced abortions than from those performed by a physician or midwife.[11]

By the 1870s and 1880s, there were several options for abortifacients for home use or as administered by a midwife or physician. Advertising in magazines and newspapers, home health guides, and stories from other women informed women about these options. Commercially available compounds and pills included "Pennyroyal Pills," "Chichester's Diamond Brand Pills," and "Tansy and Pennyroyal Compound Pills." These pills, as well as other various compounds that women could buy from druggists or obtain from abortionists, contained various herbs and plants, such as pennyroyal, tansy, ergot, snakeroot, cottonroot, and savin, which come from the juniper plant. Some concoctions featured iron as well. Advertisers often claimed that these remedies could "unblock" the menses, causing bleeding, and either restore normal periods or, if menstruation was "blocked" because of pregnancy, cause a miscarriage. More often, they caused severe vomiting, which women and druggists believed might also cause the uterus to expel a fetus. By the late nineteenth century, many regular physicians would not prescribe these compounds because they could be harmful to the mother and were seldom effective. Women still used these drugs, however, because they did not know that they were ineffective or were desperate to end an unwanted pregnancy and hoped that these remedies would work. These drugs and compounds were also likely easier to use and safer than instruments women could use at home—catheters, elm bark, knitting or crochet needles, or even scissors. In some cases, such as with Annie Roberts, abortionists provided drugs as a first strategy, then turned to instruments if these compounds failed to work, which was often the case.[12]

The women in this chapter shared more in common than dying from abortions: all were poor or working class, which made abortions dangerous for them because it was difficult to access safe, professional medical care. Poor and working-class women were also less likely than their middle and upper-class counterparts to have family physicians to create false death certificates to avoid public knowledge of the procedure. While it is impossible to determine how often physicians concealed abortions by attributing a death to another cause, it appears to have been fairly common. Not only did this practice protect the privacy of these women and their families, but it also meant that coroners would not conduct an inquest into their deaths. Besides their class positions, these women also shared similar family dynamics. Every woman was already a mother when she became pregnant for the last time, yet they were all also either separated from their husbands or unmarried. They were not adding to happy families with these pregnancies, which is why at least three were unwanted. One drank heavily, while another was married to a man who probably would have been considered an alcoholic. Two worked as prostitutes or at least in brothels—fitting the stereotype of the fallen woman who would seek an abortion, yet the press did not write sensationalistic accounts demonizing these women, instead writing brief and even somewhat sympathetic accounts. Like women who died from alcoholism or suicide, the press often treated them as victims of "bad" men, particularly Annie Roberts, who died after a physician performed an abortion at her request.[13]

Although some physicians had the primary goal of protecting the privacy of their patients who died from criminal abortions, in some cases, physicians, midwives, or others tried to hide abortions from investigating coroners to prevent being implicated in the procedures. Mrs. A. S. Miller, a midwife, tried to hide her involvement in the abortion for Mrs. Kate McClure, who died on July 24, 1881. Coroners almost never recorded the prefix "Mrs." or "Mr." in front of the deceased's name and often did so only for men and women who were prominent, indicating that thirty-year-old McClure was a respectable woman. Her good reputation sets her apart from the other women in this chapter, but otherwise, the investigation into her death is quite similar. Unlike the other women in this study, McClure's husband was likely the father of her child, but her marriage was far from happy. McClure moved to the boardinghouse of Mrs. A. S. Miller, a midwife, with her two young children several weeks before her death. Shortly after renting a furnished room, she received a letter about her husband, who worked as a butcher in Cincinnati. The letter upset McClure because it revealed that her husband had been drinking excessively recently and even risked dying. McClure then decided to terminate her pregnancy, but something went wrong and she died of complications from the procedure. Miller, the midwife and boardinghouse owner, insisted to Coroner John Frank that she did not help McClure obtain an abortion.[14]

Whether Miller did assist McClure is not known, but the coroner did not investigate Miller or the physicians who treated her, indicating that he either believed her or did not have enough evidence to investigate her. As a midwife who ran a boardinghouse, Miller could have been operating what historian James Mohr calls a "cooperative boardinghouse," in which the boardinghouse keeper provided pregnant women with a place to stay before and after they had abortions and even helped them acquire these abortions. But Coroner Frank had no concrete evidence that Miller assisted McClure with the abortion. Frank probably also believed the midwife because McClure had, in fact, performed four other abortions upon herself. She also already had had two children. When she terminated the other four pregnancies is unknown, but she could very well have done so after having these two children to limit her family size, as was fairly common practice.[15]

Miller's testimony reveals that both midwives and physicians feared facing criminal charges from assisting with or performing abortions, evidenced by the difficulty in obtaining medical treatment to help McClure after her abortion. Miller told the coroner that she had done everything possible to save McClure and had no knowledge of her abortion until after she had already begun to miscarry. On the afternoon of her death, McClure asked for Miller's help when she realized that she was experiencing a miscarriage. Although the midwife testified that she asked McClure to send for a doctor, McClure refused. Miller told Coroner Frank that she ignored McClure's request and tried to call Dr. D. W. McCarthy, but he refused to treat her because she had had an abortion. Miller then apparently called Dr. Fischel, who came twice, but then refused, claiming to be ill. In all likelihood, Fischel realized that McClure was beyond help and sought to avoid possible criminal charges from being implicated in her deadly abortion. Finally, Dr. Younkin came, but he could not save McClure from dying from metroperitonitis, an inflammation of her uterus, caused by the abortion. She died in the early morning hours of July 22, 1881. Her brother-in-law, Mr. King, took charge of her remains and notified her husband. Her remains rest in the Catholic Calvary Cemetery in St. Louis.[16]

Because McClure was a respectable married woman and had performed an abortion upon herself, the St. Louis press did not write a sensationalistic account of her death. Instead, a local reporter showed respect for her by running a brief piece about her death, buried on page three. The reporter said that McClure died from "individual malpractice" from an "operation" that she had performed on herself four times before—coded language to discuss abortion.[17]

Although no physician or midwife faced charges in McClure's death, the physicians who treated her had reason to fear such charges, as the investigation into the death of Annie Roberts, discussed in the opening story, illustrates. Perhaps the odds for a safe outcome gave Annie Roberts confidence when she sought an abortion from Metcalf and Stapp. An unwanted pregnancy had interrupted the new life that Roberts had created for herself in St. Louis. She had come to the city two years earlier, in 1876, with her one-year-old daughter, claiming to most people whom she met to be married to a husband who "was compelled to be away." But Roberts's story was a lie to protect her reputation, she confided to Carrie Stemp, the owner of the boarding-house at 3310 North Eleventh Street in which she rented a room. Roberts revealed to Stemp that she was an unwed mother, having been "seduced" by Michael O'Brien, a man from her hometown of Little Rock, Arkansas. In moving to St. Louis, Roberts had not left O'Brien behind. In fact, he had visited her at least once. Stemp later told the coroner that O'Brien "kept 'shady'" when he visited, suggesting that he did not act as a respectable man should. O'Brien apparently expected to continue his relationship with Roberts and even gave her money to move to a new residence, ostensibly so that they could avoid the disapproval of the boardinghouse keeper and the other residents. Roberts, however, had different plans. O'Brien was not the only man in her life; she was engaged to Reuben Underwood. Roberts did not tell Underwood about O'Brien. It is unknown what Roberts told Underwood about the father of her daughter, but she may have told him that she was widowed. Roberts underwent an abortion to conceal her pregnancy from Underwood, she told Stemp, because she was afraid that he would lose his "high opinion of her." If he broke off their engagement, her options would be limited, as her tarnished reputation would make it difficult to find work or to marry.[18]

Roberts had been about four months pregnant when she went to Dr. Metcalf's downtown St. Louis office, two weeks before her death. Metcalf prescribed iron pills to induce a miscarriage. Metcalf may have prescribed iron pills to build up blood in the uterus as a way to "unblock" menses. Many women sought treatment for "blocked" menses as opposed to an abortion. Physicians often prescribed medications to terminate a pregnancy and with the promise to perform a surgical operation at no additional charge if those medications failed to work, which, in Roberts's case and many others, they did. Roberts then asked the physician to perform a surgical abortion. Metcalf claimed that he did not have the necessary surgical instruments and referred her to Dr. Stapp, an obstetrician and gynecologist who performed abortions. Roberts went to Stapp's office on the afternoon of November 27 and then returned to the boardinghouse, telling Stemp and a fellow resident and casual friend, Carrie Vanderbrugge, that she "expected to be ill that evening," meaning she would soon lose the fetus because she had had an abortion. Abortions were not immediate; physicians or women used instruments or drugs to cause a miscarriage, which could take several hours.[19]

Roberts expected to recover quickly from the abortion, but the outcome of the surgery did not go as planned. Overnight, Stemp asked another resident of the boardinghouse to get Metcalf to help Roberts. She did not reveal the reason for Roberts's sickness. Metcalf came at Stemp's request and delivered Roberts's fetus at 2 A.M. Although Roberts at first appeared to be recovering after Metcalf left, her health soon declined. Stemp sent for the physician again a few days later, but this time he refused to come, claiming that he was sick. Dr. Fischel had also claimed to be sick when McClure needed treatment, indicating that pleading an illness was a tactic that physicians sometimes used to avoid being implicated in women's deaths from abortions. While Metcalf would not treat Roberts, Stapp did. He looked in on her on December 3—almost a week after her abortion. Roberts's health was growing worse, and she suffered from intense pain.[20]

Certain that she was going to die, Annie Roberts then made a startling confession: neither Reuben Underwood, her fiancé, nor Michael O'Brien, the father of her now three-year-old daughter, was the father of her unborn child. She told Stemp and Underwood that the father was a St. Louis police officer, J. W. O'Neill. Entangled in a messy love triangle, she had hoped that terminating her pregnancy would resolve at least part of her predicament by preserving her engagement. Having confessed, Roberts passed away at about ten o'clock that night from peritonitis, the result of a puncture wound to her uterus. Underwood seldom left her side; he later paid for her burial.[21]

Stemp and Stapp tried to conceal Roberts's death, but without success. Stapp created a false death certificate while Vanderbrugge and Stemp prepared the body for a quick burial, but a neighbor notified the coroner that they suspected foul play. Coroner Hugo Auler, MD, investigated Roberts's death as a potential homicide because she had died from an abortion performed by one physician and aided by another. As was typical in suspected homicides, Auler interviewed witnesses before a coroner's jury of six men. If the jury rendered a verdict of homicide, then they would also decide if Metcalf or Stapp should be charged with murder or manslaughter. Although it was possible that the coroner's jury could also hold Roberts or anyone else accountable for her death from abortion, it was highly unlikely. Missouri statutes indicated that physicians and "any other persons" would be guilty of manslaughter if they aided an abortion, or of murder if the mother died from the abortion, but "other person[s]" was understood to refer to midwives and druggists, not the patients themselves.[22]

Not only did Coroner Auler and his jury seek to determine how and why Roberts died, but they also sought to ascertain if Drs. Metcalf and Stapp should face criminal charges. The testimony of the boardinghouse keeper, Mrs. Stemp, and residents implicated both physicians in assisting with Roberts's abortion. Stemp told the coroner and his jury that she tried to dissuade Roberts from having the procedure because it could kill her. Stemp said that Roberts ignored her warning, though, and even said that "'she didn't care'" if she died because "she didn't want Mr. Underwood [her fiancé] to find out her condition, as he had a high opinion of her character." Stemp probably told the coroner's jury that she tried to prevent Roberts from having an abortion because she could have been charged with a crime as an accessory. Stemp helped Roberts recover from her abortion, acquired medical care for unexpected complications, and tried to conceal it when she died. Stemp tried to hide Roberts's abortion from other boardinghouse residents, except for one, Carrie Vanderbrugge, because she already knew about it. There is also no evidence that she helped Roberts procure an abortion. Stemp's testimony revealed that she knew about the procedure, however, and tried to avoid possible criminal charges for her involvement in it.[23]

While Mrs. Stemp told Coroner Auler and his jury that both Drs. Metcalf and Stapp treated Annie Roberts, when the two physicians took the stand, they denied having anything to do with her abortion. Dr. Metcalf claimed that he had seen Roberts two months before her death, but she was not pregnant, nor was there evidence that she had "'been intimate' with anyone." He prescribed her something at that time (probably iron pills to cause an abortion, based on other testimony), but he did not see her again until he was called to the boardinghouse, where he discovered that she was in labor. He gave her morphine to ease her pain but told her to get the help of another physician. He treated her once more and delivered a deceased fetus, and he then determined that she had had an abortion, he told the jury. In addition to trying to prove that Dr. Metcalf had assisted with the abortion, Coroner Auler also sought to determine his medical expertise—or lack thereof. Dr. Metcalf admitted before the coroner's jury that he had no medical degree "but had attended lectures." Dr. Metcalf insisted that he had nothing to do with her acquiring an abortion, nor did he refer her to Dr. Stapp. He also claimed that he did not know that Dr. Stapp was a "noted abortionist," but considering that Dr. Stapp regularly performed abortions, Dr. Metcalf was probably lying. He said that he told the women in the boardinghouse who knew about the abortion not to talk about procedure only because he did not want to be falsely accused of performing it. His testimony showed that he knew about Roberts's abortion, treated her for it, and tried to conceal it.[24]

Like Metcalf, Dr. Stapp testified that he had nothing to do with Roberts's surgery. He also claimed that he saw Roberts only after she had experienced a miscarriage. She was quite ill, especially because she had received no medical care for about a day, he told the jury. Stapp gave Roberts opium, quinine, and alcohol to ease her pain, he testified, but he never saw her before or after that date. According to Stapp, just like Metcalf, he had nothing to do with Roberts's abortion. If the testimony of both of these physicians were to be believed, another, unknown physician must have performed the abortion and Mrs. Stemp, the boardinghouse keeper, and Carrie Vanderbrugge, a resident of the boardinghouse, lied to the coroner and jury.

The coroner's jury rejected the testimony of Metcalf and Stapp. The jurors believed instead the statements of Stemp and Vanderbrugge, who testified that both physicians had treated Roberts and that Stapp had performed the abortion, and rendered a verdict of homicide. They determined that Annie Roberts had died from peritonitis, caused by a deadly injury "by the hand or hands of D. William Stapp, who . . . inflicted the above mentioned fatal injury upon the deceased with an instrument, with the intention of producing an abortion." The jury named Metcalf as an accessory to the crime. Roberts was not blamed for the abortion, even though she had gone to Metcalf for a drug-induced abortion and to Stapp for a surgical one. The coroner's jury also made no mention of the two women who knew about Roberts's abortion and tried to conceal it after she died. Metcalf and Stapp were arrested after the inquest concluded.[25]

The St. Louis press covered the inquest and vilified the physicians in a lengthy article, unlike in its accounts of women who died from abortions that they performed on themselves. Like coroners and their juries, journalists often ignored the fact that women like Roberts willingly sought abortions, treating them as victims of rogue doctors. In the case of Annie Roberts, a news reporter for the *St. Louis Globe-Democrat* sided with the coroner's jury and the grand jury in holding Stapp and Metcalf accountable for her death. Surprisingly, the reporter did not focus on Roberts's status as an unwed mother who was pregnant out of wedlock for a second time. Nor was she denigrated as a selfish woman who sought to avoid her responsibilities as a mother. The news accounts instead focused on William Stapp and Stephen Metcalf, while treating Roberts as a victim of doctors who preyed on women such as her for their own profit.

The *Globe-Democrat* attacked both physicians' professionalism, character, and even physical appearance. Their reporter claimed that Stapp's demeanor "lent an additional repulsiveness to a countenance of an exceedingly unattractive character." Even his dress and grooming reflected his immorality, as "his clothing and person were filthy in the extreme." If his supposed poor hygiene were not enough to assure readers of Stapp's guilt, the reporter added that he acted nervous when he took the stand to testify. Metcalf, like Stapp, was said to wear "shoddy and seedy" clothing. According to the news account, Metcalf was a "quack" who lacked formal medical training, gave conflicting statements, and was "unprofessional" on the stand.[26]

The reporter displayed sympathy, however, for Annie Roberts. Although the title of the *Globe-Democrat*'s article, "Sin and Death," suggests a harsh judgment of Roberts, the subtitle refers to her as an "Unhappy Woman" who "Sacrifices Herself to the Fear of Exposure." In contrast to the portrayal of the physicians, the reporter's coverage of Roberts spoke of the love that her fiancé had for her and recounted the testimony given at her inquest without remarks about her affairs, pregnancy, and abortion aside from the facts of the case. Compared to contemporary news accounts of the deaths of women who worked as prostitutes or of men and women who died by suicide, the reporter's restraint is unexpected. Reporters tended to be sympathetic toward women who had abortions, however, especially when they obtained them from midwives or physicians.[27]

The press attacks against Stapp and Metcalf were typical of news reports of deaths attributed to abortions performed by physicians. Although Stapp was a well-trained and experienced doctor, reporters treated him and his colleagues who performed abortions as professional pariahs. When the *St. Louis Post-Dispatch* and *St. Louis Globe-Democrat* wrote about the perceived problem of abortion, they named the physicians responsible and often sympathized with their patients. For example, in 1876, a *Post-Dispatch* reporter wrote that W. W. Jilz seduced a young female employee and then gave her drugs to induce an abortion when she became pregnant. In court, the prosecuting attorney, Charles P. Johnson, successfully made the case that Jilz was, in the words of the reporter, "an abortionist," "murderer," "social leper," and "destroyer of reputation." The jury convicted Jilz of criminal abortion. Other news accounts are similar, and some even note how difficult it was to get women to testify against doctors who performed abortions. Ellen Singer was one such reluctant woman. She became ill after an abortion and had to briefly stay in the Female Hospital. Shortly after the hospital released her, she was arrested and jailed to coerce her to testify against Charles A. Smith, the doctor who had performed her abortion. The *Post-Dispatch* reporter gleefully wrote that the "Doctor" was arrested and charged with manslaughter for performing an abortion on Singer, even though she did not wish to press charges and had fully recovered from the procedure. In virtually every case, the reporter focused on the misdeeds of physicians who performed abortions, not on the women who sought them. As the coverage of Smith illustrates, reporters even questioned the physicians' medical credentials, often putting the term "doctor" in quotes to indicate that they were not respectable members of the medical profession.[28]

Despite the scandalous newspaper coverage of Stapp and Metcalf's involvement in the death of Annie Roberts and a guilty verdict from the coroner's jury, neither physician served much prison time. St. Louis officials did not charge Metcalf with any crime, although Coroner Auler's jury deemed him an accessory to murder. Stapp was indicted for manslaughter, not murder, in 1879. He initially pled not guilty to the charge but then changed his plea in order to receive a shorter sentence. Stapp served sixty days in the Work House for his conviction on the charge of criminal abortion rather than the four months in the city jail he would have served for manslaughter.[29]

This outcome for Metcalf and Stapp illustrated how difficult it was to prosecute abortion cases. To convince a jury that a physician had performed a criminal abortion, a prosecutor needed to obtain evidence, which was no simple task, particularly if a woman recovered with no health issues. When officials pressed charges, investigators needed testimony that someone had provided the abortion, with the strongest statement often coming from the patient. When women became ill after an abortion and had to stay in the Female Hospital, officials encouraged or even coerced them to testify against their treating physicians. When women died from abortions, coroners interviewed witnesses to learn the names of the physicians or midwives who had performed them, as Auler did in the death of Annie Roberts.[30]

In some cases, coroners did not even investigate suspicious deaths because they simply did not have enough evidence. For example, Auler's successor as coroner, John N. Frank, sought to stop Stapp from performing abortions but struggled to find enough evidence to give to the prosecutor. Four years after Annie Roberts died, Stapp faced another coroner's investigation and possible charges. In 1882, he performed an abortion for thirty-one-year-old Rosina Eichilz, a wife and mother of six. Instead of recovering quickly from the procedure, Eichilz suffered incredible pain, which Stapp treated with morphine. He assured her husband that many women in similar instances recovered, but Eichilz's symptoms did not improve. She died a few days after the operation. Her family physician, a Dr. Ehrhardt, learned of his patient's death and became suspicious. He looked at the death certificate, which stated that Eichilz died from "congestion of the lungs." Ehrhardt told Frank about the false death certificate and demanded that he conduct an inquest, but Frank lamented that while he knew Stapp was an abortionist and wanted to "catch him" for his crimes, he did not have enough evidence to warrant an inquest. A postmortem examination would show that Eichilz had had an abortion, Frank conceded, but he had no proof that Stapp had been the person to perform the procedure. Rosina Eichilz had made no statement that implicated Stapp, no one had seen her go to his office, and Stapp had not prescribed any suspicious medications such as abortifacients. Concealing abortions, even when patients died from them, was evidently a fairly common practice in late nineteenth-century St. Louis.[31]

Coroner Frank had reason to be cautious about sending abortion cases to prosecutors: a few months earlier, he had faced a lawsuit for one zealous investigation. Coroner John Frank was one of many regular physicians who opposed the practice of medicine by unlicensed, "irregular" physicians, but unlike most physicians, he could use his position as coroner to do so. Like many other coroners in this study, Coroner John N. Frank graduated from St. Louis Medical College and worked as a practicing physician when he did not hold political office. However, while the Office of the Coroner gave him the authority to investigate suspected abortions, he did not have unlimited power, and his fervor had repercussions. In 1882, a midwife sued him after he obtained a warrant for her arrest for performing an abortion. The patient became ill after the procedure but recovered, and although she initially testified that the midwife performed an abortion, she later recanted and denied having been pregnant. Two years later, in 1884, Frank struggled to aid in the prosecution of another abortionist, a Dr. McWilliams. He interviewed a woman who became sick after receiving an abortion from McWilliams and gave the case to the prosecutor. McWilliams's defense attorney demanded a hearing and claimed that Frank had blackmailed his client because he wanted to bolster his reputation by bringing an abortionist to justice. The case ultimately went to trial, but only after a hard-fought battle.[32]

While coroners such as Frank struggled to overcome the constraints against prosecuting abortions, physicians continued to perform the procedures regularly. William Stapp was just one of many physicians who served women seeking abortions. His medical practice was listed in the St. Louis city directory from the 1870s until his death in 1892; he was not hidden. Women knew they could seek abortions from him, coroners investigated him when women died, and city officials indicted him, but he and other abortionists spent little time in jail. Like other abortion providers, Stapp hired skilled defense attorneys to defend him from criminal charges. Newspapers wrote stories about Stapp whenever he faced more charges for malpractice and performing abortions, but he continued to offer his female patients his services in both delivering their babies and terminating their unwanted pregnancies. He continued his practice well into old age, dying at eighty-one in 1892.[33]

There is no known biography of Stapp, and he and other abortion providers in St. Louis appear not to have offered any discussion in newspapers or professional journals as to why they performed these procedures. Historians can only speculate as to why William Stapp felt compelled to perform abortions sought by young women. Perhaps he sympathized with women who wanted to limit their families because his own wife gave birth to nine children. As an obstetrician and gynecologist, Stapp saw women like Annie Roberts in distress and desperate to end their pregnancies. Some became so distraught about unwanted pregnancies that they died by suicide, as one young woman, Annie Sophie Weigmann, did when the father of her unborn baby refused to marry her or even admit that he was the father. In Stapp's practice, he saw women with difficult pregnancies, women with more children than they could care for, and women for whom a pregnancy outside of wedlock would destroy their reputations and, accordingly, their opportunities for marriage, financial and emotional support from their families, or employment. Abortions performed by physicians were far safer than those performed by women on themselves, so Stapp and physicians like him may have agreed to them knowing that the women might otherwise risk their lives by taking matters into their own hands. Most of these women were wives and mothers, and their families needed them. While Stapp's exact reasons for performing abortions are unknown, it is likely that he simply wanted to help his patients. Whatever the motivation, his son, Samuel Stapp, also became an obstetrician and gynecologist who performed abortions, for which he too faced public criticism and criminal charges.[34]

Most women survived and went on with their lives after they had abortions, particularly those performed by midwives or physicians, making the cases explored in this chapter unusual. Because it was illegal in the late nineteenth century, few records document the procedure, but it was fairly common. Most women who had abortions were married and already had children, much like Mrs. Kate McClure, and most quickly recovered from the procedure, as she had several times before. Ellen Noonan, Mary Baum, and Annie Roberts were women who could have proven stereotypes about women who had abortions: they selfishly avoided motherhood, they were often unmarried, they were prostitutes, or they were victims of men who seduced them and then refused to marry them. But they gained little press attention and even sympathy, particularly Roberts, because a known abortion-providing physician ended her pregnancy and she died as a result, and the coroner's jury, prosecutor, and St. Louis press treated her as a victim—a different stereotype of women perpetuated by members of the medical profession. While physicians created abortion laws in the mid-nineteenth century to regulate their profession and protect women's health, later generations of doctors would point to cases like Baum's, McClure's, and Roberts's as evidence that antiabortion laws were not only ineffective but also harmful. Physicians like Dr. Stapp, who performed abortions and treated women who had them, listened to their women patients and helped lead a new movement in the mid-twentieth century to make abortion safe by making it legal.

CHAPTER FIVE

"I Am Afraid That You Will Beat Me to Death"

Coroners' Inquests into Domestic Homicides

ILLIE SQUIRES RESPONDED to a knock at her door around 6:00 P.M. on Friday, April 26, 1878, and was unsurprised to find her friend's common-law husband, John Cordry, waiting impatiently. Cordry asked Millie if his wife, Nellie Lee, was there. Knowing that Cordry would likely assault her friend if he knew that she was in Millie's home, she lied and told Cordry that his wife was not in her rented room. Cordry became angry and shouted, "'You g—d d—n liar, she is in there.'" He then ran into the house while Squires tried to run out of the back door. Nellie Lee was, in fact, in Millie's home, probably to hide from her husband, but perhaps also to seek care for injuries that she had just received from a fight with another woman, Pinkey Daniels. Once inside of Squires's home, Cordry asked Lee to go home with him, but she refused. Refusing to go home with Cordry did not save Lee from an assault, however, because Cordry hit her in the face, knocking her down. He then kicked and stomped on Nellie Lee. Millie Squires tried to stop him from killing her friend, yelling, "John don't hit her." Cordry threatened Squires, shouting, "Get back you black ___ or I'll beat you." Squires did as Cordry ordered, but he continued to beat her friend. He stopped, picked up his wife, and asked her, "Are you going home, Nellie?" She told him that she was not, saying, "No; I'm afraid you'll beat me,'" or possibly "'Because I am afraid that you will beat me to death.'" Cordry responded by hitting his wife "with all his force." He knocked her onto the ground and then began to kick and stomp on her, yelling, "I'll fix you."[1]

Nellie Lee never had the opportunity to leave her husband. Instead, she died on Sunday, April 28, 1878, from the injuries that he had inflicted on her.

Coroner Hugo Auler investigated the death of Nellie Lee on April 29, 1878. The inquest is remarkable for several reasons. First, because it was a homicide investigation, the coroner, rather than a deputy coroner, investigated the death. Although deputy coroners occasionally investigated homicides, most often, coroners did so. Homicide investigations invited public scrutiny and could lead to criminal charges, making these inquests of the highest importance to coroners. Second, the coroner called a large number of witnesses—fourteen—to determine how and why Nellie Lee died. He also ordered an autopsy to determine her cause of death. However, Auler did not render the verdict in the death of Nellie Lee. Because her case was a suspected homicide, Auler had less authority than in other death investigations. He summoned a coroner's jury to consider the evidence, determine a cause of death, and decide if someone else caused the death of Nellie Lee. Auler then signed off on the verdict that the jury rendered, but he had no authority to render the verdict himself.

The coroner's inquest and newspaper coverage of the murder of Nellie Lee and other women illustrate that race, class, and reputation shaped investigations into, interpretations of, and prosecutions of domestic homicides. These inquests also provide insight into the daily cruelty that was often hidden from the public but experienced by a number of women: domestic violence. Witnesses, coroners, and the press brought attention to domestic abuse into the open when these women died, however, particularly when they died at the hands of their husbands or partners. Despite the fact that these three groups acknowledged what they often called the "ill-treatment" of women, they described domestic homicides in different ways. Just as with other causes of death, race, class, gender, and reputation all shaped how witnesses, coroners, and, especially, the press described both the perpetrators and the victims of domestic homicides. In addition, a coroner's verdict of homicide could be the first step toward justice for victims of domestic homicide, who were most often women. In cases of murder-suicide, when the perpetrator would never stand trial, a verdict and acknowledgment of domestic violence could bring public recognition of the abuse.[2]

"Domestic homicide" is defined in this chapter as the historian Jeffrey Adler defines it—as a homicide between family members or intimate partners. Domestic homicides include killing parents, children, siblings, and spouses. The focus of this chapter, however, is one of the most common forms of domestic homicides: the killing of one's spouse or romantic partner. In most cases of domestic homicide, men killed their wives or lovers, often when they threatened to leave them. Adler argues that domestic violence and domestic homicide typically resulted from gender inequalities, and efforts by men to control their romantic partners and assert their dominance as men and the inquests in this chapter fit that pattern. When women committed domestic homicides, they frequently killed their husbands or companions in self-defense against domestic violence. The sample used for this study found no women who killed their husbands, however. Only three domestic homicides appear in this study, two of which were murder-suicides. All three were perpetrated by men against their romantic partners.[3]

The inquest into the death of Nellie Lee will be contrasted with another domestic homicide, a murder-suicide: Josiah Colcord's killing of his wife, Lillie, and then himself. Josiah Colcord avoided a courtroom because he died by suicide, but he was still judged for his acts, as were other men who killed their wives or partners. Coroner Hugo Auler investigated all three of these deaths. He interviewed witnesses, who detailed a history of violence perpetrated by these men against the women whom they supposedly loved. Both Nellie Lee and Lillie Colcord may have been planning to leave their husbands when they killed them—a time that was—and still is—riskiest for women with abusive partners or spouses.[4]

Although coroners' inquests into the deaths of Nellie Lee and Lillie Colcord show similar patterns of domestic violence, the press treated these women—and their male killers—quite differently. The local press covered Lee's death, while the Colcords' deaths attracted national attention as well. Because reporters did not use bylines, it is unknown which reporters wrote these various articles, but given the hiring practices common of the time, one can surmise that they were white men. These writers wrote attention-grabbing headlines and offered their own opinions of these deaths. According to the St. Louis press, John Cordry was a brutal Black man who mercilessly killed his wife. In contrast, Josiah Colcord's killing of his wife and then himself were understandable, although not justifiable, tragedies, as he had been down on his luck and was angry that his wife, a former prostitute, was having an affair. Had Josiah Colcord gone to trial, it is likely that he would have faced lesser charges and a shorter sentence than John Cordry.[5]

The inquest into the death of Nellie Lee differs from the other two domestic homicides in this study for two reasons. First, John Cordry lived to stand trial; he did not die by suicide as the men in the other two domestic homicides in this study did. Second, another person may have contributed to Lee's death, a highly unusual circumstance in homicide investigations—domestic or otherwise. The inquest into Lee's death will be compared and contrasted with the murder-suicide of Josiah and Lillie Colcord, which is more representative of a domestic homicide in this study, although the sample of three makes it more challenging to discuss patterns than with other causes of death. While Josiah's education and class standing were uncommon for perpetrators of domestic homicides, his suicide after the fact was not. Because chapter 3 provides a brief profile of Coroner Auler, this chapter features a short biography of another person whose work contributed to the Office of the Coroner: Dr. James C. Nidelet, who often performed autopsies for his brother, Coroner Sylvester L. Nidelet, and other St. Louis coroners. He also practiced medicine and, in fact, attempted to treat the Colcords for their gunshot wounds but was unable to save them.[6]

Although domestic violence was a common occurrence in the late nineteenth century—and still is—coroners investigated fewer domestic homicides than they did other forms of homicide. Of the fourteen homicides examined for this chapter, three were domestic homicides, with two of those being murder-suicides. Men overwhelmingly committed homicides in general and were the only perpetrators of domestic homicides in this study. In part, this could be because women were more likely to commit infanticide than to kill other adults, a category of homicide not examined in this project.[7] Another reason for the discrepancy is that men were—and are—much more likely than women to commit acts of violence, including domestic abuse and homicide.[8]

As with other verdicts, coroners used different terms to render a verdict of homicide and did not use the term "domestic homicide." In fact, they seldom determined that "homicide" caused a person's death. In part, this discrepancy is because coroners and their juries varied, but the primary reason is that coroners used different language to determine that someone intentionally killed another person. Coroners' juries often determined that a man or women died "as a result of injuries caused by" another individual or "at the hands of" someone else. Verdicts often added that the coroner's jury—"we the Jury"—held a specific person or people responsible for the death. In a few cases, they determined that someone died because of "justifiable homicide" or injuries that occurred "in self-defense." In cases of murder-suicide, coroners investigated without a jury and rendered the verdicts themselves, just as they did in deaths from natural causes, alcoholism, suicide, abortion, and most accidents.

Coroners noted that the men who killed their partners died by suicide afterward. For example, Coroner Hugo Auler determined that Lillie Colcord died from gunshot wounds from a revolver that "was in the hand or hands of Joseph P. Colcord" and added "the said Colcord committed suicide after the deed had been done." Because they provided evidence for potential criminal charges, homicide verdicts were especially long, detailing the type of weapon used, by whom it was used, and where, similar to the Colcord verdict.[9]

Domestic homicides are an extreme example of a common experience among women: domestic abuse. Despite its prevalence, the public seldom intervened in instances of domestic violence because they tended to see it as a family matter, not a social problem, as pointed out by the historians Linda Gordon and Elizabeth Pleck. Some women's rights advocates challenged domestic violence in the 1870s, but their efforts were short-lived, as these historians observe. Because of the ideal—and economic necessity—of a family that contained a male breadwinner and female homemaker, women's rights advocates sought limited reforms in hopes of preserving families while keeping women safe. Some women's rights advocates, such as Lucy Stone, argued for stricter laws to punish men who beat their wives, but there was little public support for such measures. The temperance movement had more support, albeit outside of St. Louis, and one of its core arguments was that alcohol should be outlawed, in part, to protect women from the violence of their drunken husbands. These efforts to reform the family—and men—were the way that most women's rights advocates challenged domestic violence in the late nineteenth century. Only the most radical activists called for increased access to divorce, and they had little support, even from women's rights advocates. Even modest reforms lost public support after the 1870s, however, as public attention turned to child abuse. Although widespread concern about family violence rose and fell in the succeeding decades, it was not until the 1960s and 1970s that feminists created the first shelters for women who sought to leave their abusive partners.[10]

The inquests in this chapter reflect these larger trends. Although friends, neighbors, and relatives told investigating coroners that these women suffered abuse, they had few resources outside of marriage. Cruelty served as grounds for divorce, but the process was difficult and highly stigmatized. Women in cities like St. Louis had more opportunities to earn wages than in other areas, but they seldom earned enough to support a family. Child care and housing were difficult to obtain if they had no family nearby. Although a few charitable organizations could help women find work and shelter in St. Louis, they were largely for widows, poor unmarried women, or, perhaps, prostitutes looking to reform their supposedly wayward ways. No organization existed specifically to help women leave abusive marriages until the late twentieth century.[11]

Like many other St. Louis women, Lillie Colcord had few opportunities outside of her marriage to Josiah Colcord, although it seems as though she may have been preparing to leave him. Before the tragic double shooting occurred, the guests and staff of St. Louis' Girard House were enjoying a quiet afternoon on August 17, 1878. Around 1:00 P.M., gunshots startled them as well as passersby near the hotel. Residents heard four shots fired in rapid succession and some also heard a body fall. A hotel clerk rushed to the locked room belonging to Josiah and Lillie Colcord, quickly followed by police officers, who heard the shots from outside. When several men forced the door open, they saw the Colcords lying on the floor. Twenty-two-year-old Lillie Colcord had three gunshot wounds: one each in her chest, stomach, and thigh. Thirty-five-year-old Josiah had a single gunshot wound to his head. Someone called Dr. James C. Nidelet, who quickly responded, in hopes of treating the pair's injuries. Josiah and Lillie Colcord died before Nidelet arrived, however, and soon, Coroner Hugo Auler was on his way to the scene.[12]

Dr. James C. Nidelet not only was a well-known physician in St. Louis but also worked closely with the Office of the Coroner and the Police Department. His brother, Sylvester Nidelet, discussed in chapter 2, served as coroner several times as well. Coroners routinely asked Dr. James C. Nidelet to perform autopsies during inquests. Nidelet was a good choice to aid the Office of the Coroner, as he was both a licensed, practicing physician as well as a former police commissioner and member of the Board of Police Commissioners in the 1870s. Controversy altered his career, however, beginning in September 1878—shortly after he was called to attempt to treat the Colcords. At this time, he served as vice president of the Board of Police Commissioners and led an effort to close down a gambling ring. However, accusations soon emerged that he had accepted bribes to notify gambling houses of upcoming raids. He soon became embroiled in a scandal, which he attributed to a backlash against his efforts to eliminate gambling. The scandal ended Nidelet's campaign to continue serving on the Board of Police Commissioners. Nidelet was not indicted, however, perhaps because there was no evidence of wrongdoing. Although James C. Nidelet's career in politics and law enforcement ended, he continued to practice medicine until his death in 1910. Coroners also continued to request that he perform autopsies during their inquests, although he did not do so for Lillie and Josiah Colcord. Coroner Auler did not need an autopsy to determine how the pair died; the gunshot wounds made the cause of death clear.[13]

Minutes after Dr. James C. Nidelet arrived to the scene of the shooting to treat the couple's injuries, only to find that the Colcords could not be saved, Coroner Hugo Auler began his inquest into the couple's deaths. The coroner did not conduct a jury inquest in this case, even though Lillie Colcord's death was a suspected homicide. In cases of murder-suicide, a coroner could—and did—investigate and render a verdict on his own, without a coroner's jury. The difference in procedure could be because the verdict would not possibly lead to an indictment because the perpetrator was deceased. Just as they did in other cases when more than one person died, such as accidents, coroners created an inquest record for each individual, even if they interviewed the same witnesses, as Coroner Auler did in the Colcord deaths. In the two murder-suicides in this study, coroners noted in their verdicts that the two deaths were connected in each verdict. In the death of Lillie Colcord, Coroner Auler determined that Lillie Colcord had died from "the effects of two gunshot wounds, inflicted upon the deceased" by Josiah Colcord and added, "the said Colcord committed suicide after the deed had been done." Similarly, he determined that Josiah Colcord died from the "effects of a gunshot wound through the right temple, inflicted by his own hands . . . after the deceased had inflicted two mortal gunshot wounds on the body of Lillie Colcord at the same place and room." Although Coroner Auler did not convene a coroner's jury and rendered similar verdicts and interviewed the same witnesses in each inquest, he and other coroners created two inquest records, making inquests into murder-suicides distinctive from both homicides and suicides.[14]

Although the Colcords' causes of death became quickly apparent, Coroner Auler investigated thoroughly, examining the bodies and interviewing nine witnesses. Auler quickly uncovered evidence of domestic violence. In addition to the gunshot wounds that killed Lillie Colcord, Coroner Auler found other injuries, including bruises on her nose, above her left eyebrow, and on her right arm. Auler interviewed witnesses who testified that they had long suspected that Josiah regularly beat his wife. Although coroners often interviewed family members first when conducting an inquest, such was not the case in the Colcord inquest, perhaps because they did not live nearby or because the couple had been isolated. Auler interviewed the staff and guests at the Girard House, however. One of the chambermaids, Lizzie Jeffries, told Coroner Auler that the bruises that he observed on Lillie's face and arm resulted from Josiah's violence. She said that the couple fought often and that Lillie had even told Jeffries that "Colcord treated her badly and she intended leaving him." Lizzie spotted an injury on Lillie's arm and asked Lillie, "'if that was the way she was treated?'" and Lillie replied, "'Yes, and worse than that sometimes.'" Other chambermaids did not know that the couple quarreled but did mention that they kept to themselves, taking meals in their rooms and not leaving much shortly before their deaths. Another witness, Conrad Farmer, who owned a local hardware store, also told Coroner Auler that Lillie complained to him "of the treatment she was receiving" and said that she planned to leave her husband. As historians of domestic homicide note, when abusive husbands killed their wives, it tended to be when they tried to leave them. It is unknown if Lillie confronted Josiah or if he suspected her plans, but it is possible that he murdered his wife, then died by suicide, because he feared that she would end their marriage.[15]

Although the press often sympathized with women in abusive relationships, local and national reporters offered almost no compassion for Lillie Colcord. The press also did not condemn Josiah for his violent acts as much as they did with other abusive men. Instead, some reporters worked to offer an explanation, even an excuse, for Josiah's acts. They even blamed Lillie for her own murder. The couple came from quite different backgrounds, and Josiah had once been a prominent attorney and legislator, although his heavy drinking and divorce had caused him to lose his social standing several years earlier. In contrast, Lillie had a bad reputation in St. Louis, having been married three times and having worked as a prostitute for a period. Initial local and national newspaper reports claimed that Josiah had killed his *mistress* and then himself because they could not believe that Josiah Colcord "would have so disgraced himself as to link his name with that of a common prostitute."[16] Reporters also immediately sought an explanation for Josiah's violence. A reporter for the *St. Louis Globe-Democrat* wrote, "He had loved, not wisely, but too well, and had atoned for his error—if atonement were possible—by slaying the object of his love, and leaping after her into the depths of eternity—a murderer and a suicide."[17] A journalist for the *Daily Rocky Mountain News* blamed Lillie for Josiah's personal and professional decline as well, writing, "ever since his connection with this woman, Colcord's course has been steadily downward."[18] This writer believed that Josiah committed the murder-suicide because the passion had faded with Lillie and Josiah regretted losing his first wife and promising career as an attorney. Lillie, this reporter believed, brought her murder on herself.[19]

Several reporters blamed intemperance for Josiah's acts, an excuse that was common in the late nineteenth century. Newspapers across the country claimed that there was rum, wine, or whiskey in the room at the time of the murder-suicide. Titles such as "Ruined by Rum," "Wine and Women," and "All the Blue-Ribbon Movements" were catchy and immediately deflected blame from Josiah to alcohol. The content of these articles also pointed to alcohol as the driving factor, and some witnesses testified that Josiah had a history of heavy drinking. He had, evidently, recently attempted to stop drinking and even joined the temperance movement but soon resumed drinking to excess. No witness testified that they observed alcohol in the couples' room on the day of the murder-suicide. Some witnesses had seen Josiah drinking on various occasions, but not drunk, while others did not know him to drink at all. None of these witnesses knew the couple well, however, so their knowledge of Josiah's drinking habits was scant. There is no evidence that Josiah had been drinking when he committed the act, so, most likely, reporters were seeking an explanation for the surprising tragedy.[20]

Although local and national reporters quickly blamed Lillie for her husband's murderous acts, in fact, Josiah had been declining personally and professionally for several years. Colcord had been a lieutenant in the Union army during the Civil War and once worked as a prominent lawyer in St. Louis. He even served in the state legislature. However, about six years earlier, his standing in the community declined as he lost his first wife to divorce and could no longer practice law, all, allegedly, because of his heavy drinking. Given his violence toward his second wife, however, it is possible that abuse as well as alcoholism caused his first wife, Mary, to divorce him. Reporters depicted Josiah Colcord as a respectable man who had been seduced and suffered a tarnished reputation because of his association with Lillie. One reporter from Denver wrote, "It was but a few years since that Josiah P. Colcord was a rising young member of the bar, universally esteemed. . . . To-day he lies cold in death, a murderer and a suicide, the victim of lust, gone red-handed into the presence of the Eternal."[21]

Another justification that the local and national press made was that Lillie had been unfaithful, prompting Josiah to become enraged with jealousy. Lillie had evidently recently traveled to Bloomington, Illinois, and some newspaper accounts suggest that she had an affair during her visit. A *St. Louis*

Globe-Democrat reporter wrote that Josiah Colcord had gone to Blooming-ton three weeks before the murder-suicide. He was "looking into some ru-mors regarding the infidelity of his wife, whose name was associated unpleasantly with a number of rakes, young and old, of this city." No news-paper offered sympathy to Lillie, and their bias casts doubt as to their accu-racy. Still, Lillie may have been having an affair. Or Josiah could have been jealous and believed that she was unfaithful, whether she was or not.[22]

Although the St. Louis press expressed mercy for Josiah, the witnesses dur-ing the inquest did not, nor did his former friends and family. Few people attended his funeral, and some of his former colleagues also requested that newspapers correct previous statements that they were associated with him. By the time of his death, Josiah Colcord had long been away from the law community. He was no longer a member of the St. Louis Bar Association. While journalists, particularly for the *Globe-Democrat* sympathized with Josiah, the people who knew him best did not.[23]

Although the press offered Lillie little to no kindness, more often, news-paper reporters offered compassion for women who were killed by their hus-bands or lovers. Coroners and witnesses did as well, as they sometimes offered "ill-treatment" by a husband as a reason for a woman's homicide or suicide. Some St. Louis coroners pointed out domestic violence in their verdicts, even if it was only suspected and not confirmed. For example, when Catharina Lielich died by suicide, Coroner Hugo Auler blamed "ill-treatment by her husband." Catharina Lielich differed from Lillie Colcord, however, as wit-nesses described her as a loving wife and mother. Her husband, however, did not properly provide for her, and he physically abused her. Lielich and other women who received pity from witnesses, coroners, and the press shared com-mon traits. Their friends, families, and neighbors understood them to be good wives and mothers, regardless of their race, class, or immigrant status. The men who abused or killed them, in contrast, often failed to protect and provide for these women in the eyes of their communities and the coroner. Many lived in disreputable neighborhoods. It made sense to many people that those "rough" men beat their wives or lovers. A once-upstanding St. Louis attorney beating his wife to death evidently did not. The press blamed Lillie Colcord for the murder-suicide because she failed to follow the gender con-ventions that society prescribed for respectable, middle-class white women.[24]

One witness acknowledged a fact that reporters overlooked: Josiah abused Lillie, and the murder-suicide was a final act of domestic violence. The murder-suicide itself suggests this, as do the bruises on Lillie and her statements to the chambermaid. Reporters eagerly sought explanations that exonerated Josiah or at least explained the violent act—namely, alcohol and Lillie herself. They pointed to a diary found in the couple's room that did not mention any violence, but this alone is far from sufficient evidence that the couple was happy. The fact that she had recently traveled and may have had an affair—perhaps part of her plans to leave him—could have triggered jealousy and violence on Josiah's part. Because of his supposed sterling reputation and her tarnished one, however, the press did not explain their deaths in this way, despite the evidence available to them. While those who saw bruises likely felt concern for Lillie, there was little they could do, even if they felt that they should intervene in what many understood to be a private, family matter. As historian Jeffrey Adler notes, because domestic violence was so common, their neighbors were often desensitized to it by the time these men killed their wives. In many cases, neighbors had often long ignored women's cries for help, typically because they felt that there was nothing they could do.[25]

The public responded to domestic violence and domestic homicide differently based on the race of the perpetrator and victim, as exemplified by the domestic homicide depicted in the opening story. When an African American man, John Cordry, beat his white wife, Nellie Lee, to death, the St. Louis press quickly depicted her as a helpless victim of a brutal Black man. Like Lillie Colcord, Nellie Lee had worked as a prostitute at one time. But her questionable reputation was overshadowed by the fact that she was beaten and killed by a Black man. John Cordry also violated the tenets of white supremacy by engaging in a common-law marriage with a white woman. And the fact that he abused and killed her represented the fears that white supremacists touted to maintain the racial hierarchy: the notion that Black men posed a danger to white women.[26]

The inquest into Nellie Lee's death revealed that the thirty-three-year-old man had physically abused his thirty-five-year-old wife for some time. Lee's friends and neighbors, Kate Seymour, Susan Miller, and Millie Squires—the friend who tried to hide Lee from Cordry—all told the coroner that Nellie Lee felt afraid to go home with John Cordry on the night of April 26, 1878. Cordry evidently came home that night and became upset because Nellie Lee was not there. He went searching for her and became angry and violent when Lee refused to go home with him. He threatened other women, notably Squires, telling her that he would beat her if she did not "get back." He then beat Nellie Lee to death when she refused to leave with him. Although witness testimony does not explicitly detail a history of domestic violence, Lee's fear of Cordry and Squires's efforts to hide her from Cordry do. Cordry's threats culminated in Lee's murder on Friday, April 26, 1878. Soon after her murder, police arrested John Cordry, and Coroner Hugo Auler launched an inquest into Lee's death.[27]

Because the evidence indicated that Nellie Lee had died from a homicide, Coroner Hugo Auler convened a coroner's jury, as mandated by Missouri law. The jury, rather than the coroner himself, rendered the verdict. In homicide cases, the coroner's inquest, including the verdict of the coroner's jury, formed the first step in the criminal justice system. While coroners examined the body and interviewed witnesses, just as they did in other kinds of deaths, they did not render the verdict themselves—with the notable exception of murder-suicides. Instead, in suspected homicides when the suspected perpetrator was still alive, a coroner's jury of six white male state residents determined the cause of death. Coroners questioned witnesses before the jury and, in many cases, ordered autopsies or toxicology analyses. But it was the coroner's jury, not the coroner, who rendered the verdict and determined how the person came to his or her death and whether anyone should be held legally responsible for taking the person's life.[28]

Even if the coroner's jury found that someone was responsible for a homicide, neither they nor the coroner had the authority to press criminal charges. A grand jury would decide whether to press charges. A verdict of homicide from a coroner's jury provided crucial evidence to the grand jury, however, as well as evidence in a criminal trial, should one be held. The coroner and his jury sought to determine the *intent* of men and women who killed other people. A coroner's jury could determine that a person intended to cause injuries with a weapon or their fists, resulting in another person's death. Or they could determine that a person acted in self-defense or justifiable homicide. Determining intent mattered because it formed the basis for criminal charges—first-degree murder, second-degree murder, or manslaughter. The accused faced a judge and jury in a criminal court to determine their legal guilt or innocence.[29]

Coroner Hugo Auler also ordered an autopsy—another common practice in cases of suspected homicide. In some cases, coroners performed autopsies themselves but often did not. Instead, they hired a licensed, practicing physician from the area to perform autopsies as needed—often Dr. James C.

Nidelet, in fact. In the death of Nellie Lee, Coroner Auler called two physicians, Dr. John M. MacDonald and Dr. Seemann, to assist with the autopsy. He may have hired two physicians instead of one because a team of medical students attended the autopsy as part of their studies. The autopsy determined that Nellie Lee died from "peritonitis and cerebral concussion," which had been caused by an assault as well as being thrown or falling on the ground. While she had a brain hemorrhage, that alone did not cause her death; John Cordry repeatedly kicking Lee and the brain injuries did. However, the autopsy did not reveal who had caused the deadly blows to Lee. In fact, she had been in a physical altercation with another woman earlier that day, Pinkey Daniels, whose assault may have contributed to Lee's death.[30]

To determine how Nellie Lee died, Coroner Auler subpoenaed fourteen witnesses to testify, which was a large number for most inquests but not uncommon for suspected homicides. Nellie Lee's neighbors, Millie Squires, Kate Seymour, and Susan Miller, told the coroner's jury that John Cordry had punched and kicked his common-law wife between 10:00 and 11:00 the night of April 26, 1878. They disagreed on some of the details, such as whether Cordry punched her once or multiple times, but all three women described a vicious beating. Millie Squires told the coroner's jury that Nellie Lee had come to her home and initially tried to convince her neighbor to return home, but she refused because she worried (and rightfully so) that he would beat her. Squires then tried to keep Cordry from finding Lee but was unable to do so. After failing to convince Lee to leave with him, Cordry then punched and kicked her until she collapsed and lay still. After she lay on the ground for nearly ten minutes, he picked her up and carried her home. The only sound that Lee made was a groan. While the details that the three women provided differed slightly, each told the coroner's jury of a deadly assault.[31]

While coroners' juries worked to determine a killer's intentions, the charges that an accused murderer received depended on the evidence presented in the case, the judge, and attorneys. An investigating coroner and his jury could determine that a man or woman intended to kill someone only to have a defense attorney convince a jury in criminal court that the person acted in self-defense or the heat of the moment. The verdicts rendered by coroners' juries were not always maintained in courts of law and, in fact, were often lowered, sometimes by prosecutors who made plea deals with defense attorneys. Race contributed to the charges and sentences of suspected murderers. African American men, such as John Cordry, were tried quickly and faced tougher charges and sentences than their white counterparts, including working-class and immigrant white men.[32]

But the coroner's jury determined that John Cordry did not kill Nellie Lee alone. In fact, a second assault earlier in the evening also caused her death, they concluded. The autopsy results, along with witness testimony, provided evidence for their verdict. Before John Cordry punched and kicked his wife on April 26, 1878, a woman named Pinkey Daniels assaulted Nellie Lee. Lee encountered Daniels in an alley and she knocked Lee onto the ground. Daniels left Lee bleeding from her left ear afterward. Lee then went to Squires's house just a few minutes later. How the fight began or ended is unknown, but the coroner's jury determined that Daniels's assault on Lee contributed to her death. The jury rendered a verdict that Nellie Lee died "from the effects of haemorrhage of the brain and gangrene of the colon" from injuries "first by the hands of Pinkey Daniels . . . and secondly by injuries received from John Gordry [*sic*]."[33]

Although the coroner's jury held two people accountable for Nellie Lee's death, the St. Louis press focused on the assault from John Cordry. In an article titled "Kicked to Death," the *St. Louis Post-Dispatch* wrote a mostly sympathetic account, referring to Nellie Lee as a "poor, abandoned" woman and a "white wife murdered by a brutal negro husband." The reporter's reference to Cordry's race was typical for press coverage of African Americans. He may have also had more sympathy for Lee because she was a white woman. However, the reporter was not entirely sympathetic to Lee, referring to her home as a "negro den." He also described her face as "swollen by habitual intemperance and hardened by exposure," which "wore an expression of animal vacuity, instead of the calm which is so frequently seen in the face of the dead." He then vividly described the bruises that covered her body, as was typical in sensational news accounts. The lengthy discussion of her physical features and commentary on her drinking were less common and show that there were limits to his sympathy. The reporter made no reference to a history of domestic violence either, another omission that shows a lack of compassion for Lee.[34]

The *St. Louis Post and Dispatch* journalist showed some understanding for Lee, however, and offered an explanation for her supposedly wayward path to prostitution. The reporter referred to Lee as "abandoned" more than once, suggesting that she turned to prostitution because her former husband, an architect named Frank Lee, left her. The reporter referred to her by her apparent alias, Clark, rather than her married name, Lee. The couple had two children.

She evidently went to work as a prostitute to support herself, as her occupation is listed in the inquest record as "prostitute." It is unknown what happened to her children, but they may have lived with relatives after her death.[35]

Both Pinkey Daniels and John Cordry faced criminal charges for the homicide of Nellie Lee, but their criminal trials differed. In January 1879, nine months after Nellie Lee's death, the district attorney of the St. Louis City Circuit Court charged Pinkey Daniels with "assault to kill," to which she pled not guilty. She stood trial in March and a jury acquitted her. While the coroner's jury believed that the evidence showed that Pinkey Daniels's attack contributed to Nellie Lee's death, the jury in the criminal trial did not believe that Daniels had assaulted with the intention of killing Lee. The court ordered Pinkey Daniels to "go home without delay." In contrast, John Cordry's trial occurred much more quickly, and he faced a stricter sentence than did Pinkey Daniels. The district attorney charged John Cordry with second-degree murder. In just two days, a jury tried and found Cordry guilty. The court sentenced him to ten years in the state penitentiary, as well as court costs. His sentence began on July 3, 1878—just over two months after he murdered his wife.[36]

Newspapers lauded Cordry's quick trial and conviction, in part because of his brutal acts, but primarily because he was a Black man. One *Post-Dispatch* reporter described Cordry as "a brutal-looking mulatto, about 30 years of age, lips thick and sensual, and covered with a small black moustache." A journalist for the *Globe-Democrat* wrote, "More of this judicial expedition would be a good thing for the criminal class." For this writer, the "criminal class" evidently referred to African Americans as well as convicted criminals because he depicted Cordry as animal-like. He claimed that Cordry killed Lee "with his heavy hoof," not his foot or his fists. The reporter considered Cordry to be essentially subhuman, this statement reveals.[37]

No reporter sought to justify or explain John Cordry's acts, as they did for Josiah Colcord. But unlike Colcord, Cordry was not a once-respectable white man who had fallen from grace. Perhaps the reporters believed it was Cordry's nature as a Black man of the supposed "criminal class" to beat and kill his wife. Or perhaps they believed that Lee's fear of his beating her showed that he was an abusive man and that explained the murder. Finally, Cordry could speak for himself and explain why he killed his wife, unlike Colcord, who died by suicide. Cordry made no statement at his trial, though. Regardless, the coverage of this murder differed from the murder-suicides because no one sought to explain, and certainly did not try to justify, Cordry's acts. Yet like

Lillie Colcord, Nellie Lee feared Cordry because he assaulted her. On the night of her death, she told both her husband and her neighbor that she feared that he would beat her to death. While St. Louis reporters offered some sympathy for Lee, they did not seek to uncover a history of domestic violence or even acknowledge that such a history probably existed. Instead, reporters cared far more about reporting the gruesome details of Lee's murder and the condition of her body than in understanding what caused her death.[38]

Domestic violence was little understood in the late nineteenth century, and finding fault with the victim was common for women with questionable or bad reputations. The press extended some sympathy to Nellie Lee despite her tarnished reputation because their own prejudices were reinforced when they learned that a Black man killed her. These same newspapers—possibly even the same reporters—likely blamed Lillie Colcord and alcohol to explain the shocking behavior of someone who once held a respected position in St. Louis. The testimony from witnesses, particularly women, in the coroners' inquests into their deaths reveal that John Cordry and Josiah Colcord were quite similar, however. Both men killed their wives after a history of physically abusing them. Both men expressed jealousy. It is possible that, like other men who committed murder-suicides in the late nineteenth century, the two men feared that their wives would leave them. Nellie Lee and Lillie Colcord both confided in women friends or acquaintances that their husbands abused them. Both women feared further assaults or even murder.

Coroner Hugo Auler uncovered similar stories in his inquests into the deaths of Josiah and Lillie Colcord and Nellie Lee. But these men were not treated as equal perpetrators, and the women were not treated as equal victims. Instead, the amount of sympathy each party received varied by race, class, reputation, and perceived adherence to gender norms. Although Lillie Colcord and Nellie Lee shared similar backgrounds, one married a white man and the other had a common-law marriage to a Black man. Nellie Lee had once had good standing in St. Louis, while Lillie Colcord had a longstanding bad reputation. Justice was not meted out in the same way in the press, nor would it have been had Colcord and Cordry lived to see criminal trials for the murders of their wives. While coroners performed the first step in the criminal justice system in deaths caused by homicide, that system was an unequal one.

CHAPTER SIX

"No One Was Blamed"

Coroners' Inquests into Deadly Workplace Accidents

THIRTY-NINE-YEAR-OLD John Brennan arrived to work as a foreman at the Collier White Lead and Oil Company on the evening of
June 4, 1876, probably expecting an ordinary overnight shift. That
night proved to be far from ordinary, however. Brennan worked in the boiler
room overnight, and around 2:00 A.M., the boiler pressure suddenly fell in
one of the three boilers that were operating. Steam also began to come from
an unusual spot. A coworker, Henry Kief, alerted Brennan to the issue, but
he assured Kief that the company's fireman and acting engineer that night,
Nicholas Degendorf, monitored the boilers closely. About fifteen minutes
later, the boiler exploded and injured several workers, including Brennan.
The blast shook much of the neighborhood, ruined a large part of the building, and scattered debris for blocks. The explosion caused a fire in the
building, and several employees, including Brennan, were unable to escape.
Degendorf suffered internal injuries, burns, and bruises. City firemen rushed
to the scene to extinguish the flames and rescue the men who worked there.
Initially, Brennan's injuries did not appear life-threatening, but the explosion had caused more damage to his body than his treating physicians realized. Brennan died at 8:00 P.M. on the day after the explosion.[1]

On June 6, Coroner George F. Dudley, MD, began a two-day inquest to
determine the cause of the explosion—the source of the company's sixth fire.
Dudley interviewed fifteen witnesses, many of whom were engineers, to determine if any individual caused the explosion or if the owners of the Collier
White Lead and Oil Company were to blame. Because John Brennan's death
was a potential homicide, Dudley convened a coroner's jury, as required by
Missouri law. A coroner's jury found that the company was not to blame, but

an individual was: Nicholas Degendorf, the acting engineer during that shift. Witnesses who were coworkers of Brennan's told the coroner and his jury that Degendorf had been drinking before he showed up for work, and while Brennan and the engineer from the previous shift, John Kauffman, believed that Degendorf was "able to attend his duties," other coworkers disagreed. The coroner's jury held Degendorf responsible for the explosion and claimed that he was guilty of "negligence." St. Louis officials did not file charges against Degendorf, however, although the verdict could have prompted charges of criminal negligence, manslaughter, or possibly even homicide. In addition, the Collier White Lead and Oil Company escaped blame. Neither the jury nor the press held the company's owners responsible for Brennan's death, even though they hired Degendorf and their company had had five previous fires. In fact, an absence of blame for a company and a lack of criminal charges against an individual were both typical in cases of deaths that coroners determined to be accidental. Coroners' juries seldom determined that an individual was responsible for a death in the case of a workplace accident, making their verdict that Nicholas Degendorf's negligence contributed to the death of John Brennan remarkable.[2]

Dangerous workplaces caused many deadly accidents in late nineteenth-century cities like St. Louis. Coroners had an important task when conducting investigations into deaths that occurred in workplaces. They acted as death investigators as well as stewards of public health and safety. Coroners and their juries had to determine whether an employer or another individual, often a coworker, caused or contributed to accidental deaths in the workplace, such as equipment malfunctions, falls, and vehicular accidents. A verdict from a coroner's jury that determined that someone caused a death either deliberately or because of negligence could be the first step toward criminal charges, a trial, and prison time or a fine. Criminal negligence and manslaughter were lesser charges than homicide but serious nonetheless. In addition, if a coroner's jury found an employer to be at fault, it could cost the company a substantial fine or, possibly, prompt new workplace safety regulations. Despite these possibilities, however, coroners' juries almost never found employers accountable for deadly workplace accidents. The ten years between 1875 and 1885 marked an era in which some workplace safety laws were in effect in Missouri and nationwide, but they were far less substantial than those that would be enacted during the early twentieth century. Progressive reformers sought these laws because of the workplaces dangers that existed and the regularity in which deadly accidents, such as the boiler explosion that killed John Brennan, occurred. In cases of accidental deaths, coroners and their juries typically determined that no one was responsible for a person's death, even though in some cases, employers, the deceased, or others took actions that caused these accidents.[3]

The inquest into the death of John Brennan differs from most other accidental deaths because it was a potential homicide and the coroner's jury held someone liable. More often, a coroner and/or a deputy coroner investigated accidental deaths on their own, without needing to convene a coroner's jury, because they did not anticipate charges of homicide, manslaughter, or criminal negligence to follow their inquests. Brennan's case will be contrasted with one of these more typical inquests, that of Henry Diekhoener, who died when an overloaded elevator collapsed. The chapter will also feature a brief biography of Deputy Coroner Herman Praedicow, who assisted Coroner John Frank in investigating Diekhoener's untimely death.

John Brennan's death is just one of thirty-three accidental deaths examined in this study and one of only two accidental deaths in which a coroner's jury held someone else accountable. Unlike in homicide cases, however, accountability did not mean intent to kill or killing someone in the heat of passion. Intent did not necessarily mean engaging in criminal negligence, either. Instead, coroners' juries determined that another person's actions unintentionally caused a death, typically because of carelessness or negligence. They still determined these deaths to be accidental, however. While the actions of others caused or contributed to these accidents, coroners' juries did not find that they *intended* to cause harm. Officials declined to file criminal charges in part because of this lack of intent. More often, coroners and their juries did not hold anyone responsible for these deaths, although in some cases, employers, the deceased, or others took actions that caused these accidents. However, Missouri law and coroners' juries did not equate a failure to exercise due caution with an intention to take another's life.[4]

The thirty-three cases examined include a variety of accidental deaths, including those caused by falls, drowning, burns, medical accidents, poisoning, and train and buggy accidents. Several other types of accidents were examined in the original data sample of 868 cases, and at least one male and one female from each type of accidental death were selected to analyze. Victims of accidents differ from those who died from those who died from other causes examined in this book. First, they tended to be older—many between ages forty and fifty—and German immigrants are overrepresented. Many worked as laborers and, like the other men and women in this study, were working class. Most of these men and women were respected members of their communities. Many also died in public, rather than at home, particularly because many of these accidents occurred at workplaces. For this reason, men died in accidents more often than women, although women often died while at home—typically their workplace—or while in public running errands or tending to other business. A final difference is that although several accidents may have been caused, in part, by alcohol use, the coroner did not add references to alcohol in his verdict, distinguishing these cases from those discussed in chapter 2.

Coroners were particularly thorough in cases of accidents that took place when the deceased was at work because they had to determine if the deceased, an employer, or another person caused the death. Coroners called witnesses and sought to uncover every detail of the events that led to the accidents to determine what happened and if anyone caused the accident, meaning, if it was potentially a homicide or, in some cases, a suicide. Coroners and, in some cases, their juries examined evidence to decide if another person acted with malice or negligence to cause these deaths. Despite Missouri laws that made it necessary for coroners to potentially assign blame in accidental deaths, few laws held individuals or companies responsible for deadly negligence or dangerous workplaces. In late nineteenth-century St. Louis, no workers' compensation laws existed, life insurance was rare, and few laws regulated workplaces, making it nearly impossible for coroners to hold employers accountable for the accidental deaths that they investigated, even if their actions contributed to or caused those deaths.[5]

The potential consequences of a coroner's verdict in cases of accidental deaths were significant because a verdict could lead to criminal charges. Coroners investigated most of these deaths themselves, rather than allowing deputy coroners to do so alone. In some cases, deputies assisted coroners in these investigations, with both interviewing witnesses to determine the causes of these deaths. Coroners interviewed between one and fifteen witnesses in cases of accidental deaths but often questioned at least five witnesses for accidental deaths that occurred in public, including workplace accidents. They interviewed more witnesses than they typically did for suspected suicides, alcohol-related deaths, abortions, or natural deaths because part of their job was to determine if other people or an employer was responsible for these deaths. Inquests into accidental deaths resembled investigations into suspected homicides in this way. Witnesses, including people who saw these men and women die, recounted the facts in as much detail as possible and often told the coroner what they believed caused the accident. In some cases, they had different accounts of what happened—such as the speed of a striking vehicle or, in the death of John Brennan, the condition of the boilers. Newspapers provided more coverage for large accidents in public places than for accidents at home or those that killed one person. Newspaper reporters recounted the gruesome details of the accidents but seemed to be more concerned with the insurance of damaged buildings and the estimated cost of the damages than aiding the victims and their families. Newspapers seldom mentioned the liability of building owners in cases of explosions and fires, although some laws existed that held them liable. In some cases, witnesses and the press blamed the victims of accidents for their deaths, especially at work.[6]

As with other causes of death, coroners especially valued testimony from members of the deceased's family. Coroners interviewed relatives even when they were not present when their loved ones died. They also generally placed their testimony first in the inquest record, whether or not they were first interviewed, indicating that coroners considered the statements of relatives to be the most important. The St. Louis press also focused on the families. Newspapers depicted deaths from workplace accidents as especially tragic because they left relatives behind. Reporters noted when victims had spouses and children who survived the deceased, even in short articles. If a family struggled after a loved one died in an accident, reporters sometimes mentioned that too and suggested that they needed charity. Although civil lawsuits for damages were possible, families of accident victims seldom went this route, probably because they did not expect to be successful. Historian Donald W. Rogers argues that in the late nineteenth century, employees were understood to engage in contracts with their employers and knowingly took on workplace risks. While employers were expected to exercise "due care" and provide safe environments, few laws and policies forced them to, and courts seldom favored employees over employers. Another likely reason is because few could afford attorneys to do so.[7]

The workplace accident that left John Brennan's wife a widow initially had unknown causes. The deadly explosion at the Collier White Lead and Oil Company occurred around 2:00 A.M. on June 5, 1876. Although several workers were injured, John Brennan was the only one who died in the blaze.

Over the course of two days, Coroner George F. Dudley interviewed fifteen witnesses before a coroner's jury of six men over the age of eighteen, so that they could evaluate the evidence and determine whether someone should be charged with homicide, manslaughter, or criminal negligence. Fifteen was a large number of witnesses to interview in an accidental death, even for one that could lead to possible criminal charges. These witnesses included Brennan's coworkers as well as several engineers who investigated the remnants of the boiler after it exploded. Interestingly, Dudley did not interview John Brennan's wife, which differed from most inquests, regardless of cause of death. It is possible that she felt too distraught to testify. Coroner Dudley interviewed fifteen other people to determine what caused the boiler to explode as well as whether a crime had been committed.[8]

The coroner and his jury learned that Brennan and several other men worked the overnight shift, and operations ran normally until around 11:30 P.M. on June 4, 1876, when an issue with the boilers first became apparent. William H. Singer, a licensed stationary engineer, told Coroner Dudley and his jury that the boilers were running well, except for a tile that was out of place on one of them. Singer repaired the tile, and all of the machinery was running well when he performed his last inspection before leaving at midnight. Singer left Degendorf in charge of the machinery, telling him to watch the three boilers at their workplace and ensure that they had enough water. Singer felt confident that Degendorf would manage the boilers well, as he had been employed at the Collier White Lead and Oil Company between eight and ten months and had served as engineer in Singer's stead before. However, soon after Singer left, the boilers began to have issues again.[9]

Between 1:00 and 2:00 on the morning of the explosion, Henry Kief and other coworkers became concerned about the boiler. Kief stated that he heard one of the coal passers on duty say, "Let her go to hell" or "Let her blow to hell," which prompted Kief to check the boilers himself. Kief believed that one of the boilers had stopped and shared his concerns with Brennan, who assured Kief that Degendorf was sober and managing the machines. Soon after, the boiler began running again, but quickly—"like hell and damnation," Kief said. About fifteen minutes before the explosion, Kief saw steam coming from a place on the boiler that did not usually produce it. Kief saw Brennan go to tend the boilers approximately five minutes before they exploded. After the explosion, between 2:00 A.M. and 3:00 A.M., Engineer William H. Singer returned to work, only to find the aftermath of the blast and a small fire burning. The boilers, evidently, were not running as well as he thought when he left earlier that night. It was also possible that Degendorf did not tend the boilers properly.[10]

In addition to interviewing witnesses to detail the events of the explosion as accurately as possible, the coroner also had to assess whether or not the workers, particularly the engineers on duty that night, possessed the requisite qualifications to manage the boilers. The city of St. Louis required that engineers who worked in factories or for railroads hold licenses to do so. Coroner Dudley interviewed several engineers, including Albert Stephenson, who testified that he was a member of the Board of Engineers of St. Louis City. Stephenson said that Singer was "well qualified" and demonstrated "steadiness and sobriety" in his work. He testified that he did not know whether Degendorf held the requisite license, however, and added that one would have to check for a record of it at the Office of the Boiler Inspector. Although Singer trusted Degendorf enough to let him oversee the boilers in his stead, witness testimony did not make it clear whether he held the necessary credentials.[11]

Another crucial factor in determining whether anyone was legally responsible for Brennan's death was the cause of the boiler explosion. Coroner Dudley devoted most of his inquest to interviewing witnesses about the details of the accident. The coroner interviewed seven engineers, but they disagreed as to the cause of the blast. According to Missouri statutes in the late nineteenth century, an engineer had to manage boilers, which is probably why the coroner interviewed so many of them to determine the cause of the explosion. Three engineers explained that the boiler did not have enough water in it at the time of the explosion, and they believed that this is what caused the deadly accident. Four other engineers disagreed, claiming that a recent hydrostatic test strained the boiler and led to the explosion. Still others argued that thin material in some areas or simply poor construction of the boilers contributed to the blast. It seems that the recent hydrostatic test, in addition to an examination of the boilers after the fire, did not provide conclusive answers to the cause of the deadly fire.[12]

Other witnesses claimed that an inebriated engineer contributed to the explosion, as he could not properly tend to the machinery in his condition. Two witnesses testified that Nicholas Degendorf had been drinking before arriving for his shift. John Kauffman, a fireman at the Collier White Lead and Oil Company and colleague of Brennan's, testified that the engineer "was under the influence of Liquor that night, but he was able to attend to his duties." Another coworker, Henry Kief, disagreed, testifying not only that Degendorf was drunk but that his showing up to work under the influence of alcohol had worried him for some time. Kief testified that Degendorf was "under the influence of Liquor as he passed us." Kief and another coworker, Wagner, "remarked to each other at the time . . . that we did not think he was in a fit condition to take charge of the Engine." It was not the first time that Kief had noticed that Degendorf had arrived to work under the influence of alcohol. He testified, "I had not felt safe for some time when Nick was in charge of the engines" because he had come to work drunk before. In fact, Kief had confronted Degendorf about the lack of water at least one time prior to the explosion.[13]

Kief and Singer both offered explanations for the explosion as well. Kief emphasized his warnings about the boiler operating improperly and his concerns about Degendorf's intoxication. In contrast, Singer concluded that a hydrostatic test caused the explosion, not a failure by Degendorf to ensure the right amount of water was in the boiler. Given Singer's trust in Degendorf, however, he may have been inclined to believe that the man he left in charge did not neglect his duties.[14]

Dudley's experience as a physician and a coroner aided him as he oversaw the inquest and questioned witnesses before the coroner's jury, but ultimately, the jury rendered a verdict. The coroner's jury took the evidence presented into account, including Nicholas Degendorf's inattentiveness, drunkenness, and the condition of the boiler. The jury concluded that it was Nicholas Degendorf's negligence to provide ample water in the boilers that caused the accident.[15] The verdict read, in part: "And the Jury further find that the Burns and Scalds of the said Brennan were caused by an Explosion of the Steam Boilers at about 2 o'clock A.M. June 5th, 1876 . . . and the Jury further say that the cause of the said Explosion was an over pressure of Steam Superinduced by a scarcity of water in the Boilers, as the result of the negligence of one Nicholas Degendorf acting Engineer at the time of the explosion."[16]

The jury's verdict placed blame on an individual rather than the company. First, the jury's verdict indicates that they believed the two witnesses who testified that Degendorf had been drinking before he came to work. The jury also evidently believed that too little water, not a recent test or thin material, caused the explosion, another factor that was the responsibility of a careless employee and not the company. Finally, the jury did not hear testimony about the five previous fires that occurred at the Collier White Lead and Oil Company and may not have known about them, another likely reason that they did not hold the company responsible. The lack of accountability attributed to the Collier White Lead and Oil Company is not surprising. Dangerous workplaces were a fact of life in the late nineteenth century, so holding a company or its owners responsible would be highly unusual, as well as difficult to prove. Despite the fact that the coroner's jury determined that an employee was ultimately responsible for the death of John Brennan, rather than the company itself, the verdict was significant because it held someone liable—a rare occurrence. In addition, because the verdict from the coroner's jury determined that Nicholas Degendorf was negligent, he faced potential charges of fourth-degree manslaughter.[17]

Reporters for the *St. Louis Globe-Democrat* and *St. Louis Post-Dispatch* agreed with the coroner's jury—that Nicholas Degendorf alone was to blame for the explosion. They expressed more concern for the company's losses than Brennan's family as well. The newspapers wrote several articles about the explosion, fire, and inquest. The *Globe-Democrat* noted that the "immense establishment has burned down half a dozen times," named the people who were injured (including Brennan), explained the details of the blast, and concluded by estimating the financial amount of damages as well as the company's insurance. Despite the company's multiple fires, the reporter did not place blame on the company, probably because they did not believe that blame rested with the company. Despite the company's numerous fires, there were few newspaper articles about them and, evidently, no suspicion of negligence or malice. The *Milwaukee Daily Sentinel* and *St. Louis Post-Dispatch* did not blame the company either, writing only about the details of the injuries and the inquest into Brennan's death. The *Post-Dispatch* concluded its last article about the explosion by noting that photographs were taken of the ruins so that other companies could insure their own businesses and equipment appropriately. Although reporters for these three newspapers expressed concern about the financial damages that the Collier White Lead and Oil Company experienced, as well as their insurance, they did not indicate whether John Brennan had life insurance, even though he was fairly young at age thirty-nine and had a wife to support.[18]

The absence of condemnation for Brennan's employer was typical in the late nineteenth century because the law and many ordinary people believed that workers agreed to take on certain risks when they chose to work in a given profession, as observed by historians Nate Holdren and Donald Rogers. Holdren refers to this expectation as an "assumption of risk."[19] As Rogers points out, employees were expected to exercise "due care" at work, meaning appropriate caution—a somewhat vague definition, but one that likely included being sober at work.[20] In cases of workplace injuries or deaths, in order to hold an employer liable, often in a lawsuit, evidence had to prove that an employee was in no way at fault for their injury. The "fellow servant rule" could also absolve a company of responsibility, meaning that a company was not liable for a workplace injury or death if another employee was to blame for the accident. If it could be proven that an employee exercised prudence but was injured or killed at work because the employer did not maintain appropriate safety standards, then the employer could be found negligent in a court of law or civil court. It was nearly impossible to meet that standard, however.[21]

In the death of John Brennan, it appears that the coroner's jury observed the fellow servant rule, which held that Nicholas Degendorf, not the Collier White Lead and Oil Company, was to blame for his death. Drinking alcohol before or during work, as Degendorf likely did, violated expectations of exercising appropriate caution. The company likely paid for Brennan's funeral, but no other costs. Workers' compensation laws did not exist until the early twentieth century, and life insurance was rare. The 1870s marked a turning point nationwide, however, as lawmakers and workers began to expect employers to protect employees against dangers that a "reasonably prudent man" would encounter. The trend accelerated after the infamous Triangle Shirtwaist Factory Fire in New York killed 146 people in 1911—most of them women—prompting state legislatures to pass more stringent workplace safety laws. After that workplace disaster, lawmakers and ordinary people across the country decided that it was "common sense" that employers were responsible for workplace safety.[22]

The state of Missouri followed national trends by expanding its requirements for public safety, including workplace safety, in the 1870s. By 1879, three years after John Brennan died, Missouri published its updated *Revised Statutes* with an expanded section regarding "Public Safety." The new statutes not only required that engineers pass an examination and hold a professional license but also added detailed requirements for engineers of any steam engine to maintain certain qualifications to perform their jobs. Stationary engineers had to demonstrate that they had both the "knowledge and ability" to maintain the safety of workers as well as property in order to manage steam boilers or other machinery. The state required that engineers in any city pass an examination before they could be employed. In fact, acting as an engineer without the proper qualifications could result in being charged and convicted of a misdemeanor. Both the state of Missouri and the city of St. Louis required that engineers in any city pass an examination given by "a committee of examiners," which, in St. Louis, was the Board of Engineers. The revised laws also increased the potential charges for workplace negligence. In 1879, a negligent engineer could face charges of third-degree manslaughter, rather than the fourth-degree manslaughter charges mandated by the earlier laws that were in place when John Brennan died because of Nicholas Degendorf's—and his employer's—negligence.[23]

Even after the state of Missouri added new requirements for workplace safety and liability in 1879, deadly workplace accidents persisted without employers being held legally accountable. Such was the case in the death of Henry Diekhoener, whom Coroner John N. Frank and Deputy Coroner H. Praedicow investigated. It was unusual for both a coroner and his deputy to investigate a death together, but they may have done so because Diekhoener died in a public place. They may have been especially thorough because the inquest would have garnered public attention and, perhaps, public criticism. Another possibility is that Coroner Frank did not trust his deputy coroner to investigate alone. Unlike the death of John Brennan, the coroner and the deputy coroner did not suspect that Diekhoener may have been murdered, so they did not have to convene a coroner's jury. Instead, they investigated together, with Coroner Frank rendering the official verdict.[24]

Critics of the coroner system often argued that the men who conducted inquests and rendered verdicts were untrained and, therefore, unqualified to hold office as coroners and deputy coroners. Deputy coroners like Herman Praedicow provided evidence to support their arguments. Deputy Coroner Praedicow, sometimes called "Peculiar Praedicow" by the St. Louis press, was serving his third (nonconsecutive) term as deputy coroner when he helped Coroner Frank investigate the death of Henry Diekhoener in 1881. Unlike some deputy coroners, Praedicow had ample training for the Office of the Coroner, having learned the trade under his father, who worked as a surgeon and coroner in Germany. Like many other coroners and their deputies, Praedicow served in the Civil War for the Union, although he was discharged for a disability almost one year after joining the war effort. Although most coroners practiced as physicians even when they did not hold office, it varied among deputy coroners. Praedicow only practiced medicine when he served as deputy coroner, a position that he was appointed to four times by three coroners between 1875 and his death in 1891.[25]

Praedicow created his share of personal and professional scandals. Coroners fired him from the position of deputy coroner almost as often as they appointed him. Praedicow's appointments to the roles of deputy coroner and superintendent of the morgue appear to be based on party politics as well as his substantial experience, as newspaper articles suggest that he held these positions for long periods of time, except when Democrats held office and appointed men from their party. During one of his terms as a deputy coroner, Praedicow allegedly impersonated his supervising coroner, Hugo Auler, and bribed witnesses. He also reportedly pulled a gun to intimidate a witness, an accusation that has merit because he had a history of using firearms. He even allegedly fired a gun at his brother-in-law during an argument. His behavior had consequences. Republican Coroner Auler forced him to resign in 1878 for insubordination because he shouted and cursed at Auler in addition to the aforementioned impersonations of Auler during inquests. Despite these controversies, Coroner Frank appointed Praedicow to serve as deputy coroner once more in 1880, likely because he was an experienced deputy but also because the two were related by marriage. The appointment was opposed by former Coroner Auler and Dr. James C. Nidelet, the physician who often performed autopsies for the Office of the Coroner and served on the Board of Police Commissioners. Frank ignored their concerns and appointed Praedicow to the position anyway.[26]

Praedicow also served as superintendent of the morgue several times between 1871 and 1891, and he created scandals in this role as well. His odd behavior in this position seems to have been what earned him the moniker "Peculiar Praedicow." On at least one occasion, he allegedly took a corpse to a saloon, pretending that he was tired or did not drink. He also evidently enjoyed arranging corpses so that when someone walked into the room, they would be touched by a corpse's hand (and he would invite people into the room for this purpose). Some claimed that he held parties in the morgue. The *St. Louis Post-Dispatch* reported that he "had made the dead-house the scene of drunken revels and debauchery." Critics claimed that Praedicow and his allies created a monopoly and did not allow all undertakers to care for and bury bodies. Although Republican coroners often appointed Praedicow to these positions, party alignments did not guarantee his position. Coroner

Frank suspended him for thirty days when he served as superintendent of the morgue after he mishandled the clothing of a deceased person in his care. Although the St. Louis press may have exaggerated some of these events, there is likely some truth to them. Other coroners expressed concerns about his fitness, yet they also continued to appoint him to roles in which he handled the dead and investigated their causes of death. "Peculiar Praedicow" rendered verdicts that impacted people's lives.[27]

Despite Deputy Coroner Praedicow's sometimes strange behavior, there is no evidence that he did anything inappropriate in the death investigation of Henry Diekhoener, in which he assisted Coroner John N. Frank. Unlike in the death investigation of John Brennan, in the inquest into the death of Henry Diekhoener, as in most cases of accidental deaths that occurred in the workplace, the coroner held no individual or company responsible. In some cases, they determined that these deaths resulted from accidents, while in others, including the death of Diekhoener, they indicated that the deceased themselves bore at least part of the blame. Coroner John N. Frank and Deputy Coroner H. Praedicow determined that Diekhoener died from "an accidental fall of an overloaded elevator." Diekhoener was pulling up lead pigs (a crudely shaped chunk of lead that would be melted down for another use, such as making bullets) at the St. Louis Shot Tower Company, where he worked on the afternoon of July 21, 1881, when he suffered a deadly accident. The pigs that he loaded onto the elevator were supposed to go into the tower, where they would be liquified and made into bullets. The elevator made three stops, as usual, but suddenly came crashing down. The sudden fall crushed Diekhoener's head, killing him. Frank and Praedicow interviewed only four witnesses and did not convene a jury inquest because they did not suspect a homicide. The absence of a coroner's jury was not unusual, but a coroner investigating a death alongside his deputy coroner was. More often, deputy coroners and coroners each investigated cases alone, with deputies often conducting inquests into seemingly easy-to-solve cases alone while coroners investigated more challenging cases, as well as some routine ones, depending on the day's workload.[28]

Although Henry Diekhoener died at work, making it a more visible case, the coroner and deputy did not suspect homicide, and it was unlikely that they would hold Diekhoener's employer liable for his death. Frank and Praedicow recorded the testimony of Maria Diekhoener, Henry's wife, first in their inquest record. Although Maria Diekhoener did not witness her husband's death or was at his place of work, as his nearest relative, the coroner and deputy coroner found her testimony to be valuable. Maria Diekhoener told investigators that her husband was "in good health" when he left for work that morning, evidence that the accident alone killed him. She also provided biographical information that was often included in inquest records—his age (forty-one), place of birth (Germany), and family status (married and a father of five children). The coroners devoted most of their inquest to interviewing Diekhoener's coworkers. His supervisor, Orville Rule, who worked as a superintendent at the St. Louis Shot Tower Company, testified that Diekhoener had failed to follow instructions by overloading the elevator with more weight than he should have. He stated that he had instructed Diekhoener to only bring up seventeen to eighteen pigs of lead, but the deceased had instead loaded the elevator with twenty. The excess weight is what caused the elevator to suddenly crash and fall, he said. As Diekhoener's supervisor, however, Rule had reason to absolve himself of any blame. If he had failed to warn Diekhoener about the excess weight or even instructed him to load the elevator with twenty pigs, then he could have been held liable in the coroners' verdict, as Nicholas Degendorf had been in the death of John Brennan.[29]

In fact, there was some evidence in the inquest that Diekhoener was not entirely to blame for the accident and his own death. A coworker, Julius Gastrow, testified that Diekhoener had told him that the elevator was not working properly earlier that day. Gastrow had run the elevator for a few years for the company, generally trading off with Diekhoener. Diekhoener told Gastrow on the afternoon of the accident, "What's the matter, she runs hard." Gastrow had not had problems running the elevator the previous night and morning, however, he told the coroners. He noticed that the elevator was falling after Diekhoener went up the final time and tried to grasp the rope to stop the rapidly declining elevator but could not. A final witness, Officer Robert White, could not speak to the accident itself but told the coroners about the condition that Diekhoener was in when he responded to the call and his efforts to call an ambulance to save him. Those efforts were futile.[30]

After interviewing four witnesses, Coroner John Frank determined that Henry Diekhoener had died because of an "accidental fall of an overloaded elevator." Ultimately, he and Deputy Coroner Praedicow believed that employee carelessness caused the deadly accident. Unlike John Brennan, the evidence presented to the coroner suggested that Henry Diekhoener unintentionally caused the elevator that he was using to come crashing down. In order for another person, such as Diekhoener's supervisor or the St. Louis Shot Tower Company, to be liable for his death, there had to be evidence that Diekhoener bore *no* responsibility. He evidently ignored his own knowledge of the elevator's weight limit as well as his supervisor's instructions when he added two extra lead pigs to the machine.[31]

Both the *St. Louis Post-Dispatch* and the *St. Louis Globe-Democrat* attributed Diekhoener's death to his overloading the elevator. The *Post-Dispatch* wrote a brief article, noting that Diekhoener fell 156 feet to his death after putting more weight on the elevator than the maximum allowed. The *Globe-Democrat* wrote a more sensationalistic piece, as it often did, referring to the death as "the most horrifying accident that has happened in St. Louis for many years." The reporter referred to Diekhoener's body as "mangled," adding that it was the most badly damaged body that the superintendent of the morgue had ever seen. The account noted that Coroner Frank planned to investigate the elevator the day after the inquest to help determine the cause of death but, if he did so, did not include that investigation in the inquest record. Both reporters concluded that it was the overloaded elevator that caused the fall.[32]

Because Diekhoener's death was determined to be an accident and no one, except perhaps the deceased himself, was to blame, no criminal charges followed the coroner's inquest. The newspapers ended their coverage after his verdict. Unlike in the death of John Brennan, the press did not recount a history of tragic accidents at the St. Louis Shot Tower Company. The press treated Diekhoener's death as a single tragedy, rather than part of a pattern.

Deadly elevator falls were somewhat common in the late nineteenth century, however, as were other deadly workplace accidents—fires, burns, scalds, and falls—in general. St. Louis and the state of Missouri had some workplace safety laws in place as well as professional standards, such as examinations, licenses, and certificates, to maintain the safety of workers, but they were just beginning. Despite these regulations, John Brennan, Henry Diekhoener, and numerous other men and women died from workplace accidents, and such deaths were an unfortunate reality of late nineteenth-century industries in St. Louis and other cities. Despite possibly holding a license to work as an engineer, an intoxicated Nicholas Degendorf was still permitted to manage the boilers at the Collier White Lead and Oil Company. And while Missouri laws increased the requirements for some workers, such as engineers, no legislation or workplace regulations prevented a lone worker from loading a heavy elevator to a height of 180 feet—an elevator guided only by a rope.

John Brennan and Henry Diekhoener left behind wives, children, and other relatives, just as did other men and women who died from accidents. Newspapers and coroners often highlighted the losses that these families experienced, but few provisions existed for those who were left behind after an accident. Coroners and their juries seldom held employers accountable for deaths that they may have contributed to, and families had few resources to help them cope financially outside of charities. While companies had insurance to protect their financial losses from fires and explosions, they did not have to provide for a worker's family after an employee died from those same fires or explosions, save for funeral expenses in most cases. Newspaper reporters lamented the deaths of men who were breadwinners, but at the same time, they did not believe that a system that allowed dangerous workplaces to exist that caused some of these deaths were at fault. People took risks when they went to work, and although it was tragic if they died doing those things, most men and women did not believe that it was a failure of the system. It was not until the early twentieth century that popular opinion changed to believe that employers, the city, and others should protect people's safety, and progressive reformers worked to change laws to do so. In St. Louis between 1875 and 1885, most men and women believed that no one was to blame in these tragedies—preventable or not.

The Importance of Death Investigations
in the Past and Present

A S ST. LOUIS EXPANDED between 1875 and 1885 and beyond, the city created new opportunities for work and leisure but also poverty, racism and segregation, violent crime, addiction, and other social problems, as these coroners' inquests illustrate. Violent deaths were a daily occurrence, particularly among the urban poor and working class. The few benevolent societies in St. Louis could not assist all of the city's residents, and many helped only respectable white men and women. Mental illness and alcoholism were poorly understood, leaving even wealthier residents of the city, such as Estelle Johnson, with limited options for treatment. The poor, working-class, immigrant, and Black populations of the city had few opportunities to enter growing white-collar, professional work. Many worked long hours in the city's factories, which paid little and had a host of dangers, some of them deadly. Women had few options for wage work and even fewer options to leave an abusive marriage or prevent or abort an unwanted pregnancy.

Arguments for protective legislation, resources and education for the poor, safer workplaces, and regulations and training for government officials, including coroners, became more widespread between the 1880s and 1910s. Progressive reformers in cities across the country used statistics, including mortality records, to argue for government regulations to mitigate the dangers of industrial capitalism. These reformers challenged the notion that poverty, alcoholism, government corruption, and dangerous workplaces were simply a part of life. They sought government solutions to these social problems. Progressive reformers advocated for stricter workplace safety laws, shorter work hours, Prohibition, civil service examinations for government employees, education to help the poor achieve middle-class status, and the vote for women, which they believed would further ensure protective measures for women and children. Most did not challenge gender and racial inequalities, however, and did not advocate for women's full equality with men or an end to segregation. Some of their proposed reforms succeeded and created a foundation for additional measures, such as worker safety. Other reforms, such as Prohibition, failed to curb alcoholism and even worsened crime in urban areas as an illegal trade in alcohol emerged. Progressives took no measures specifically against domestic violence, although some hoped that Prohibition would curb it. Contraception and abortion were too radical to discuss, even for most suffragists, and only became central to women's rights advocates in the 1960s and 1970s, with the advent of second-wave feminism.

Progressive reformers also argued for a shift to a medical examiner system as part of a larger effort to rely on scientific and professional expertise. The Office of the Coroner slowly declined in the late nineteenth and twentieth centuries, particularly in large urban areas. A medical examiner system separated the medical and legal operations of the coroner, and the position was appointed, rather than elected. Medical examiners were trained physicians, often specialists in pathology, unlike many coroners, who could be physicians but may also have had no medical or legal training. Some physicians, attorneys, former coroners, and medical examiners in Missouri and across the country charged that poor training and outdated state regulations for coroners resulted in incompetence, corruption, and injustice from the mid-nineteenth to the early twentieth centuries. Massachusetts created the first medical examiner office in 1877, but it took decades for large-scale change to occur because of political, medical, and logistical barriers.[1]

In the twentieth century, more states began to require increased regulations, licensing, and education for death investigators, who tended to be medical examiners rather than coroners. The transition occurred gradually, however. By 1900, only Massachusetts, Maryland, and Rhode Island had medical examiner systems. In 1909, Dr. Rutherford Gradwohl, an early forensic scientist who occasionally worked as a physician for the St. Louis Office of the Coroner, argued in a groundbreaking paper that Missouri should follow Massachusetts' lead. Determining how a person came to his or her death required different skills than a criminal investigation, he argued. Gradwohl soon became one of the country's leading forensic scientists, but few cities and states heeded his call, including Missouri. In 1918, New York

City created a medical examiner system, and other cities and states followed suit, but slowly. Opposition from politicians, some physicians, and even state constitutions that mandated a coroner's office limited the possibility of reform. It was not until the 1930s that physicians came to dominate death investigations. By this time, coroners and medical examiners relied on autopsies to determine most causes of death, as opposed to witness testimony. In the next decades, the authority of coroners declined gradually and physicians gained more authority. By the 1940s, St. Louis coroners still held inquests in suspicious deaths or deaths of unknown people, but physicians had to sign the death certificate. The St. Louis Office of the Coroner officially became the Office of the Medical Examiner in 1977 and remains to this day.[2]

The medical examiner system is more private and based on scientific analysis, as opposed to a public coroners' system, which relied heavily on witness testimony. Today, medical examiners in the city of St. Louis and across the country are medical doctors who often specialize in forensic and anatomical pathology. The St. Louis Office of the Medical Examiner still conducts investigations into deaths that are unexpected, suspicious, a result of violence, a crime, or neglect or occur when the deceased is not being treated by a physician, much as the coroner did in the late nineteenth century. Medical examiners are still medicolegal professionals, but they are appointed rather than elected, and their primary purpose is to serve public health. However, autopsies are routine rather than rare, and investigations are performed in the Office of the Medical Examiner, away from friends, neighbors, and relatives. Instead of convening a jury, as coroners in St. Louis and elsewhere did in some cases, medical examiners conduct their investigations and render their verdicts based on information gathered from the scene of death, the deceased's medical history, laboratory tests, and an autopsy. Medical examiners no longer have to defer some verdicts to juries, as coroners did, a change that has decreased the likelihood of inaccurate verdicts. Many of their records are closed to the public, although the files are available to family members of the deceased, and relatives can ask questions about the process. The Office of the Medical Examiner also saves tissue samples in case relatives need it in the future. The public and press no longer witness death investigations.[3]

Death investigations in St. Louis and throughout the country have changed substantially since the late nineteenth century, but many of the issues from that era are still concerns today. Early, unexpected, and violent deaths are, unfortunately, still a daily occurrence. Access to safe abortions is once more a central topic of public debate and policy. Death investigators still examine early and suspicious deaths from a variety of causes and determine what they understand to be a manner of death, which may be the first step in the criminal justice system. While St. Louis shifted from a coroner's office to a medical examiner system in the 1970s, many counties in Missouri and across the nation have not. Fourteen states have a county-, parish-, or district-based coroner system, including many midwestern and western states, such as Kansas, Nebraska, the Dakotas, and Montana. Another fourteen states have a mixture of a coroner and medical examiner system, including Missouri and Illinois. Twenty-two states have a centralized or county- or district-based medical examiner system, particularly New England and the mid-Atlantic region. In the twenty-first century, Missouri still has a coroner system throughout much of the state, and in some counties, officeholders have little medical training or experience. Other states use coroner systems as well. The work of medical examiners and coroners is not conducted in a vacuum; they are subject to pressure from families and, in some cases, the public. Occasionally, coroners alter their verdicts on their reports and death certificates, particularly in stigmatized causes of death such as suicide, deaths from addiction, and even Covid-19. City offices are still a part of political systems, although politics and death investigations have changed since the 1870s and 1880s. Criticisms of death investigators and the nation's criminal justice system remain as well.[4]

Newspaper reports of unexpected deaths are also more private in the twenty-first century than they were in the late nineteenth century. Instead of reading sensationalistic stories of suicides and deaths from alcohol or drugs, newspapers often conceal these deaths by using phrases such as "died unexpectedly" or "died at home." The press is more respectful of the privacy of the family as well as of the deceased in the twenty-first century. The press often prints obituaries written by family members, and some use them as an opportunity to educate others about addiction, suicide, and other struggles that many people experience. Others prefer to focus on the life of the loved one, rather than the cause of death, whether they died from an illness, an accident, or suicide or addiction.

The ongoing Covid-19 pandemic has created a new public health crisis and exacerbated other existing ones, such as suicide and addiction. Even before the pandemic, public health officials expressed concern about a "suicide epidemic" and an "opioid epidemic." A recent increase in violent crime is also worrisome. Many psychologists, sociologists, and policymakers note that "deaths of despair," particularly those from suicide and addiction, as well as increased violence toward others, result from decreased social connections. Suicides began to increase in the twenty-first century, particularly among middle-aged white men. Although the pandemic seems to be worsening depression and addiction, evidently, suicides are not increasing, although public health officials note that it will take time to fully understand the mental health toll of the pandemic. While men and women in the late nineteenth century could become addicted to morphine, laudanum, or opium, today many use prescription painkillers and heroin. Alcohol was also a commonly used substance in the late nineteenth and twenty-first centuries, and some evidence suggests that alcohol addiction is increasing, particularly among women. While it is easier for women to seek treatment for alcoholism today, there is still a chapter "for the wives" in the "Big Book," the guidebook for the popular twelve-step Alcoholics Anonymous program. There is no chapter specifically for husbands of alcoholics.[5]

Women also still struggle to find safe, accessible abortions, especially as many states are recriminalizing the procedure in 2022, after the Supreme Court overturned the *Roe v. Wade* decision of 1973. Even before the overturning of that decision, the procedure had become more difficult to access, particularly for the working class and poor, just as it was in the late nineteenth century. Just as they did in the 1870s and 1880s, antiabortion activists often treat women as the hapless victims of abortion providers. Finally, violent deaths and homicides in general are still national problems, particularly those from gun violence. Domestic violence also increased during the pandemic, and shelter-in-place orders made it difficult to find relief or escape from abuse.[6]

Finally, activists point out the disproportionate number of African American men and women killed by police—often when unarmed and during routine traffic stops. Police violence against African Americans is not new, nor is racism, as is apparent in the coroners' inquests into the deaths of Black men and women in the 1870s and 1880s. But the attention to this problem is new. A verdict rendered by a coroner or a medical examiner is often still the first step in the criminal justice system. For instance, the medical examiner for Hennepin County, Minnesota, determined that George Floyd's death was a homicide in June 2020, a ruling that supported video evidence against Derek Chauvin, the police officer who kneeled on Floyd's neck, killing him.

Chauvin subsequently faced criminal charges and a conviction for the homicide.[7]

Violence and early deaths continue to be problems for individuals, their families, and society. Coroners and medical examiners still investigate unexpected and early deaths to determine how and why a person died. Their determination of a manner of death may still be the first step in the criminal justice system if the death investigator determines that another person was at fault. In cases in which criminal charges are not at stake, a determination of a manner of death provides meaning for the families of the deceased. These rulings also provide crucial data for social scientists (and historians) to better understand phenomena like addiction, suicide, workplace safety, and homicide.

It is important to understand the histories of women and men like Lillie Colcord, who was killed by her husband, Josiah, before he took his own life, and John Brennan, who died because a supervisor neglected to maintain workplace safety. Their stories, while more than a hundred years old, help illuminate present-day problems and, hopefully, can help create solutions, such as the need for policies to protect the health and safety of workers, survivors of domestic violence, people with mental illnesses and addictions, and those seeking abortions. An expanded social safety net, affordable and accessible health care, and safe jobs and housing improve the quality of life and can extend one's life.[8]

NOTES
BIBLIOGRAPHY
INDEX

List of Abbreviations

STL Coroner: St. Louis City Office of the Coroner—Inquests, 1845–1900
MSA: Missouri State Archives, Jefferson City, Missouri
DI: Digital Image

Introduction

1. J. W. McElvain Inquest, July 11, 1881, Case No. 226, Folder 27, Box 26 (MSA microfilm roll C31278), STL Coroner. Hereafter, the record will be referred to as "McElvain Inquest." Subsequent inquests will follow the same citation pattern.

2. McElvain Inquest.

3. For historical works regarding how coroners and medical examiners conducted death investigations, see J. Maxwell Atkinson, *Discovering Suicide: Studies in the Social Organization of Sudden Death* (Pittsburgh: University of Pittsburgh Press, 1978); James C. Mohr, *Doctors and the Law: Medical Jurisprudence in Nineteenth-Century America* (New York: Oxford University Press, 1993); Michelle McGoff-McCann, *Melancholy Madness: A Coroner's Casebook* (Douglas Village, Cork: Mercier Press, 2003); Stefan Timmermans, *Postmortem: How Medical Examiners Explain Suspicious Deaths* (Chicago: University of Chicago Press, 2006); Jeffrey M. Jentzen, *Death Investigation in America: Coroners, Medical Examiners, and the Pursuit of Medical Certainty* (Cambridge, Mass.: Harvard University Press, 2009).

4. *First Annual Report of the Health Department of the City of St. Louis, 1877, under the Provisions of the New Charter for Fiscal Year Ending April 10, 1878* (St. Louis, Mo.: The Printing House, 1878).

5. STL Coroner, in the "Coroner's Inquest Database," MSA, http://www.sos.mo.gov/archives/resources/coroners/, accessed September 1, 2017; *First Annual Report of the Health Department of the City of St. Louis, 1877, under the Provisions of the New Charter for Fiscal Year Ending April 10, 1878* (St. Louis, Mo.: The Printing House, 1878).

6. Wesley Morrell Inquest, May 16, 1883 Case No. 102, Folder 101, Box 33 (MSA microfilm roll C31280), STL Coroner.

7. "A New Deputy Coroner," *St. Louis Post-Dispatch*, May 7, 1883, 2; "The Coroner's Assistants," *St. Louis Globe-Democrat*, November 28, 1880, 13; Sylvester Nidelet, *Directory of Deceased American Physicians, 1804–1929*, DI, Ancestry.com, accessed May 29, 2019; "Well-Known St. Louisans," *St. Louis Post-Dispatch*, July 28, 1896, 4.

8. Max Aaron Goldstein, ed., *One Hundred Years of Medicine and Surgery in Missouri: Historical and Biographical Review of the Physicians and Surgeons of the State of Missouri and Sketches of Some of Its Notable Medical Institutions* (St. Louis, Mo.: St. Louis Star, 1900); *The Mayor's Message with Accompanying Documents, to the Municipal Assembly of the City of St. Louis, for the Fiscal Year Ending April 12th, 1897*, printed for the Municipal Assembly, 1898, 702. Information regarding coroners and their deputies was found using census data, death certificates, and city directories, which listed few as physicians by trade. U.S. Census 1850, 1860, 1870, 1880, 1890, 1900, 1910, and 1920; Missouri Death Certificates, Missouri State Archives, Jefferson City, Missouri, accessed online: http://www.sos.mo.gov/archives /resources/deathcertificates/default.asp, accessed July 10, 2011.

9. Gerald J. Baldasty, *The Commercialization of News in the Nineteenth Century* (Madison: University of Wisconsin Press, 1992), 96.

10. Joseph A. Dacus and James W. Buel, *A Tour of St. Louis: or, The Inside Life of a Great City* (St. Louis, Mo.: Western Publishing Co., 1878), 536–537; "St. Louis Globe-Democrat Announces It Will Close This Year," *The New York Times*, November 8, 1983, section A, 27. The *St. Louis Globe-Democrat* ceased publication in 1983. The *St. Louis Post-Dispatch* is still in operation in 2022.

11. "St. Louis Globe-Democrat Announces It Will Close This Year"; Baldasty, *Commercialization of News*, 128; Dacus and Buel, *Tour of St. Louis*, 542–544, 547–549; "St. Louis Globe-Democrat Announces It Will Close This Year"; "Happy Anniversary to Us," St. Louis Today.com, https://www.stltoday.com /news/archives/happy-anniversary-to-us-take-a-journey-through-history-with -the-post-dispatch/collection_ca197e6f-b80a-552c-bd89-564d42efe172.html, accessed June 28, 2022.

12. See, for example, local press accounts of the murder-suicide of Josiah and Lillie Colcord. "Wine and Women," *Daily Rocky Mountain News*, August 18, 1878, 1; "Post Mortem Points," *St. Louis Globe-Democrat*, August 20, 1878, 4; "Under the Sod," *St. Louis Globe-Democrat*, August 19, 1878, 8; "Post Office Corners," *St. Louis Globe-Democrat*, August 19, 1878, 4; "Funeral Notice," *St. Louis Globe-Democrat*, August 21, 1878, 5; "St. Louis in Splinters," *St. Louis Globe-Democrat*, August 21, 1878, 8; "Funeral of Lillie Colcord," *St. Louis Globe-Democrat*, August 22, 1878, 8.

13. "A Fatal Blow," *St. Louis Globe-Democrat*, March 8, 1885, 20; "A Cold-Blooded Murder," *St. Louis Globe-Democrat*, December 23, 1882, 12; "Kicked to Death," *St. Louis Post and Dispatch*, April 29, 1878, 4; "A Devilish Deed," *St. Louis*

Globe-Democrat, October 9, 1883, n.p.; "Local Brevities," *St. Louis Globe-Democrat*, October 11, 1883, 4.

14. "The Political Field," *St. Louis Globe-Democrat*, August 4, 1878, 8.

15. Stefan Timmermans, *Postmortem: How Medical Examiners Explain Suspicious Deaths* (Chicago: University of Chicago Press, 2006), 4; John M. McIlroy Jr., "The Coroner v. the Medical Examiner in Missouri," *Missouri Law Review* 34, no. 2 (1969): 221; Allen E. Wagner, *Good Order and Safety: A History of the Metropolitan Police Department, 1861–1906* (St. Louis: Missouri History Museum, 2008), xvi, 447; "The Phalanx Forming," *St. Louis Globe-Democrat*, June 23, 1876; James C. Mohr, *Doctors and the Law: Medical Jurisprudence in Nineteenth-Century America* (Baltimore: Johns Hopkins University Press, 1993), 217; "Andy Brown's Contract," *St. Louis Post-Dispatch*, September 1, 1881, 4; "Undertakers Complain," *St. Louis Post-Dispatch*, April 18, 1889, 2; "Morgue Combination," *St. Louis Post-Dispatch*, April 20, 1889, 3.

16. "The Coroner's Assistants," *St. Louis Globe-Democrat*, November 28, 1880, 13; "Getting Ready to Vacate," *St. Louis Post-Dispatch*, November 15, 1888, 2; "A Row Over Spoils," *St. Louis Post-Dispatch*, November 22, 1888, 2; "You Stand Charged: Democratic Officials to Be Tried by the Hendricks Association," *St. Louis Post-Dispatch*, January 24, 1888, 2; "Praedicow Will be Suspended," *St. Louis Post-Dispatch*, January 30, 1890, 8; John C. Burnham, *Health Care in America: A History* (Baltimore: Johns Hopkins University Press, 2015), 127; Rebecca Edwards, *New Spirits: Americans in the Gilded Age, 1865 to 1905* (New York: Oxford University Press, 2011), 72.

17. Edwards, *New Spirits*, 17; Katharine T. Corbett, *In Her Place: a Guide to St. Louis Women's History* (St. Louis: Missouri Historical Press, 1999), 101.

18. Edwards, *New Spirits*, 17; Corbett, *In Her Place*, 101.

19. "Our Criminal Code," *St. Louis Globe-Democrat*, January 6, 1879, 3; R. B. H. Gradwohl, "The Office of the Coroner: Its Past, Its Present, and Its Advisability of Its Abolishment in the Commonwealth of Missouri," *Journal of the American Medical Association* 54 (March 12, 1910): 842–846; Jeffrey M. Jentzen, *Death Investigation in America: Coroners, Medical Examiners, and the Pursuit of Medical Certainty* (Cambridge, Mass.: Harvard University Press, 2009), 23–25; Herbert S. Breyfogle, "The Laws of Missouri Relating to Inquests and Coroners," *Missouri Law Review* 10 (1945): 36–37, 59–60, 63; Randy Hanzlick and Debra Combs, "Medical Examiner and Coroner Systems: History and Trends," *Journal of the American Medical Association* 279, no. 11 (1998): 870–871; Timmermans, *Postmortem*, 5, 36; Oscar T. Schultz and E. M. Morgan, "The Coroner and the Medical Examiner," *Bulletin of the National Research Council* 64–66 (1928): 23–24; John M. McIlroy Jr., "The Coroner v. the Medical Examiner in Missouri," *Missouri Law Review* 34, no. 2 (1969): 219, 221–222; Baxter W. Leisure Jr., Executive Assistant of the Office of the Medical Examiner of St. Louis, Interview by Author, St. Louis, Missouri, August 13, 2015.

20. John C. Burnham, *Health Care in America: A History* (Baltimore: Johns Hopkins University Press, 2015); Paul Starr, *The Social Transformation of American Medicine: The Rise of a Sovereign Profession and the Making of a Vast Industry*, Updated Edition (New York: Basic Books, 2017), 79–80, 102–105, 127; *First Annual Report of the Health Department of the City of St. Louis, 1877, under the Provisions of the New Charter for Fiscal Year Ending April 10, 1878* (St. Louis, Mo.: The Printing House, 1878), 3.

21. Mohr, *Doctors and the Law*, xiii; Allen E. Wagner, *Good Order and Safety: A History of the Metropolitan Police Department, 1861–1906* (St. Louis: Missouri History Museum, 2008), xvi.

22. Dacus and Buel, *Tour of St. Louis*, 533–535; Wagner, *Good Order and Safety*, xvi, 85, 120–122, 253, 449; "A Surprise," *St. Louis Post-Dispatch*, August 11, 1883, 2; "Noland's Cases," *St. Louis Post-Dispatch*, August 16, 1879, 2.

23. Roger Lane, *Violent Death in the City: Suicide, Accident & Murder in 19th Century Philadelphia* (Cambridge, Mass.: Harvard University Press, 1979), 1; Jeffrey S. Adler, *First in Violence, Deepest in Dirt: Homicide in Chicago, 1875–1920* (Cambridge, Mass.: Harvard University Press, 2006); Stephen Berry, "The Historian as Death Investigator," in *Weirding the War: Stories from the Civil War's Ragged Edges*, ed. Stephen Berry (Athens: University of Georgia Press, 2011): 176–188; Stephen Berry, *Count the Dead: Coroners, Quants, and the Birth of Death as We Know It* (Chapel Hill: University of North Carolina Press, 2022), 84; "CSI: Dixie," Claudio Saunt and Stephen Berry, https://csidixie.org/, accessed August 4, 2021.

24. Berry, "Historian as Death Investigator," 186; Berry, *Count the Dead*, 109.

25. Berry, "Historian as Death Investigator," 186; "Drunkard's Deaths: The High Sounding Titles Given by the Physicians," *St. Louis Post-Dispatch*, September 22, 1882, 1; "Many Such: Sad Case of Abortion and Morphine Poisoning," *St. Louis Post-Dispatch*, September 5, 1882, 7; Mary Scott Inquest, January 27, 1883, Case No. 1331, Folder 59, Box 32 (MSA microfilm roll C31280), STL Coroner; Mary Harris Inquest, June 18, 1880, Case No. 2087, Folder 38, Box 22 (MSA microfilm roll C31276), STL Coroner; "Was It Suicide?" *St Louis Globe-Democrat*, June 19, 1880, 8; "The Coroner," *St. Louis Globe-Democrat*, June 20, 1880, 4; Timmermans, *Postmortem*, 4; McGoff-McCann, *Melancholy Madness*, 34.

26. Of my original sample of 868 cases, 106 were conducted into the deaths of African Americans, 272 into the deaths of native-born whites, 54 into the deaths of men and women whose race or ethnicity I could not determine, and 436 into the deaths of a variety of immigrant men and women, including men and women from Canada, Sweden, Switzerland, France, and Italy, but primarily from Germany and Ireland.

27. Corbett, *In Her Place*, 101–102.

28. Corbett, *In Her Place*, 102.

1. Not as Simple as Disease

1. Kate Williamson Inquest, September 15, 1880, Case No. 408, Folder 59, Box 35 (MSA microfilm roll C31280), STL Coroner.

2. Williamson Inquest. Peck was the deputy coroner under Coroner Sylvester L. Nidelet. Dr. James Nidelet was Sylvester's brother and routinely performed autopsies for the coroner's office.

3. Of the fourteen cases that were selected for this chapter, seven were inquests into the deaths of men and seven were for women. The men and women were older than those who died by suicide, abortion, alcoholism, and homicides, ranging in age from thirty to forty-seven. Only three were native-born white men and women, while five were Black, and the rest were born in Europe (two from Ireland, one Switzerland, one Wales, and one Germany). Similar cases to those discussed in this chapter will be footnoted throughout.

4. Herbert S. Breyfogle, "The Laws of Missouri Relating to Inquests and Coroners," *Missouri Law Review* 10 (1945): 38; *The Statutes of the State of Missouri*, compiled by David Wagner (St. Louis, Mo.: W. J. Gilbert, Law Book Publisher, 1872), 283; R. B. H. Gradwohl, "The Office of the Coroner: Its Past, Its Present, and Its Advisability of Its Abolishment in the Commonwealth of Missouri," *Journal of the American Medical Association* 54 (March 12, 1910): 844.

5. Breyfogle, "Laws of Missouri," 38–39, 51; Gradwohl, "Office of the Coroner," 844. Missouri coroners could also place witnesses in jail if they refused to testify.

6. Breyfogle, "Laws of Missouri," 43–45, 52; *The Statutes of the State of Missouri*, compiled by David Wagner, 285; Stefan Timmermans, *Postmortem: How Medical Examiners Explain Suspicious Deaths* (Chicago: University of Chicago Press, 2006), 109–110.

7. Timmermans, *Postmortem*, 5; St. Louis City Office of the Coroner, Inquests, 1845 to 1900, https://s1.sos.mo.gov/records/archives/archivesdb/coroners/Results.aspx, accessed July 2, 2021.

8. For examples, see Mary Maher Inquest, July 11, 1881, Case No. 225, Folder 26, Box 26 (MSA microfilm roll C31278), STL Coroner; David Kelleher Inquest, July 11, 1881, Case No. 224, Folder 25, Box 26 (MSA microfilm roll C31278), STL Coroner; J. W. McElvain Inquest, July 11, 1881, Case No. 226, Folder 27, Box 26 (MSA microfilm roll C31278), STL Coroner; "Hot as Hades," *St. Louis Post-Dispatch*, July 8, 1881, 4; "The Sun's Sufferers," *St. Louis Globe-Democrat*, July 11, 1881, 5; "Slaughtered by the Sun," *St. Louis Post-Dispatch*, July 12, 1881, 5; "Coroner's Cases. Crowded Condition of the City Morgue during the Hot Spell," *St. Louis Post-Dispatch*, July 13, 1881, 4; "Killed by Heat," *St. Louis Post-Dispatch*, July 14, 1881, 1; "The Heat," *St. Louis Post-Dispatch*, July 15, 1881, 4; "The Weather," *St. Louis Post-Dispatch*, July 22, 1881, 8.

9. *Statutes of the State of Missouri*, compiled by David Wagner, 284.

10. Carl A. McCandless, *Government, Politics and Administration in Missouri* (St. Louis, Mo.: Educational Publishers, Inc., 1949), 147; Breyfogle, "The Laws of Missouri," 54–56, 58–59; Gradwohl, "Office of the Coroner," 843; *Statutes of the State of Missouri*, compiled by David Wagner, 286.

11. Breyfogle, "Laws of Missouri," 39.

12. Breyfogle, "Laws of Missouri," 36–37; Allen E. Wagner, *Good Order and Safety: A History of the Metropolitan Police Department, 1861–1906* (St. Louis: Missouri History Museum, 2008), 137.

13. Deputy Coroners Charles T. Noland and Cornelius MacBride worked as attorneys. Deputy Coroner Thomas Hennessy became a judge later in this career. Deputy Coroners William H. Renick and George W. Peck both worked as physicians.

14. William Herbert Renick, *U.S. School Catalogs, 1765–1935*, DI, ancestry.com, accessed June 2, 2022; "Coroner Nidelet," *St. Louis Post-Dispatch*, December 1, 1882, 2; William H. Renick, *U.S. Returns from Military Posts, 1806–1916*, DI, ancestry .com, accessed June 2, 2022; William Renick, U.S. Civil War Pension Index: General Index to Pension Files, 1861–1934, DI, ancestry.com, accessed June 18, 2020; U.S. Census, 1880; Sandra (Renick) Stark, "Dr William Herbert Renick," https://www .findagrave.com/memorial/44564798/william-herbert-renick, accessed June 2, 2022; "The Weekly Report of the Smallpox Hospital," *St. Louis Post-Dispatch*, November 27, 1876, 3; "Life in St. Louis," *St. Louis Post-Dispatch*, October 8, 1877, 2; "Board of Health," *St. Louis Post-Dispatch*, November 1, 1877, 3; "Baring Their Arms," *St. Louis Post-Dispatch*, December 26, 1881, 5; "Life in St. Louis," *St. Louis Post-Dispatch*, October 8, 1877, 2; "A New Deputy Coroner," *St. Louis Post-Dispatch*, May 7, 1883, 2; "Renick," *St. Louis Post-Dispatch*, April 27, 1889, 5; George Peck, U.S. Census 1870, 1880; "The Coroner's Deputy Resigns," *St. Louis Post-Dispatch*, February 19, 1884, 5; "Local Politics," *St. Louis Globe-Democrat*, September 24, 1884, 8.

15. "About Town," *St. Louis Post-Dispatch*, December 22, 1882, 2. The *Post-Dispatch* noted that Laddy was not attended by a physician when she died; Josephine Laddy Inquest, December 22, 1882, Case No. 1250 Folder 150, Box 31 (MSA microfilm roll C31279), STL Coroner.

16. Laddy Inquest.

17. Laddy Inquest.

18. Laddy Inquest.

19. Laddy Inquest.

20. See, for example, Matilda Reynolds Inquest, May 11, 1885, Case No. 84, Folder 40, Box 123 (MSA microfilm roll C31300), STL Coroner.

21. See, for examples, Reynolds Inquest; Lucinda Adams Inquest, January 3, 1883, Case No. 1280, Folder 8, Box 32 (MSA microfilm roll C31280), STL Coroner;

George Vanderheide Inquest, October 17, 1880, Case No. 2332, Folder 13, Box 24 (MSA microfilm roll C31277), STL Coroner.

22. "A Cold-Blooded Murder," *St. Louis Globe-Democrat*, December 23, 1882, 12; "About Town," *St. Louis Post-Dispatch*, December 22, 1882, 2.

23. James C. Nidelet also served on the Board of Police Commissioners in the 1870s. See Wagner, *Good Order and Safety*, 121–122, 155–162. For the other two natural deaths that were initially suspected homicides, see Frank Anderson Inquest, October 25 and 26, 1880, Case No. 2356, Folder 37, Box 24 (MSA microfilm roll C31277), STL Coroner; "Coroner's Cases," *St. Louis Globe-Democrat*, October 26, 1880, 4.

24. Williamson Inquest.

25. Williamson Inquest.

26. Williamson Inquest.

27. Williamson Inquest.

28. Williamson Inquest; "Was It Murder?" *St. Louis Post-Dispatch*, September 14, 1883, 2; "The Williamson Inquest," *St. Louis Post-Dispatch*, September 15, 1883, 4; "A Suspicious Case," *St. Louis Globe-Democrat*, September 15, 1883, 12; "Died," *St. Louis Globe-Democrat*, September 16, 1883, 8; "Released from Custody," in "Multiple News Items," *St. Louis Globe-Democrat*, September 16, 1883, 16; "City News," *St. Louis Post-Dispatch*, September 17, 1883, 8.

29. "Was It Murder?" *St. Louis Post-Dispatch*, September 14, 1883, 2; "Released from Custody," in "Multiple News Items," *St. Louis Globe-Democrat*, September 16, 1883, 16.

2. "She Was a Hard Drinker"

1. Ann Donahoe Inquest, February 2, 1884, Case No. 752, Folder 110, Box 37 (MSA microfilm roll C31281) and Folder 258, Box 120 (MSA microfilm roll C31308), STL Coroner.

2. Donahoe Inquest.

3. Donahoe Inquest.

4. Although this study focuses on inquests conducted between 1875 and 1885, there are records for the Office of the Coroner from 1845 to 1900. Ann Donahoe's verdict is the only verdict of dipsomania in the entire database.

5. Michelle L. McClellan, *Lady Lushes: Gender, Alcoholism, and Medicine in Modern America* (New Brunswick, N.J.: Rutgers University Press, 2017), 24, 32; Sarah W. Tracy, *Alcoholism in America: From Reconstruction to Prohibition* (Baltimore: Johns Hopkins University Press, 2005), 32. Historians and documents from the period

show a consensus about the characteristics of dipsomania, although some claimed it was related to insanity, while others said it was a form of insanity. For more information, see Gerry Johnstone, "From Vice to Disease? The Concepts of Dipsomania and Inebriety, 1860–1908," *Social and Legal Studies* 5 (1996): 37–56; Patricia E. Prestwich, "Female Alcoholism in Paris, 1870–1920: The Response of Psychiatrists and of Families," *History of Psychiatry* 14, no. 3 (2003): 321–336; "Dipsomania," in "Clinical Notes and Comments," *Quarterly Journal of Inebriety* 4, no. 1 (1880): 51–52; "Dipsomania and Heredity," in "Clinical Notes and Comments," *Quarterly Journal of Inebriety* 10 (1888): 395–397; Norman Kerr, "The Treatment of Female Inebriety," "Dipsomania and Heredity," in "Clinical Notes and Comments," *Quarterly Journal of Inebriety* 10 (1888): 68–76; Dr. E. Decaisne, "Dipsomania in Women," *Quarterly Journal of Inebriety* 11 (1889): 247–252; "Drugs That Enslave: Words of Good Advice and Encouragement for Their Victims," *St. Louis Post-Dispatch*, June 2, 1889, 17; "Drunkards and Dipsomaniacs," *St. Louis Post-Dispatch*, May 19, 1881, 2.

6. Stefan Timmermans, *Postmortem: How Medical Examiners Explain Suspicious Deaths* (Chicago: University of Chicago Press, 2006), 55–56; For examples, see Martha J. Thomas Inquest, April 22, 1882, Case No. 805, Folder 56, Box 29 (MSA microfilm roll C31279), STL Coroner; Bridget Tracy Inquest, July 6, 1885, Case No. 180, Folder 50, Box 43 (MSA microfilm roll C31283), STL Coroner.

7. For examples, see James Hardy Inquest, June 3, 1880, Case No. 2056, Folder 7, Box 22 (MSA microfilm roll C31276), STL Coroner; Johanna Hamilton Inquest, April 29, 1882, Case No. 819, Folder 70, Box 29 (MSA microfilm roll C31279), STL Coroner; Ellen Maloney Inquest, July 12, 1881, Case No. 241, Folder 42, Box 26 (MSA microfilm roll C31278), STL Coroner; Jacob Blumenthal Inquest, November 25 and 26, 1877, Case No. 18, Folder 157, Box 12 (MSA microfilm roll C31274), STL Coroner.

8. Both Tracy and Michelle McClellan note that the term "alcoholism" did not come into common use by specialists until the 1890s and 1900s. Tracy, *Alcoholism in America*, 27–28; McClellan, *Lady Lushes*, 24. For additional works about alcoholism in the United States, see Harry Gene Levine, "The Discovery of Addiction: Changing Conceptions of Habitual Drunkenness in America," *Journal of Studies on Alcohol* 39, no. 1 (1978): 143–174; William J. Rorabaugh, *The Alcoholic Republic: An American Tradition* (New York: Oxford University Press, 1979); Mark Lender, "A Special Stigma: Women and Alcoholism in the Late 19th and Early 20th Centuries," in *Alcohol Interventions: Historical and Sociocultural Approaches*, ed. David L. Strug, S. Priyadarsini, and Merton M. Hyman (New York: Haworth Press, 1986), 41–57; Catherine Gilbert Murdock, *Domesticating Drink: Women, Men and Alcohol in America, 1870–1940* (Baltimore: Johns Hopkins University Press, 1998); Sarah W.

Tracy and Caroline Jean Acker, *Altering American Consciousness: The History of Alcohol and Drug Use in the United States, 1800–2000* (Amherst: University of Michigan Press, 2004); Scott C. Martin, *Devil of the Domestic Sphere: Temperance, Gender, and Middle-Class Ideology, 1800–1860* (DeKalb: Northern Illinois University Press, 2008).

9. Timmermans, *Postmortem*, 55–56, 84.

10. John Grady Inquest, July 6, 1885, Case No. 177, Folder 47, Box 43 (MSA microfilm roll C31283), STL Coroner. For two similar cases, see John Nicely Inquest, June 3, 1880, Case No. 2059, Folder 10, Box 22 (MSA microfilm roll C31276), STL Coroner; "The Coroner's Temperance Lecture," *St. Louis Daily Globe-Democrat*, June 4, 1880, 8; Andrew Conlin Inquest, July 14, 1881, Case No. 250, Folder 51, Box 26 (MSA microfilm roll C31278), STL Coroner; "Coroner's Cases," *St. Louis Daily Globe-Democrat*, July 6, 1885, 10.

11. John Grady, Missouri, Death Records, 1834–1910, DI, ancestry.com, accessed May 27, 2015. A coroner ordered an autopsy in one other alcohol-related death. See J. C. Pinger Inquest, July 25, 1881, Case No. 94, Folder 243, Box 11 (MSA microfilm roll C31278), STL Coroner.

12. In the original sample of 868 cases, thirty-five men and women died from alcohol-related deaths at home, while eleven died in various public places and others died at work, in hospitals, out of state, or in locations not listed in the inquest record. Forty-seven men died from alcohol-related deaths, while eighteen women did. Alcohol-related deaths comprised about 7 percent of all cases. In contrast, 135 St. Louisans died from suicide, or about 16 percent of all cases.

13. "Coroner's Cases," *St. Louis Daily Globe-Democrat*, July 6, 1885, 10.

14. "Died Drunk," in "Coroner's Cases," *St. Louis Daily Globe-Democrat*, June 28, 1880; "The Coroner's Temperance Lecture," *St. Louis Daily Globe-Democrat*, June 4, 1880, 8; Hardy Inquest; James Hardy, *Missouri, Death Records, 1834–1910*, DI, ancestry.com, accessed June 1, 2015; James Grady, *St. Louis City Death Records, 1850–1902*, DI, ancestry.com, accessed June 1, 2015.

15. Dacus and Buel, *A Tour of St. Louis: or, The Inside Life of a Great City* (St. Louis, Mo.: Western Publishing Co., 1878), 462.

16. Dacus and Buel, *A Tour of St. Louis*, 461–467, 478–481.

17. Tracy, *Alcoholism in America*, 46, 51–52; Lender, "A Special Stigma," 42; Kerr, "The Treatment of Female Inebriety," 71–72; "Badly Needed: A Sanitarium for the Treatment of Confirmed Drunkards," *St. Louis Post-Dispatch*, March 20, 1882, 3. An ad in the *St. Louis Post-Dispatch* offered treatment at a Jerseyville, Illinois, facility: Display Ad 2, No Title, *St. Louis Post-Dispatch*, June 27, 1900, 2.

18. "Ready for the Nominations," *St. Louis Post-Dispatch*, September 20, 1896, 11; *Directory of Deceased American Physicians, 1804–1929*, DI, ancestry.com, accessed

May 29, 2019; "Well-Known St. Louisans," *St. Louis Post-Dispatch*, July 28, 1896, 4; U.S. Census 1850; National Park Service, *U.S. Civil War Soldiers, 1861–1865*, DI, ancestry.com, accessed May 29, 2019; "Eminent Drs. S.L. and J.C. Nidelet," *St. Louis Post-Dispatch*, July 11, 1881, 8; "The Veil Is Rent," *St. Louis Post-Dispatch*, February 18, 1879, 1; "The Lottery Ring," *St. Louis Post-Dispatch*, March 4, 1879, 4; "Sylvester L. Nidelet," Missouri Death Records, DI, ancestry.com, accessed June 18, 2019.

19. Matilda Reynolds Inquest, May 11, 1885, Case No. 84, Folder 40, Box 123 (MSA microfilm roll C31300), STL Coroner.

20. Maggie Tyler Inquest, May 18, 1883, Case No. 113, Folder 112, Box 33 (MSA microfilm roll C31280), STL Coroner; "City News," *St. Louis Post-Dispatch*, May 19, 1883, Supplement, 10; "Local Brevities," *St. Louis Daily Globe-Democrat*, May 19, 1883, 8. Similar cases include Ellen Collins Inquest, January 23, 1883, Case No. 1325, Folder 53, Box 32 (MSA microfilm roll C31280), STL Coroner. Nidelet also investigated Collins's death. An example of another St. Louis woman, "Mollie," or "Old Moll," known for her drinking and prostitution, repeatedly served time in both the Work House and jail can be found in this brief article: "Jokelets," *St. Louis Post-Dispatch*, July 11, 1895, 4.

21. Donahoe Inquest; U.S. Census 1870, 1880. For additional inquests into verdicts of alcoholism for women, see Margaret Doyle Inquest, June 27, 1880, Case No. 2099, Folder 50, Box 22 (MSA microfilm roll C31276), STL Coroner; "Died Drunk," in "Coroner's Cases," *St. Louis Daily Globe-Democrat*, June 28, 1880, 8; Martha J. Thomas Inquest, April 22, 1882, Case No. 805, Folder 56, Box 29 (MSA microfilm roll C31279), STL Coroner; Johanna Hamilton Inquest, April 29, 1882 Case No. 819, Folder 70, Box 29 (MSA microfilm roll C31279), STL Coroner.

22. Donahoe Inquest.

23. Donahoe Inquest; U.S. Census 1880.

24. Donahoe Inquest; Sarah Tracy notes that concerns about intemperance were related to fears of "newcomers," or immigrants. Tracy, *Alcoholism in America*, 7; McClellan, *Lady Lushes*, 31. In the original sample of 868 inquests, coroners rendered verdicts of alcohol as a cause or contributor to a death for eighteen native-born white men and women and eighteen Irish men and women. Twelve people with German ancestry received such verdicts. The numbers were much smaller for those with other ethnicities.

25. Donahoe Inquest; Missouri Death Records, DI, ancestry.com, accessed August 3, 2016; U.S. Census 1880.

26. Lender, "A Special Stigma," 41; Prestwich, "Female Alcoholism in Paris," 330; McClellan, *Lady Lushes*, 3.

27. Corbett, *In Her Place*, 102–103; McClellan, *Lady Lushes*, 5, 7, 10, 36, 45. Norman Kerr, "The Treatment of Female Inebriety," 66, 69; Murdock, *Domesticating*

Drink, 4, 48; Lender, "A Special Stigma," 41–44, 46–48; Tracy, *Alcoholism in America*, 46; McClellan, "'Lady Tipplers,'" 281; Martin, *Devil of the Domestic Sphere*, 39; Decaisne, "Dipsomania in Women."

28. Tracy, *Alcoholism in America*, 23; Levine, "The Discovery of Addiction," 143–144; Katharine A. Chavigny, "Reforming Drunkards in Nineteenth-Century America: Religion, Medicine, Therapy," in *Altering American Consciousness: the History of Alcohol and Drug Use in the United States, 1800–2000*, ed. Sarah W. Tracy and Caroline Jean Acker (Amherst: University of Michigan Press, 2004), 117–118; Sarah W. Tracy, "Building a Boozatorium: State Medical Reform for Iowa's Inebriates, 1902–1920," in *Altering American Consciousness*, ed. Sarah W. Tracy and Caroline Jean Acker (Amherst: University of Michigan Press, 2004), 138–140.

29. McClellan, *Lady Lushes*, 17, 24; "Dipsomania," in "Clinical Notes and Comments," *Quarterly Journal of Inebriety* 4, no. 1 (1880): 51–52; Decaisne, "Dipsomania in Women"; "Dipsomania and Heredity," in "Clinical Notes and Comments," *Quarterly Journal of Inebriety* 10 (1888): 395–397; Prestwich, "Female Alcoholism in Paris," 329; Tracy, *Alcoholism in America*, 31–33.

30. McClellan, *Lady Lushes*, 31; Corbett, *In Her Place*, 106.

31. Doyle Inquest; Johanna Hamilton Inquest, April 29, 1882 Case No. 819, Folder 70, Box 29 (MSA microfilm roll C31279), STL Coroner.

3. "Whilst Laboring under Mental Derangement"

1. Estell Johnson Inquest, September 3, 1879, Case No. 1576, Folder 77, Box 18 (MSA microfilm roll C31275), STL Coroner.

2. Johnson Inquest.

3. These two cases were selected from twenty-nine cases from the total sample of 120 cases. Of the twenty-nine cases, eighteen feature qualified verdicts, an intentional oversampling.

4. Roger Lane, *Violent Death in the City: Suicide, Accident & Murder in 19th Century Philadelphia* (Cambridge, Mass.: Harvard University Press, 1979), 32; Howard I. Kushner, *American Suicide: A Psychocultural Exploration* (New Brunswick, N.J.: Rutgers University Press, 1991), 64–65; Maria Teresa Brancaccio, Eric J. Engstrom, and David Lederer, "The Politics of Suicide: Historical Perspectives on Suicidology before Durkheim. An Introduction," *Journal of Social History* 46, no. 3 (2013): 612; Georgina Laragy, "'A Peculiar Species of Felony': Suicide, Medicine, and the Law in Victorian Britain and Ireland," *Journal of Social History* 46, no. 3 (2013): 732–743; Nancy Tomes, *A Generous Confidence: Thomas Kirkbride and the Art of Asylum-Keeping, 1840–1883* (Cambridge: Cambridge University

Press, 1984), 91–92. For more on histories of suicide, see J. Maxwell Atkinson, *Discovering Suicide: Studies in the Social Organization of Sudden Death* (Pittsburgh: University of Pittsburgh Press, 1978); Howard I. Kushner, "Immigrant Suicide in the United States: Toward a Psycho-Social History," *Journal of Social History* 18, no. 1 (1984): 3–24; Howard I. Kushner, "Women and Suicide in Historical Perspective," *Signs* 10, no. 3 (1985): 537–552; Howard I. Kushner, "Biochemistry, Suicide, and History: Possibilities and Problems," *Journal of Interdisciplinary History* 16, no. 1 (1985): 69–85; Jennifer M. Lehmann, "Durkheim's Response to Feminism: Prescriptions for Women," *Sociological Theory* 8, no. 2 (1990): 163–187; Howard I. Kushner, "Suicide, Gender, and the Fear of Modernity in Nineteenth-Century Medical and Social Thought," *Journal of Social History* 26, no. 3 (1993): 461–490; Jennifer Lehmann, "Durkheim's Theories of Deviance and Suicide: A Feminist Reconsideration," *American Journal of Sociology* 100, no. 4 (1995): 904–930; Georges Minois, *History of Suicide: Voluntary Death in Western Culture*, translated by Lydia G. Cochrane (Baltimore: Johns Hopkins University Press, 1999); Ronald M. and Stephen T. Holmes, *Suicide: Theory, Practice, and Investigation* (Thousand Oaks, Calif.: SAGE, 2005); John C. Weaver and David Wright, eds., *Histories of Suicide: International Perspectives on Self-Destruction in the Modern World* (Toronto: University of Toronto Press, 2008); John C. Weaver, *A Sadly Troubled History: The Meanings of Suicide in the Modern Age* (Montreal: McGill-Queen's University Press, 2009); David Silkenat, *Moments of Despair: Suicide, Divorce, and Debt in Civil War Era North Carolina* (Chapel Hill: University of North Carolina Press, 2011); Diane Miller Sommerville, "'A Burden Too Heavy to Bear': War Trauma, Suicide, and Confederate Soldiers," *Civil War History* 59, no. 4 (2013): 453–491; Craig Thompson Friend and Lorri Glover, *Death and the American South* (New York: Cambridge University Press, 2014); Diane Miller Sommerville, *Aberration of Mind: Suicide and Suffering in the Civil War-Era South* (Chapel Hill: University of North Carolina Press, 2018). See also *Journal of Social History* 46, no. 3 (2013). This entire issue of *Journal of Social History* is devoted to a transnational history of suicide across time.

5. Stefan Timmermans explains that death investigators today look for evidence that a death resulted from injuries that were both intentional and inflicted upon oneself. Stefan Timmermans, *Postmortem: How Medical Examiners Explain Suspicious Deaths* (Chicago: University of Chicago Press, 2006), 5–6, 8, 84–85.

6. "Suicide Statistics," *St. Louis Post-Dispatch*, March 18, 1882, 5; Terri L. Snyder, "What Historians Talk about When They Talk about Suicide: The View from Early Modern British North America," *History Compass* 5, no. 2 (2007): 659; "Suicide Statistics," *St. Louis Post-Dispatch*, March 18, 1882, 5; Sommerville, "'A Burden Too Heavy to Bear,'" 481; Lane, *Violent Death in the City*, 30; Kushner, "Immigrant Suicide in the United States," 15.

7. See also Carrie Kuhnle Inquest, July 5, 1885, Case No. 174, Folder 44, Box 43 (MSA microfilm roll C31283), STL Coroner; Johanna Toelke Inquest, July 9, 1881, Case No. 209, Folder 10, Box 26 (MSA microfilm roll C31278), STL Coroner; Emma C. Tuggy Inquest, July 21, 1881, Case No. 268, Folder 69, Box 26 (MSA microfilm roll C31278), STL Coroner.

8. In the original sample of 868 cases, there were 111 men and 24 women who died by suicide. Kushner, "Women and Suicide," 543–547; Kushner, "Suicide, Gender, and the Fear of Modernity," 461; Sommerville, *Aberration of Mind*, 8, 50–51, 53.

9. Katharine T. Corbett, *In Her Place: A Guide to St. Louis Women's History* (St. Louis: Missouri Historical Press, 1999), 102; Clarence Ward Inquest, September 15, 1875, Case No. 452, Folder 53, Box 7 (MSA microfilm roll C31272), STL Coroner; Mary Harris Inquest, June 18, 1880, Case No. 2087, Folder 38, Box 22 (MSA microfilm roll C31276), STL Coroner; "Was It Suicide?" *St Louis Globe-Democrat*, June 19, 1880, 8; "The Coroner," *St. Louis Globe-Democrat*, June 20, 1880, 4; Wesley Morrell Inquest, May 16, 1883, Case No. 102, Folder 101, Box 33 (MSA microfilm roll C31280), STL Coroner; "Singular Suicides," *St. Louis Post-Dispatch*, February 9, 1882, 5; "Suicide Statistics," *St. Louis Post-Dispatch*, March 18, 1882, 5; "Death's Doings," *St. Louis Post-Dispatch*, May 4, 1883, 8; "Matters of Mystery," *St. Louis Post-Dispatch*, December 16, 1884, 8; "Colored Cussedness: Josephine Howard Attempts Suicide by Taking Morphine," *St. Louis Post-Dispatch*, September 18, 1877, 1; "Fannie Robinson's Suicide," *St. Louis Post-Dispatch*, May 29, 1877, 4; "An Overdose of Civil Rights," *St. Louis Post-Dispatch*, March 23, 1875, 2. Other historians have also found few records of the suicides of African Americans, notably Diane Miller Sommerville and David Silkenat, who have written about suicide after the Civil War. Sommerville, *Aberration of Mind*, 145–146; Silkenat, *Moments of Despair*, 40.

10. "Intelligence by Mail," *The Galveston Daily News*, April 4, 1878; Hugo Auler, 1890 U.S. Veterans Schedules, DI, ancestry.com, accessed May 25, 2020; St. Louis, Missouri Directories 1889–1890, DI, ancestry.com, accessed May 25, 2020; U.S. Census 1850, 1870, 1880; Gerald Grob, *Mental Illness and American Society, 1875–1940* (Princeton, N.J.: Princeton University Press, 1983), 30–31.

11. Franz Kurrus, Missouri Death Records, DI, ancestry.com, accessed May 25, 2020; Joanna or Johanna Toelke, Missouri Death Records, 1850–1931, DI, ancestry.com, accessed May 25, 2020; Joseph Krs, Missouri Death Records, DI, ancestry.com, accessed May 25, 2020; Dr. V. Hugo Auler, Missouri Death Records, DI, ancestry.com, accessed May 29, 2020; "Intelligence by Mail," *The Galveston Daily News*, April 4, 1878; Hugo Auler, 1890 Veterans Schedules, DI, ancestry.com, accessed May 25, 2020; Hugo Auler, *U.S. City Directories, 1822–1995*. DI, ancestry.com, accessed May 25, 2020; U.S. Census 1850, 1870, 1880.

12. "Suicide Statistics," *St. Louis Post-Dispatch*, March 18, 1882, 5; "Disgusted with Herself," *St. Louis Globe-Democrat*, June 8, 1881, 5; Mary A. Kengon Inquest, September 3, 1875, Case No. 435, Folder 36, Box 7 (MSA microfilm roll C31272), STL Coroner. For more on coroners' inquests into the alleged suicides of prostitutes, see Sarah Lirley McCune, "Death of a Prostitute: Suicide and Respectability in St. Louis, 1875 to 1900," *The Missouri Historical Review* 109, no. 2 (2015): 108–127.

13. Robin E. Gearing and Dana Lizardi, "Religion and Suicide," *Journal of Religion and Health* 48, no. 3 (2009): 334, 337; Brancaccio et al., "The Politics of Suicide," 611; Snyder, "What Historians Talk about When They Talk about Suicide." See also: Brancaccio et al., "The Politics of Suicide," 608; Kushner, "Immigrant Suicide in the United States," 14; Sommerville, *Aberration of Mind*, 241; Silkenat, *Moments of Despair*, 13–14; Kushner, *American Suicide*, 37–38.

14. A person's faith was determined by church membership, if noted in an obituary, as well as the cemetery in which they were buried, if death records could be found. Leon Boucher Inquest, October 11, 1880, Case No. 2321, Folder 2, Box 24 (MSA microfilm roll C31277), STL Coroner; Frank Bingham Inquest, November 25, 1885, Case No. 513, Folder 6, Box 45 (MSA microfilm roll C31283), STL Coroner; Charles Hobbs Inquest, October 6, 1884, Case No. 1251, Folder 52, Box 40 (MSA microfilm roll C31282 and Folder 142, Box 122, Reel C31308), STL Coroner; George Kienker Inquest, February 17 and 18, 1880, Case No. 1869, Folder 23, Box 26 (MSA microfilm roll C31276), STL Coroner; Gearing and Lizardi, "Religion and Suicide," 334.

15. Franz H. Kurrus Inquest, October 29, 1884, Case No. 1294, Folder 95, Box 40 (MSA microfilm roll C31282 and 31308), STL Coroner.

16. Kurrus Inquest.

17. Kurrus Inquest; Death Record for Friedrika Kurrus, *Missouri, Death Records, 1834–1910*, DI, ancestry.com, accessed December 10, 2014; Kurrus, Fredericka, St. Louis City Wills, DI, ancestry.com, accessed December 10, 2014.

18. Kurrus Inquest.

19. Franz Kurrus was buried in Old St. Markus Cemetery. Franz Kurrus, Missouri Death Records, DI, ancestry.com, accessed May 25, 2020.

20. Kurrus Inquest.

21. Kurrus Inquest.

22. Kurrus Inquest; "A Cooper's Suicide," in "Coroner's Cases," *St. Louis Globe-Democrat*, October 29, 1884, 12; "Why He Killed Himself," *St. Louis Post-Dispatch*, October 29, 1884.

23. Naturalization Record, Herman Kurrus, http://www.sos.mo.gov/Records/Archives/ArchivesDb/naturalization/Detail.aspx?id=147887, accessed May 28, 2020; Kushner, "Immigrant Suicide in the United States," 11; Christian Stemipf Inquest, February 10, 1880, Case No. 1856, Folder 87, Box 20 (MSA microfilm roll

C31276), STL Coroner; "A Deliberate Suicide," *St. Louis Globe-Democrat*, February 10, 1880, 8; Stemipf Inquest; U.S. Census 1860, 1870, 1880; Jerome Perry Buckley Inquest, May 14, 1883, Case No. 96, Folder 95, Box 26 (MSA microfilm roll C31280), STL Coroner.

24. Johnson Inquest; "A Sad Death," *St. Louis Post-Dispatch*, September 3, 1879, 1; "Died," *St. Louis Post-Dispatch*, September 4, 1879, 4; "Reunited," *St. Louis Daily Globe-Democrat*, September 4, 1879, 8.

25. Johnson Inquest; Papers, Johnson, Charles P. (1836–1920), (Collection CA6380), The State Historical Society of Missouri, University of Missouri, Columbia, Missouri; Death Certificate for Ralph Johnson, Missouri Secretary of State, DI, http://www.sos.mo.gov/images/archives/deathcerts/1920/1920_00018750.PDF, accessed December 1, 2014; "A Sad Death," *St. Louis Post-Dispatch*, September 3, 1879, 1; "Died," *St. Louis Post-Dispatch*, September 4, 1879, 4; "Reunited," *St. Louis Daily Globe-Democrat*, September 4, 1879, 8; "Suicide from Grief," *New-York Tribune*, September 4, 1879; *Chronicling America: Historic American Newspapers*, Library of Congress, http://chroniclingamerica.loc.gov/lccn/sn83030214/1879-09-04/ed-1/seq-1/, accessed December 5, 2014.

26. Johnson Inquest; Charles P. Johnson Papers; "A Sad Death," *St. Louis Post-Dispatch*, September 3, 1879, 1; "Died," *St. Louis Post-Dispatch*, September 4, 1879, 4; "Reunited," *St. Louis Daily Globe-Democrat*, September 4, 1879, 8.

27. Johnson Inquest, Charles P. Johnson Papers; Ralph Johnson Death Certificate; "A Sad Death," *St. Louis Post-Dispatch*, September 3, 1879, 1; "Died," *St. Louis Post-Dispatch*, September 4, 1879, 4; "Reunited," *St. Louis Daily Globe-Democrat*, September 4, 1879, 8; "Suicide from Grief," *New-York Tribune*, September 4, 1879; *Chronicling America: Historic American Newspapers*, Library of Congress; Kimberley Zittel, *Postpartum Mood Disorders: A Guide for Medical, Mental Health, and Other Support Providers* (Washington, DC: National Association of Social Work Press, 2010), 7; Laura J. Miller, "Postpartum Depression," *Journal of the American Medical Association* 287, no. 6 (2002): 762.

28. Johnson Inquest; Charles P. Johnson Papers; Akihito Suzuki, *Madness at Home: The Psychiatrist, the Patient, and the Family in England, 1820–1860* (Berkeley: University of California Press, 2006), 106.

29. Johnson Inquest; Charles P. Johnson Papers.

30. Johnson Inquest; "Reunited," *St. Louis Daily Globe-Democrat*, September 4, 1879, 8.

31. Johnson Inquest; "A Sad Death," *St. Louis Post-Dispatch*, September 3, 1879, 1; "Died," *St. Louis Post-Dispatch*, September 4, 1879, 4; "Reunited," *St. Louis Daily Globe-Democrat*, September 4, 1879, 8. For a similar case in which Auler rendered a qualified verdict, in this case, "ill-treatment" by her husband, see Catherina

Lielich Inquest, June 14, 1880, Case No. 2077, Folder 28, Box 22 (MSA microfilm roll C31280), STL Coroner; "Suicide of the Mother of a Family, Caused by Poverty and Hunger," *St. Louis Daily Globe-Democrat*, June 15, 1880, 4.

32. Johnson Inquest.

33. "A Sad Death," *St. Louis Post-Dispatch*, September 3, 1879, 1.

34. The couple's son, Ralph Johnson, also died by suicide in 1920, at age forty-six. He was seven when his mother died. Death Certificate; Death Certificate for Ralph Johnson, Missouri Secretary of State, http://www.sos.mo.gov/images /archives/deathcerts/1920/1920_00018750.PDF, accessed December 1, 2014.

4. "With the Intention of Producing an Abortion"

1. Material in this chapter was published as Sarah Lirley McCune, "The Untimely Death of Annie Roberts and the Politics of Abortion in Late Nineteenth-Century St. Louis," *Missouri Historical Review* 111, no. 3 (2017): 189–203, and appears here by permission of the State Historical Society of Missouri.

2. Annie E. Roberts Inquest, December 6 and 7, 1878, Case No. 044, Folder 23, Box 13 (MSA microfilm roll C31274), STL Coroner. Hereafter the case will be referred to as "Roberts Inquest." The testimony is missing from Roberts's inquest, but the *St. Louis Globe-Democrat* reprinted much of it verbatim. "Sin and Death," *St. Louis Globe-Democrat*, December 7, 1878, 2.

3. Roberts Inquest; "Sin and Death," *St. Louis Globe-Democrat*, December 7, 1878, 2; "At the Four C's," *St. Louis Globe-Democrat*, December 10, 1878, 8; "St. Louis in Splinters," *St. Louis Globe-Democrat*, January 15, 1879, 8; "An Unhappy Pair," *St. Louis Globe-Democrat*, February 1, 1879, 3; "Four Courts Notes," *St. Louis Globe-Democrat*, July 15, 1879, 4; St. Louis City Circuit Court, *Criminal Court Record Book* 20: 203, 205; Leslie J. Reagan, *When Abortion Was a Crime: Women, Medicine, and the Law in the United States, 1867–1973* (Berkeley: University of California Press, 1997), 21–23.

4. Reagan, *When Abortion Was a Crime*, 24. She draws on Mohr's definition of abortion as "the intentional termination of gestation by any means and at any time during pregnancy from conception to full term." James C. Mohr, *Abortion in America: The Origins and Evolution of National Policy, 1800–1900* (New York: Oxford University Press, 1978), viii.

5. Reagan, *When Abortion Was a Crime*, 24, 54; Mohr, *Abortion in America: The Origins and Evolution of National Policy, 1800–1900* (New York: Oxford University Press, 1978), 230–233. Reagan's and Mohr's works are foundational for the historical study of abortion. Other works about abortion policy, practice, rhetoric, and debates include Kristin Luker, *Abortion and the Politics of Motherhood* (Berkeley: University of

California Press, 1984); Rosalind Pollack Petchesky, *Abortion and Woman's Choice: The State, Sexuality, and Reproductive Freedom* (New York: Longman, 1984); Janet Farrell Brodie, *Contraception and Abortion in Nineteenth-Century America* (Ithaca, N.Y.: Cornell University Press, 1994); Nathan Stormer, *Articulating Life's Memory: US Medical Rhetoric about Abortion in the Nineteenth Century* (Lanham, Md.: Lexington Books, 2002); Rickie Solinger, *Pregnancy and Power: A Short History of Reproductive Politics in America* (New York: New York University Press, 2005); Sara Dubow, *Ourselves Unborn: A History of the Fetus in Modern America* (New York: Oxford University Press, 2011); Nathan Stormer, *Sign of Pathology: US Medical Rhetoric on Abortion, 1800s–1960s* (University Park: Pennsylvania State University Press, 2015); Mary Ziegler, *Dollars for Life: the Anti-Abortion Movement and the Fall of the Republican Establishment* (New Haven, Conn.: Yale University Press, 2022).

6. J. Berger, "A Fatal Fashion," *St. Louis Medical Journal* 12, no. 7 (1885): 289–296; Mary A. Dixon-Jones, "Criminal Abortion: Its Evil and Sad Consequences," *Medical Record* 46 (1894): 9–16; William B. Ely, "The Ethics of Criminal Abortion," *Western Medical Review* 10, no. 3 (1905): 97–102; Everett W. Burdett, "The Medical Jurisprudence of Criminal Abortion," *New England Medical Gazette* 18 (1883): 200–214; Raymond M. Spivy, "The Control and Treatment of Criminal Abortion," *Journal of the Missouri State Medical Association* 15, no. 1 (1918): 1–5; C. S. Bacon, "The Duty of the Medical Profession in Relation to Criminal Abortion," *Illinois Medical Journal* 7 (1905): 18–24.

7. Mohr, *Abortion in America*, 21, 22, 25; Reagan, *When Abortion Was a Crime*, 8.

8. "Race Suicide (Criminal Abortion)," in "Correspondence," *Journal of the American Medical Association* 46, no. 13 (1906): 972; Dixon-Jones, "Criminal Abortion."

9. Reagan, *When Abortion Was a Crime*, 4–5.

10. Mohr, *Abortion in America*, 25; *Laws of the State of Missouri* (St. Louis, Mo.: E. Charless, 1825), 283; *Revised Statutes of the State of Missouri* (St. Louis, Mo.: Argus Office, 1835), 168; *Revised Statutes of the State of Missouri* (St. Louis, Mo.: J. W. Dougherty, 1845), 351. The law specified such a punishment for either a drug- or instrument-induced abortion. *Statutes of the State of Missouri*, 3rd ed. (St. Louis, Mo.: W. J. Gilbert, 1872), 1:445–447; *General Statutes of the State of Missouri* (Jefferson City, Mo.: Emory S. Foster, 1866), 781; Hockaday, John A., Thomas H. Parrish, Benjamin F. McDaniel, and Daniel H. McIntyre, committee, eds, *Revised Statutes of the State of Missouri* (Jefferson City, Mo.: Carter and Regan, 1879), 1:219–220; David R. Francis, Stephen H. Claycomb, and Joseph J. Russell, eds, *Revised Statutes of the State of Missouri* (Jefferson City, Mo.: Tribune Printing Co., 1889), 1:849–850. As was noted by physicians, Missouri continued to have some of the strongest laws in the nation in the early twentieth century. See "Criminal Abortion in Its Broadest Sense," *Journal of the American Medical Association* 51, no. 12 (1908): 957–961.

11. St. Louis City Office of the Coroner, Inquests, 1845 to 1900, https://s1.sos.mo
.gov/records/archives/archivesdb/coroners/Results.aspx, accessed August 5, 2016;
Reagan, *When Abortion Was a Crime*, 8, 24, 77; Mohr, *Abortion in America*, 18–19.

12. Reagan, *When Abortion Was a Crime*, 9, 43–44; Mohr, *Abortion in America*,
7–8, 60–62.

13. Ellen Noonan Inquest, August 30, 1882, Case No. 1046, Folder 147, Box 30
(MSA microfilm roll C31279), STL Coroner; "The Noonan Inquest," *St. Louis
Globe-Democrat*, August 29, 1882, 10; "A Very Distressing Case," *St. Louis Globe-
Democrat*, August 31, 1882, 12; St. Louis City Death Records, Death Record for In-
fant of Ellen Noonan, DI, ancestry.com [accessed January 20, 2016]; "Many Such:
Sad Case of Abortion and Morphine Poisoning," *St. Louis Post-Dispatch*, Septem-
ber 5, 1882, 7; Reagan, *When Abortion Was a Crime*, 40–41, 73.

14. Mrs. Kate McClure Inquest, July 24, 1881, Case No. 277, Folder 78, Box 26
(MSA microfilm roll C31278), STL Coroner.

15. Mohr, *Abortion in America*, 96–97; Reagan, *When Abortion Was a Crime*, 40.

16. Whether or not King was a prominent St. Louisan is not yet known, but if
so, it could explain why McClure was treated with more respect than other
men and women; Ancestry.com, *St. Louis, Missouri, Burial Index, Archdiocese of
St. Louis, 1700–2010* [database online]. Provo, UT, USA: ancestry.com Operations, Inc., 2011, accessed January 20, 2016; Ancestry.com, *Missouri, Death Records, 1834–1910* [database online]. Provo, UT, USA: Ancestry.com Operations,
Inc., 2008, accessed January 20, 2016.

17. "Splinters," *St. Louis Globe-Democrat*, July 30, 1881, 3.

18. Roberts Inquest; "Sin and Death," *St. Louis Globe-Democrat*, December 7,
1878, 2.

19. Mohr, *Abortion in America*, 97; "Sin and Death," *St. Louis Globe-Democrat*,
December 7, 1878, 2; *Directory of Physicians, Dentists and Druggists of Missouri,
1889* (St. Louis, Mo.: G. Gonser & Co., 1889), 105; Roberts Inquest; Mary Baum
Inquest, November 3, 1881, Case No. 516, Folder 117, Box 27 (MSA microfilm roll
C31278), STL Coroner; Mrs. Kate McClure Inquest, July 24, 1881, Case No. 277,
Folder 78, Box 26 (MSA microfilm roll C31278), STL Coroner.

20. Roberts Inquest; "Sin and Death," *St. Louis Globe-Democrat*, December 7,
1878, 2.

21. Roberts Inquest; "Sin and Death," *St. Louis Globe-Democrat*, December 7,
1878, 2.

22. *Statutes of the State of Missouri* (1872), 3:445–450; *Revised Statutes of the State of
Missouri* (1879), 1:219–220; *Revised Statutes of the State of Missouri* (1889) 1:849–850.
Even into the early twentieth century, women seldom faced convictions for abortion.
The Missouri State Penitentiary Records show only one woman, Frances Spinner, an

African American, who served a sentence for abortion (presumably for performing one upon herself, but perhaps on another woman). A judge commuted Spinner's three-year sentence because she was ill. Frances Spinner, page 228, Volume DD, Reel S230, Missouri State Penitentiary Database, MSA. http://s1.sos.mo.gov/records/archives /archivesdb/msp/Detail.aspx?id=35156, accessed December 20, 2016.

23. "Sin and Death," *St. Louis Globe-Democrat*, December 7, 1878, 2; Roberts Inquest.

24. "Sin and Death," *St. Louis Globe-Democrat*, December 7, 1878, 2.

25. Roberts Inquest; "Sin and Death," *St. Louis Globe-Democrat*, December 7, 1878, 2.

26. "Sin and Death," *St. Louis Globe-Democrat*, December 7, 1878, 2.

27. "Sin and Death," *St. Louis Globe-Democrat*, December 7, 1878, 2; Mary Baum Inquest, November 3, 1881, Case No. 516, Folder 117, Box 27 (MSA micro-film roll C31278), STL Coroner; "Locals in Brief," *St. Louis Globe-Democrat*, November 3, 1881, 6; Lucy Baird Inquest, July 10, 1898, Case No. 302, Folder 103, Box 110 (MSA microfilm roll C31304), STL Coroner; "Veil Lifted at Death," *St. Louis Post-Dispatch*, July 10, 1898, 8; "Cora Kirk's Suicide," *St. Louis Globe-Democrat*, July 10, 1898, 24; *Missouri Death Records, 1834–1910*, Ancestry.com; McClure Inquest; "Splinters," *St. Louis Globe-Democrat*, July 30, 1881, 3.

28. "Justice at Last: Jilz, the Abortionist, behind the Bars of the County Jail," *St. Louis Post-Dispatch*, August 9, 1876, 2; "Charged with Manslaughter: Doctor Charles A. Smith's Criminal Malpractice—Interview with the Prisoner," *St. Louis Post-Dispatch*, December 17, 1879, 4; "Obscene Literature: The Secret Circulation of Vile Books in St. Louis," *St. Louis Evening Post*, March 6, 1878, 2; "The Truant Witness: Ellen Singer, the Missing Witness in the Dr. Smith Case, Safely Caged," *St. Louis Post-Dispatch*, January 17, 1880, 8.

29. St. Louis City Circuit Court, *Criminal Court Record Book* 20: 203, 205.

30. Roberts Inquest; "Charged with Manslaughter: Doctor Charles A. Smith's Criminal Malpractice—Interview with the Prisoner," *St. Louis Post-Dispatch*, December 17, 1879, 4; "Hard to See: How Dr. Fitzporter Manages to Evade the Law's Clutches," *St. Louis Post-Dispatch*, October 17, 1884, 2; "A Serious Charge: Coroner Nidelet Swears to the Warrant against Dr. Rutledge," *St. Louis Post-Dispatch*, December 31, 1884, 5; "The Secret Twelve: Subjects to Which Their Attention Will Be Called by Judge Laughlin," *St. Louis Post-Dispatch*, May 16, 1882, 4; Mohr, *Abortion in America*, 120–124; Reagan, *When Abortion Was a Crime*, 114–118.

31. "Many Such: Sad Case of Abortion and Morphine Poisoning," *St. Louis Post-Dispatch*, September 5, 1882, 7.

32. *The Book of Missourians: The Achievements and Personnel of Notable Living*, St. Louis, MO, John N. Frank, DI, ancestry.com, accessed July 2, 2019; "Case against

the Coroner," *St. Louis Post-Dispatch*, January 3, 1882, 2; "The McWilliams Case: A Heated Discussion between the Coroner and an Attorney," *St. Louis Post-Dispatch*, August 1, 1882, 4.

33. *Gould & Aldrich's Annual Directory of the City of St. Louis, for 1872* (St. Louis, Mo.: Review Steam Press, 1872), 716; *Gould's St. Louis Directory for 1874* (St. Louis, Mo.: David B. Gould, 1874), 847; *Gould's St. Louis Directory for 1880* (St. Louis, Mo.: David B. Gould, 1880), 981; *Gould's St. Louis Directory for 1889* (St. Louis, Mo.: Gould's Directory Co., 1889), 1209; *Gould's St. Louis Directory for 1892* (St. Louis, Mo.: Gould's Directory Co., 1892), 1462; "The New Grand Jury: It Is Sworn in This Morning and Mr. Nathan Cole Made Foreman," *St. Louis Post-Dispatch*, July 7, 1890, 3; "Trials for Homicide: Fourteen of Them Docketed for the Coming Term," *St. Louis Post-Dispatch*, January 4, 1891, 11. Interestingly, Charles P. Johnson, who had prosecuted a known abortionist, W. W. Jilz, in 1876, defended Stapp in the 1890s. "Justice at Last: Jilz, the Abortionist, Behind the Bars of the County Jail," *St. Louis Post-Dispatch*, August 9, 1876, 2; "Four Courts Notes," *St. Louis Globe-Democrat*, Tuesday, July 15, 1879, 4; *Missouri, Death Records, 1834–1910*, DI, ancestry.com, accessed January 23, 2016. He is buried in Bellefontaine Cemetery. Randal Nicholads, "Dr William Stapp," http://www.findagrave.com/cgibin/fg.cgi?page=gr&GSln=Stapp&GSiman=1&GSst=26&GSob=c&GRid=151266260&, accessed January 23, 2016.

34. "Sin and Death," *St. Louis Globe-Democrat*, December 7, 1878, 2; U.S. Census, 1850, 1860, 1880; Annie Sophie Weigmann Inquest, July 23, 1884, Case No. 1079, Folder 79, Box 39 (MSA microfilm roll C31282), STL Coroner; "News from Missouri," *Potosi Journal*, March 1–3, 1902, 1. Samuel Stapp was arrested in March 1902 for performing an abortion on seventeen-year-old Essie Howard.

5. "I Am Afraid That You Will Beat Me to Death"

1. "Kicked to Death," *St. Louis Post and Dispatch*, April 29, 1878, 4; "A Brutal Crime," *St. Louis Post-Dispatch*, July 3, 1878, 1; Nellie Lee Inquest, April 29, 1878, Case No. 29, Folder 8, Box 13 (MSA microfilm roll C31276), STL Coroner.

2. Elizabeth Pleck, *Domestic Tyranny: The Making of Social Policy against Family Violence from Colonial Times to the Present* (New York: Oxford University Press, 1987), 7. For more on domestic violence and domestic homicide, see Linda Gordon, *Heroes of Their Own Lives: The Politics and History of Family Violence: Boston, 1880–1960* (New York: Viking, 1988); Pamela Haag, "The 'Ill-Use of a Wife': Patterns of Working-Class Violence in Domestic and Public New York City, 1860–1880," *Journal of Social History* 25, no. 3 (1992): 447–477; Jeffrey Adler, "'If

We Can't Live in Peace, We Might as Well Die': Homicide-Suicide in Chicago, 1875–1910," *Journal of Urban History* 26, no. 3 (1999): 3–21; Jeffrey Adler, "'We've Got a Right to Fight; We're Married': Domestic Homicide in Chicago, 1875–1920," *Journal of Interdisciplinary History* 34, no. 1 (2003): 27–48; Kirsten S. Rambo, *"Trivial Complaints": The Role of Privacy in Domestic Violence Law and Activism in the U.S.* (New York: Columbia University Press, 2009); Ashley Baggett, *Intimate Partner Violence in New Orleans: Gender, Race, and Reform, 1840–1900* (Jackson: University Press of Mississippi, 2017).

3. Jeffrey Adler, "I Loved Joe, but I Had to Shoot Him': Homicide by Women in Turn-of-the-Century Chicago," *Journal of Criminal Law and Criminology* 92, no. 3/4 (2002): 873; Adler, "'We've Got a Right to Fight,'" 27; Jeffrey Adler, *First in Violence, Deepest in Dirt: Homicide in Chicago, 1875–1920* (Cambridge, Mass.: Harvard University Press, 2002), 51, 55. Much has been written about the history of homicide. For important monographs in the field, see Roger Lane, *Violent Death in the City: Suicide, Accident, and Murder in Nineteenth Century Philadelphia* (Cambridge, Mass.: Harvard University Press, 1979); Adler, *First in Violence*; Randolph Roth, *American Homicide* (Cambridge, Mass.: Belknap Press of Harvard University Press, 2009).

4. Adler, *First in Violence*, 68–69; "Why Do Victims Stay?" National Coalition Against Domestic Violence, https://ncadv.org/why-do-victims-stay, accessed August 2, 2021.

5. Michael Schudson, *Discovering the News: A Social History of American Newspapers* (New York: Basic Books, 1978), 145; Gerald J. Baldasty, *The Commercialization of News in the Nineteenth Century* (Madison: University of Wisconsin Press, 1992), 126–127. See "A Fatal Blow," *St. Louis Globe-Democrat*, March 8, 1885, 20; "A Devilish Deed," *St. Louis Globe-Democrat*, October 9, 1883, n.p.; "Local Brevities," *St. Louis Globe-Democrat*, October 11, 1883, 4; Peletiah Jenks Inquest, October 9, 1883, Case No. 462, Folder 113, Box 35 (MSA microfilm roll C31281), STL Coroner.

6. Adler, *First in Violence*, 51, 55; Maria Sutton Inquest, September 15, 1875, Case No. 453, Folder 54, Box 7 (MSA microfilm roll C31272), STL Coroner; Clarence Ward Inquest, September 15, 1875, Case No. 452, Folder 53, Box 7 (MSA microfilm roll C31272), STL Coroner; "Love's Madness," *St. Louis Globe-Democrat*, September 16, 1875, 8; "John Finley's Story," *St. Louis Globe-Democrat*, September 16, 1875, 4; "St. Louis in Splinters," *St. Louis Globe-Democrat*, September 17, 1975, 4; "The Courts," *St. Louis Globe-Democrat*, September, 17, 1875, 3; "Murder and Suicide," *St. Louis Globe-Democrat*, September 15, 1875, 4; "Clarence A. Ward," Ancestry.com, *Missouri, Death Records, 1834–1910*; "Clarence A. Ward," St. Louis County, Missouri, Probate Court, *Probate Case Files, 1802–1876*, ancestry.com, accessed September 25, 2016.

7. Adler, "'I Loved Joe,'" 871–877. Jeffrey Adler examines women who killed their children and the reasons they did so in this article. Adler also points out that when women did kill other adults, it was often their husbands, typically because they were abusive.

8. Adler, "'I Loved Joe,'" 871–877.

9. John Walton Inquest, June 20, 1876 Case No. 790, Folder 169, Box 9 (MSA microfilm roll C31273), STL Coroner; Lillie Colcord Inquest, August 14, 1878, Case No. 878, Folder 64, Box 15 (MSA microfilm roll C31274), STL Coroner.

10. Pleck, *Domestic Tyranny*, 7, 69, 90–91, 96–97, 99, 102, 187–192; Gordon, *Heroes of Their Own Lives*, 3–4, 7, 27–30. Nationwide, in 2022, approximately one in four women and one in nine men experienced domestic violence. In 2021 in St. Louis, there were 2,200 reported instances of domestic assaults per day. Given the lack of resources available to people in abusive relationships, those numbers were likely much higher in the 1870s and 1880s.

11. Catherine Corbett describes some of these benevolent organizations in *In Her Place*, 135–143.

12. Lillie Colcord Inquest; Josiah P. Colcord Inquest, August 14, 1878, Case No. 877, Folder 63, Box 15 (MSA microfilm roll C31274), STL Coroner; Dm Wms, "Mrs. Lillie Southfield," http://www.findagrave.com/memorial/102048673 /Lillie-southfield, accessed July 19, 2021. The memorial page features a newspaper article about the murder-suicide.

13. Allen E. Wagner, *Good Order and Safety: A History of the Metropolitan Police Department, 1861–1906* (St. Louis: Missouri History Museum, 2008), 155, 158, 161, 249; J. Thomas Scharf, *History of St. Louis and County, from the Earliest Periods to the Present Day: Including Biographical Sketches of Representative Men, Volume II* (Philadelphia: Louis H. Everts & Co., 1883), 1540–1541; "Well-Known St. Louisans," *St. Louis Post-Dispatch*, July 28, 1896, 4. For more on the scandal with the gambling ring: "A Few Facts," *St. Louis Post-Dispatch*, September 7, 1878, 1; "Nidelet's Nightmare," *St. Louis Post-Dispatch*, December 28, 1878, 5; "Governor Phelps Speaks," *St. Louis Post-Dispatch*, February 17, 1879, 2; "The Veil Is Rent," *St. Louis Post-Dispatch*, February 18, 1879, 1; "The Lottery Ring," *St. Louis Post-Dispatch*, March 4, 1879, 4; "A New Indictment," *St. Louis Post-Dispatch*, April 29, 1879, 4; "A Bombshell," *St. Louis Post-Dispatch*, May 1, 1879, 1; "The Wakefield-Nidelet Telegrams," *St. Louis Post-Dispatch*, November 7, 1879, 4.

14. Lillie Colcord Inquest; Josiah P. Colcord Inquest; "Wine and Women," *Daily Rocky Mountain News*, August 18, 1878, 1.

15. "Wine and Women," *Daily Rocky Mountain News*, August 18, 1878, 1; Adler, *First in Violence*, 68–69.

16. "Wine and Women," *Daily Rocky Mountain News*, August 18, 1878, 1.

17. "The Dead Lawyer," *St. Louis Globe-Democrat*, August 21, 1878, 7.

18. "Wine and Women," *Daily Rocky Mountain News*, August 18, 1878, 1.

19. "The Dead Lawyer," *St. Louis Globe-Democrat*, August 21, 1878, 7; "Wine and Women," *Daily Rocky Mountain News*, August 18, 1878, 1; "Post Mortem Points," *St. Louis Globe-Democrat*, August 20, 1878, 4; "Under the Sod," *St. Louis Globe-Democrat*, August 19, 1878, 8; "Post Office Corners," *St. Louis Globe-Democrat*, August 19, 1878, 4; "Funeral Notice," *St. Louis Globe-Democrat*, August 21, 1878, 5; "St. Louis in Splinters," *St. Louis Globe-Democrat*, August 21, 1878, 8; "Funeral of Lillie Colcord," *St. Louis Globe-Democrat*, August 22, 1878, 8; Marriage of Lillie I. Gibbons and Josiah P. Colcord, 9 May, 1877, *Missouri, U.S. Marriage Records, 1805–2002*, DI, ancestry.com, accessed July 19, 2021 (the record shows the name "Joriah" instead of "Josiah").

20. Pleck, *Domestic Tyranny*, 98–101; "All the Blue-Ribbon Movements...," *St. Louis Globe-Democrat*, August 18, 1878, 4; "Personal Intelligence," *The North American*, August 19, 1878, 1; "Ruined by Rum," *St. Louis Globe-Democrat*, August 18, 1878, 1; "Wine and Women," *Daily Rocky Mountain News*, August 18, 1878, 1.

21. "Wine and Women," *Daily Rocky Mountain News*, August 18, 1878, 1; "Ruined by Rum," *St. Louis Globe-Democrat*, August 18, 1878, 1; "Post Office Corners," *St. Louis Globe-Democrat*, August 19, 1878, 4; "Post Mortem Points," *St. Louis Globe-Democrat*, August 20, 1878, 4; "J. P. Colcord," *St. Louis Globe-Democrat*, August 23, 1878, 3; "The Dead Lawyer," *St. Louis Globe-Democrat*, August 21, 1878, 7.

22. "Post Mortem Points," *St. Louis Globe-Democrat*, August 20, 1878, 4.

23. "A Card," *St. Louis Globe-Democrat*, August 20, 1878, 7; "The Dead Lawyer," *St. Louis Globe-Democrat*, August 21, 1878, 7; "Under the Sod," *St. Louis Globe-Democrat*, August 19, 1878, 8; "St. Louis in Splinters," *St. Louis Globe-Democrat*, August 21, 1878, 8; "Funeral of Lillie Colcord," *St. Louis Globe-Democrat*, August 22, 1878, 8; Dm Wms, "Col Josiah Perham Colcord," http://www.findagrave.com/memorial/102047617/Josiah-perham-colcord, accessed July 19, 2021; Dm Wms, "Mrs. Lillie Southfield," http://www.findagrave.com/memorial/102048673/Lillie-southfield, accessed July 19, 2021.

24. Catherina Lielich Inquest, June 14, 1880, Case No. 2077, Folder 28, Box 22 (MSA microfilm roll C31280), STL Coroner. This is just one example of such a verdict; "Wine and Women," *Daily Rocky Mountain News*, August 18, 1878, 1; "Under the Sod," *St. Louis Globe-Democrat*, August 19, 1878, 8.

25. "Wine and Women," *Daily Rocky Mountain News*, August 18, 1878, 1; Adler, *First in Violence*, 55–56.

26. "Kicked to Death," *St. Louis Post and Dispatch*, April 29, 1878, 4; "A Brutal Crime," *St. Louis Post-Dispatch*, July 3, 1878, 1.

27. "A Brutal Crime," *St. Louis Post-Dispatch*, July 3, 1878, 1; "Kicked to Death," *St. Louis Post and Dispatch*, April 29, 1878, 4; Lee Inquest.

28. For more on coroners' juries and the office in general, see Herbert S. Breyfogle, "The Laws of Missouri Relating to Inquests and Coroners," *Missouri Law Review* 10 (1945): 34–63; R. B. H. Gradwohl, "The Office of the Coroner: Its Past, Its Present, and Its Advisability of Its Abolishment in the Commonwealth of Missouri," *Journal of the American Medical Association* 54 (1910): 842–846; *General Statutes of the State of Missouri* (Jefferson City, Mo.: Emory S. Foster, 1866); John A. Hockaday, Thomas H. Parrish, Benjamin F. McDaniel, and Daniel H. McIntyre, committee, eds, *Revised Statutes of the State of Missouri* (Jefferson City, Mo.: Carter and Regan, 1879); David R. Francis, Stephen H. Claycomb, and Joseph J. Russell, eds., *Revised Statutes of the State of Missouri* (Jefferson City, Mo.: Tribune Printing Co., 1889); *The Statutes of the State of Missouri*, compiled by David Wagner (St. Louis, Mo.: W. J. Gilbert, Law Book Publisher, 1872).

29. For an example of a homicide that the coroner's jury determined was in self-defense, see John Walton Inquest, June 20, 1876 Case No. 790, Folder 169, Box 9 (MSA microfilm roll C31273), STL Coroner; for a justifiable homicide, committed in the course of duty as a police officer, see George Stevens Inquest, August 2, 1877 Case No. 36, Folder 7, Box 123 (MSA microfilm roll C31309), STL Coroner; Roger Lane observes that most shootings committed by police officers during the course of duty were ruled as "justifiable" homicides in the twentieth century, but they were investigated more carefully in the nineteenth century. Lane, *Violent Death in the City*, 88.

30. "Kicked to Death," *St. Louis Post and Dispatch*, April 29, 1878, 4; Lee Inquest.

31. "Kicked to Death," *St. Louis Post and Dispatch*, April 29, 1878, 4.

32. For example, a judge reduced charges against Charles Koebel from first-degree murder to third-degree manslaughter. He died of bronchitis while awaiting his trial but had faced up to three years in the state penitentiary if he had been convicted. Charles Meyers Inquest, February 2, 1884, Case No. 708, Folder 66, Box 37 (MSA microfilm roll C31281), STL Coroner; Albin Berger Inquest, February 7, 1884, Case No. 718, Folder 76, Box 37 (MSA microfilm roll C31281), STL Coroner; "It Is a Murder," *St. Louis Post-Dispatch*, February 1, 1884, 3; "The Second Victim," *St. Louis Globe-Democrat*, February 7, 1884, 12; "A Fatal Affray," *St. Louis Globe-Democrat*, January 31, 1884, 12; "Stabbed to Death," *The Milwaukee Sentinel*, January 31, 1884, 2; "The Twelfth Street Tragedy," *St. Louis Globe-Democrat*, February 1, 1884, 10; "The Criminal Courts," *St. Louis Globe-Democrat*, February 8, 1884, 9; "The Criminal Courts," *St. Louis Globe-Democrat*, March 8, 1884, 12; "Criminal Court," *St. Louis Post-Dispatch*, May 4, 1885, 7. Similarly, Frank Randeland, also known as "Desperado Rande," was sentenced to serve life in prison for killing police officer John White. He died by suicide while in prison

several years later. John White Inquest, November 19, 1877, Case No. 17, Folder 156, Box 12 (MSA microfilm roll C31274), STL Coroner; "Frank Rande Suicides," *Rocky Mountain News*, March 8, 1884, n.p.; White Inquest; "The St. Elmo Murderer," *Inter Ocean*, November 19, 1877, 5.

33. Lee Inquest; "A Brutal Crime," *St. Louis Post-Dispatch*, July 3, 1878, 1; "Charges of Crime," *St. Louis Globe-Democrat*, December 11, 1878, 7; "The Courts," *St. Louis Globe-Democrat*, January 22, 1879, 7; "Walked Away from Suicide," *St. Louis Globe-Democrat*, January 28, 1880, 8; "City Criminalities," *The Daily Inter Ocean*, June 19, 1882, 8.

34. "Kicked to Death," *St. Louis Post and Dispatch*, April 29, 1878, 4.

35. "Kicked to Death," *St. Louis Post and Dispatch*, April 29, 1878, 4; Lee Inquest; U.S. Census, 1870.

36. "The Courts," *St. Louis Globe-Democrat*, January 22, 1879, 7; City of St. Louis, Mo., Circuit Court Case 5, "State of Missouri vs. Pinkey Daniels," April 29, 1879, Indictment for Assault to Kill, *Criminal Court Record Book* 20: 112, Missouri State Archives, St. Louis; City of St. Louis, Mo., Circuit Court Case 5, "State of Missouri vs. Pinkey Daniels," April 29, 1879, Case Continuance, *Criminal Court Record Book* 20: 139, Missouri State Archives, St. Louis; City of St. Louis, Mo., Circuit Court Case 5, "State of Missouri vs. Pinkey Daniels," March 7, 1879, Assault to Kill, *Criminal Court Record Book* 20: 179–180, Missouri State Archives, St. Louis; "A Brutal Crime," *St. Louis Post-Dispatch*, July 3, 1878, 1; Entry for Inmate Jno Cordry, aged 31 years, colored, born Michigan 1847; Volume G, Register of Inmates Received, 1836–1931, p. 31; Missouri State Penitentiary, Reel S216, Register No. 928, Missouri State Archives, Jefferson City.

37. "Sharp Work," *St. Louis Globe-Democrat*, July 4, 1878, 5; "Kicked to Death," *St. Louis Post and Dispatch*, April 29, 1878, 4.

38. "Kicked to Death," *St. Louis Post and Dispatch*, April 29, 1878, 4.

6. "No One Was Blamed"

1. John Brennan Inquest, June 6 and 7, 1876, Case No. 113, Folder 117, Box 8 (MSA microfilm roll C31273), STL Coroner.

2. Brennan Inquest; "Terrific Explosion," *St. Louis Globe-Democrat*, June 5, 1876, 5; "Casualties," *Milwaukee Daily Sentinel*, June 6, 1876, 5; Burst Boilers," *St. Louis Globe-Democrat*, June 7, 1876, 8; "Want of Water," *St. Louis Globe-Democrat*, June 8, 1876, 3; "The Recent Explosion—Progress of the Inquest," *St. Louis Post-Dispatch*, June 7, 1876, 4; "Blown Up: Terrible Explosion at the Collier White Lead Works," *St. Louis Post-Dispatch*, June 5, 1876, 4; *The Statutes of the State of Missouri*, compiled

by David Wagner (St. Louis, Mo.: W. J. Gilbert, Law Book Publisher, 1872), 284. There was at least one fire five years later as well. See "Investigating: The Fire Department and the Management of the Collier Fire," *St. Louis Post-Dispatch*, October 17, 1881, 4; "'Not Guilty Enough': The Mayor's Qualified Decision in Regard to the Collier Fire," *St. Louis Post-Dispatch*, October 22, 1881, 4.

3. The other case in which a coroner's jury held someone accountable in the verdict was a railroad accident, and these were quite common in the late nineteenth century. See Thomas Sullivan Inquest, July 9, 1881, Case No. 203, Folder 4, Box 26 (MSA microfilm roll C31278), STL Coroner; Roger Lane, *Violent Death in the City: Suicide, Accident & Murder in 19th Century Philadelphia* (Cambridge, Mass.: Harvard University Press, 1979), 37, 39; Jeffrey M. Jentzen, *Death Investigation in America: Coroners, Medical Examiners, and the Pursuit of Medical Certainty* (Cambridge, Mass.: Harvard University Press, 2009), 139.

4. Judith Green, "Accidents: The Remnants of a Modern Classificatory System," in *Accidents in History: Injuries Fatalities and Social Relations*, ed. Roger Cooter and Bill Luckin (Amsterdam: Editions Rodopi B.V., 1997), 35–58. Vehicular and train accidents also gained a lot of press attention and lengthy inquests. For examples, see Friedrich Brueckner Inquest, August 13 and 14, 1882, Case No. 1024, Folder 125, Box 30 (MSA microfilm roll C31279), STL Coroner; "Brueckner's Death," *St. Louis Post-Dispatch*, August 14, 1882, 5; "The Brueckner Inquest," *St. Louis Globe-Democrat*, August 15, 1882, 10; George Grasser Inquest, April 26 and 27, 1882, Case No. 814, Folder 65, Box 29 (MSA microfilm roll C31279), STL Coroner; "A Sad Accident," *St. Louis Globe-Democrat*, April 25, 1882, 8; "Casualties," *The Daily Inter Ocean*, April 27, 1882, 5; "Relief in Death," *St. Louis Globe-Democrat*, April 27, 1882, 6; "The Late Judge Grasser," *St. Louis Globe-Democrat*, April 28, 1882, 8; "The Grasser Inquest," *St. Louis Globe-Democrat*, April 30, 1882, 2; "Judge Grasser," *St. Louis Post Dispatch*, April 26, 1882, 7; "Judge Grasser's Death," *St. Louis Post Dispatch*, April 27, 1882, 4.

5. Lane, *Violent Death in the City*, 37–39. For three cases of possible suicides in which coroners determined they were accidents, see Mary Harris Inquest, June 18, 1880, Case No. 2087, Folder 38, Box 22 (MSA microfilm roll C31276), STL Coroner; "Was It Suicide?" *St Louis Globe-Democrat*, June 19, 1880, 8; "The Coroner," *St. Louis Globe-Democrat*, June 20, 1880, 4; Mary Scott Inquest, January 27, 1883, Case No. 1331, Folder 59, Box 32 (MSA microfilm roll C31280), STL Coroner; Timothy O'Keefe Inquest, October 28, 1884, Case No. 1293, Folder 94, Box 40 (MSA microfilm roll C31282 and C31308), STL Coroner.

6. Henry Diekhoener Inquest, July 21, 1881, Case No. 272, Folder 73, Box 26 (MSA microfilm roll C31278), STL Coroner; Mary Harris Inquest, June 18, 1880, Case No. 2087, Folder 38, Box 22 (MSA microfilm roll C31276), STL Coroner.

7. Donald W. Rogers, *Making Capitalism Safe: Work Safety and Health Regulation in America, 1880–1940* (Urbana: University of Illinois Press, 2009), 12–15.

8. Brennan Inquest. It is possible that he did interview Brennan's wife, but the testimony was not recorded in the inquest record. Of the fifteen witnesses on the cover sheet for the inquest, testimony was recorded for only nine of them.

9. Brennan Inquest.

10. Brennan Inquest; "Terrific Explosion," *St. Louis Globe-Democrat*, June 5, 1876, 5.

11. Brennan Inquest.

12. Brennan Inquest; John A. Hockaday, Thomas H. Parrish, Benjamin F. Mc-Daniel, and Daniel H. McIntyre, committee, eds., *Revised Statutes of the State of Missouri, Volume I* (Jefferson City, Mo.: Carter and Regan, State Printers and Binders, 1879), 1298.

13. Brennan Inquest.

14. Brennan Inquest.

15. David R. Francis, Stephen H. Claycomb, and Joseph J. Russell, eds., *Revised Statutes of the State of Missouri, Volume I* (Jefferson City, Mo.: Tribune Printing Company, State Printers and Binders, 1889), 1714.

16. Brennan Inquest; Hockaday et al., *Revised Statutes of the State of Missouri, Volume I*; Francis et al., *Revised Statutes of the State of Missouri, Volume I*; David Wagner, ed., *The Statutes of the State of Missouri, Volumes I and II* (St. Louis, Mo.: W. J. Gilbert, Law Book Publisher, 1872), 447–448.

17. Brennan Inquest; "Terrific Explosion," *St. Louis Globe-Democrat*, June 5, 1876, 5.

18. Brennan Inquest; "Terrific Explosion," *St. Louis Globe-Democrat*, June 5, 1876, 5; "Casualties," *Milwaukee Sentinel*, June 6, 1876, 5; "Burst Boilers," *St. Louis Globe-Democrat*, June 7, 1876, 8; "Want of Water," *St. Louis Globe-Democrat*, June 8, 1876, 3; "The Recent Explosion—Progress of the Inquest," *St. Louis Post-Dispatch*, June 7, 1876, 4; "Blown Up: Terrible Explosion at the Collier White Lead Works," *St. Louis Post-Dispatch*, June 5, 1876, 4; "Investigating: The Fire Department and the Management of the Collier Fire," *St. Louis Post-Dispatch*, October 17, 1881, 4; "'Not Guilty Enough': The Mayor's Qualified Decision in Regard to the Collier Fire," *St. Louis Post-Dispatch*, October 22, 1881, 4.

19. Nate Holdren, *Injury Impoverished: Workplace Accidents, Capitalism, and Law in the Progressive Era* (Cambridge: Cambridge University Press, 2020), 20.

20. Rogers, *Making Capitalism Safe*, 12, 15.

21. Holdren, *Injury Impoverished*, 19–20; Rogers, *Making Capitalism Safe, 1880–1940*, 12, 15.

22. Rogers, *Making Capitalism Safe, 1880–1940*, 28–29; Holdren, *Injury Impoverished*, 99–100. See also John Fabian Witt, *The Accidental Republic: Crippled Workingmen, Destitute Widows, and the Remaking of American* Law (Cambridge, Mass.: Harvard University Press, 2004).

23. Hoackday et al., *Revised Statutes of the State of Missouri* (Jefferson City, Mo.: Carter and Regan, 1879), 1298, 220; Brennan Inquest.

24. Diekhoener Inquest.

25. Herman Praedicow, 1890 U.S. Veterans Schedules, DI, ancestry.com [accessed May 25, 2020]; U.S. Census 1870, 1880; "Peculiar Praedicow," *St. Louis Post-Dispatch*, January 12, 1891, 5; "The Lounger," *St. Louis Post-Dispatch*, March 28, 1883, 4. He served from 1875–1877, 1877–1878, 1881–1882, and 1890 to his death in 1891. Coroners George Dudley, Hugo Auler, and John Frank appointed him to the position.

26. "The Charges against Praedicow," *St. Louis Post-Dispatch*, December 18, 1880, 4; "Taking the Testimony," *St. Louis Globe-Democrat*, December 18, 1880, 7; "Undertakers Complain," *St. Louis Post-Dispatch*, April 18, 1889, 2; "Morgue Combination," *St. Louis Post-Dispatch*, April 20, 1889, 3; "Praedicow Will Be Suspended," *St. Louis Post-Dispatch*, January 30, 1890, 8; "Peculiar Praedicow," *St. Louis Post-Dispatch*, January 12, 1891, 5; "Trouble with the Mayor," *St. Louis Post-Dispatch*, December 4, 1888, 2; "Praedicow's Predicament," *St. Louis Post-Dispatch*, October 4, 1882, 3; "A Lively Row," *St. Louis Post-Dispatch*, December 20, 1878, 1.

27. "Praedicow Will Be Suspended," *St. Louis Post-Dispatch*, January 30, 1890, 8; "The Lounger," *St. Louis Post-Dispatch*, March 28, 1883, 4; "Peculiar Praedicow," *St. Louis Post-Dispatch*, January 12, 1891, 5; "Peculiar Praedicow," *St. Louis Post-Dispatch*, January 12, 1891, 5.

28. Diekhoener Inquest.

29. Diekhoener Inquest. According to Carl Gersuny, workplace regulations and practices were often contradictory. Carl Gersuny, *Work Hazards and Industrial Conflict* (Hanover, N.H.: University Press of New England, 1981), 27.

30. Diekhoener Inquest.

31. Diekhoener Inquest.

32. "Broken Bones," *St. Louis Globe-Democrat*, July 22, 1881, 3; Diekhoener Inquest; "Local Brevities," *St. Louis Post-Dispatch*, July 22, 1881, 3.

Conclusion

1. Jeffrey M. Jentzen, *Death Investigation in America: Coroners, Medical Examiners, and the Pursuit of Medical Certainty* (Cambridge, Mass.: Harvard University Press, 2009), 25–30; James C. Mohr, *Doctors and the Law: Medical Jurisprudence*

in Nineteenth-Century America (New York: Oxford University Press, 1993), 213–216, 235–236; Stefan Timmermans, *Postmortem: How Medical Examiners Explain Suspicious Deaths* (Chicago: University of Chicago Press, 2006), 5; Oscar T. Schultz and E. M. Morgan, "The Coroner and the Medical Examiner," *Bulletin of the National Research Council* 64–66 (1928): 5.

2. Mohr, *Doctors and the Law*, 213–218, 235–236; B. H. Gradwohl, "The Office of the Coroner: Its Past, Its Present, and Its Advisability of Its Abolishment in the Commonwealth of Missouri," *Journal of the American Medical Association* 54 (1910): 842–843; Jentzen, *Death Investigation in America*, 4, 23–24, 26–30; Timmermans, *Postmortem*, 36; Randy Hanzlick and Debra Combs, "Medical Examiner and Coroner Systems: History and Trends," *Journal of the American Medical Association* 279, no. 11 (1998): 872–873; Schultz and Morgan, "The Coroner and the Medical Examiner," 5; Herbert S. Breyfogle, "The Laws of Missouri Relating to Inquests and Coroners," *Missouri Law Review* 10 (1945): 34–63. An article from March 12, 1951, describes Gradwohl's groundbreaking work in forensic science. See "Medicine: Crime Doctor," Time.com, https://content.time.com/time/subscriber /article/0,33009,805849,00.html, accessed August 1, 2022.

3. Timmermans, *Postmortem*, 5, 270; St. Louis University School of Medicine, "Medicolegal Death Investigators Training," https://www.slu.edu/medicine /pathology/medicolegal-death-investigators-training/index.php, accessed July 20, 2022; St. Louis City Office of the Medical Examiner, "Information for Family and Friends," March 22, 2021, https://www.stlouis-mo.gov/government/departments /medical-examiner/documents/information-family-friends.cfm, accessed July 20, 2022; Baxter W. Leisure Jr., Executive Assistant of the Office of the Medical Examiner of St. Louis, Interview by Author, St. Louis, Missouri, August 13, 2015.

4. Timmermans, *Postmortem*, 16, 21; Centers for Disease Control and Prevention, "Death Investigation Systems," https://www.cdc.gov/phlp/publications /coroner/death.html, accessed September 26, 2021; Centers for Disease Control and Prevention, "Missouri Coroner/Medical Examiner Laws," https://www.cdc .gov/phlp/publications/coroner/missouri.html, accessed August 9, 2021; Andrew Jeong, "Missouri County Coroner Removed Covid from Death Certificates to 'Please' Grieving Families," The Washington Post.com, https://www.washingtonpost .com/nation/2021/08/04/covid-missouri-macon-deaths/, accessed August 1, 2022; Gradwohl, "The Office of the Coroner," 842–846; John M. McIlroy Jr., "The Coroner v. The Medical Examiner in Missouri," *Missouri Law Review* 34, no. 2 (1969): 219–235; Missouri Coroners' and Medical Examiners' Association, http://www.mcmea.org/index.html, accessed July 20, 2022; Office of the Medical Examiner, http://www.stlouisco.com/HealthandWellness/MedicalExaminer, accessed July 20, 2022; Jennifer E. Laurin, "Remapping the Path Forward: Toward a

Systemic View of Forensic Science Reform and Oversight," *Texas Law Review* 91, no. 246 (2013): 1051–1118; Avery Everett, "Target 8 Update: Howard County Coroner Faces Opposition This Election," KOMU.com, https://www.komu.com /news/target-8-update-howard-county-coroner-faces-opposition-this-election /article_22d6d90d-b00d-5d9e-8147-372930f8e8b0.html, accessed August 1, 2022.

5. *The New York Times* cites historian of homicide Randolph Roth in this piece: David Leonhardt, "Nine Mass Shootings," The New York Times.com, https://www .nytimes.com/2022/03/23/briefing/crime-shootings-anomie-america.html, accessed August 1, 2022; Nicholas Nissen, "Despite Increase in Depression During Pandemic, Suicides May Have Decreased: Studies," ABCNews.com, https://abcnews.go.com /Health/increase-depression-pandemic-suicides-decreased-studies/story?id =77039876, accessed August 9, 2021; Atul Gawande, "Why Americans Are Dying from Despair," The New Yorker.com, https://www.newyorker.com/magazine/2020 /03/23/why-americans-are-dying-from-despair, accessed August 9, 2021; Rajan Menon, "Suicide Is Becoming America's Latest Epidemic," The Nation.com, https:// www.thenation.com/article/archive/suicide-rate-americas-latest-epidemic/, accessed August 9, 2021; Paige Williams, "The Wrong Way to Fight the Opioid Crisis," The New Yorker.com, February 3, 2020, https://www.newyorker.com/magazine/2020 /02/10/the-wrong-way-to-fight-the-opioid-crisis, accessed August 9, 2021]; Maria Fabrizio, "'Off the Charts' Rise in Alcoholic Liver Disease in Young Women," National Public Radio, https://www.npr.org/2021/05/21/999071685/off-the-charts-rise -in-alcoholic-liver-disease-among-young-women, accessed August 9, 2021; National Institute on Drug Abuse, "Opioid Overdose Crisis," https://www.drugabuse.gov /drug-topics/opioids/opioid-overdose-crisis, accessed August 9, 2021.

6. National Public Radio, "Understanding 2021's Rise in Gun Violence," https:// www.npr.org/2021/06/19/1008304493/understanding-2021s-rise-in-gun-violence, accessed August 9, 2021; Chloe Atkins, "What U.S. Abortion Access Looks Like, in Graphics," NBC News.com, https://www.nbcnews.com/news/us-news/what-u-s -abortion-access-looks-graphics-n1274859, accessed August 9, 2021; Jeffrey Kluger, "Domestic Violence Is a Pandemic within the Covid-19 Pandemic," Time.com, https://time.com/5928539/domestic-violence-covid-19, accessed August 9, 2021. This page is about why victims stay, noting the danger of leaving: National Coalition Against Domestic Violence, "Why Do Victims Stay?" https://ncadv.org /why-do-victims-stay, accessed August 9, 2021.

7. National Public Radio, "Fatal Police Shootings of Unarmed Black People Reveal Troubling Patterns," https://www.npr.org/2021/01/25/956177021/fatal-police -shootings-of-unarmed-black-people-reveal-troubling-patterns, accessed August 9, 2021; "Medical Examiner Who Ruled George Floyd's Death a Homicide Blames

Police Pressure for His Death," NBC News, https://www.nbcnews.com/news/us-news/medical-examiner-who-ruled-george-floyd-s-death-homicide-blames-n1263670, accessed August 9, 2021; "Medical Examiner's Autopsy Reveals George Floyd Had Positive Test for Coronavirus," NPR, https://www.npr.org/sections/live-updates-protests-for-racial-justice/2020/06/04/869278494/medical-examiners-autopsy-reveals-george-floyd-had-positive-test-for-coronavirus, accessed August 9, 2021; "Derek Chauvin Guilty in Death of George Floyd," CNN.com, https://www.cnn.com/us/live-news/derek-chauvin-trial-04-20-21/index.html, accessed August 9, 2021.

8. *Alcoholics Anonymous*, 4th ed. (New York City, Alcoholics Anonymous World Services, Inc., 2002).

Primary Sources—Published

Articles

Bacon, C. S. "The Duty of the Medical Profession in Relation to Criminal Abortion." *Illinois Medical Journal* 7 (1905): 18–24.

Berger, J. "A Fatal Fashion." *St. Louis Medical Journal* 12, no. 7 (July 1885): 289–296.

Burdett, Everett W. "The Medical Jurisprudence of Criminal Abortion." *New England Medical Gazette* 18 (July 1883): 200–214.

"Criminal Abortion in Its Broadest Sense." *Journal of the American Medical Association* 51, no. 12 (1908): 957–961.

Decaisne, Dr. E. "Dipsomania in Women." *Quarterly Journal of Inebriety* 11 (1889): 247–252.

"Dipsomania," in "Clinical Notes and Comments." *Quarterly Journal of Inebriety* 4, no. 1 (1880): 51–52.

"Dipsomania and Heredity," in "Clinical Notes and Comments." *Quarterly Journal of Inebriety* 10 (1888): 395–397.

Dixon-Jones, Mary A. "Criminal Abortion: Its Evil and Sad Consequences." *Medical Record* 46 (1894): 9–16.

Ely, William B. "The Ethics of Criminal Abortion." *Western Medical Review* 10, no. 3 (1905): 97–102.

Fisher, T. W. "Insane Drunkards—Their Medico-Legal Relations," in "Clinical Notes and Comments." *Quarterly Journal of Inebriety* 4, no. 1 (1880): 18.

Gradwohl, R. B. H. "The Office of the Coroner: Its Past, Its Present, and Its Advisability of Its Abolishment in the Commonwealth of Missouri." *Journal of the American Medical Association* 54 (1910): 842–846.

Gross, Charles. "The Early History and Influence of the Office of Coroner." *Political Science Quarterly* 7 (1892): 656–672.

Kerr, Norman. "The Treatment of Female Inebriety," "Dipsomania and Heredity," in "Clinical Notes and Comments." *Quarterly Journal of Inebriety* 10 (1888): 68–76.

The Mayor's Message with Accompanying Documents, to the Municipal Assembly of the City of St. Louis, for the Fiscal Year Ending April 12th, 1897, printed for the Municipal Assembly, 1898.

Pringle, Robert. "Homicidal and Suicidal Inebriety." *Quarterly Journal of Inebriety* 9 (1887): 156–164.

"Race Suicide (Criminal Abortion)," in "Correspondence." *Journal of the American Medical Association* 46, no. 13 (1906): 972.

Schultz, Oscar T., and E. M. Morgan. "The Coroner and the Medical Examiner." *Bulletin of the National Research Council* 64–66 (1928).

Spivy, Raymond M. "The Control and Treatment of Criminal Abortion." *Journal of the Missouri State Medical Association* 15, no. 1 (1918): 1–5.

Books

Alcoholics Anonymous, 4th ed. New York City: Alcoholics Anonymous World Services, Inc., 2002.

Ancestry.com. *The Book of Missourians: The Achievements and Personnel of Notable Living*. Accessed online: ancestry.com.

Ancestry.com. *Directory of Deceased American Physicians, 1804–1929*. Accessed online: ancestry.com.

Ancestry.com. National Park Service. *U.S. Civil War Soldiers, 1861–1865*. Accessed online: ancestry.com.

Ancestry.com. St. Louis County, Missouri, Probate Court. *Probate Case Files, 1802–1876*. Accessed online: ancestry.com.

Ancestry.com. *St. Louis, Missouri, Burial Index, Archdiocese of St. Louis, 1700–2010*. Accessed online: ancestry.com.

Ancestry.com. *U.S., City Directories, 1822–1995*. Accessed online: ancestry.com.

Ancestry.com. *U.S. Returns from Military Posts, 1806–1916*. Accessed online: ancestry.com.

Ancestry.com. *U.S. School Catalogs, 1765–1935*. Accessed online: ancestry.com.

Annual Report of the Health Commissioner of the City of St. Louis, Fiscal Year Ending April 9, 1883, with Accompanying Documents and Tabular Statements. St. Louis, Mo.: A. Ungar and Company, Printers and Binders, 1883.

Annual Report of the Health Commissioner of the City of St. Louis. For the Fiscal Year 1879–1880. St. Louis, Mo.: Woodward, Tiernan, and Hale, Printers and Binders, 1880.

Annual Report of the Health Commissioner for the Fiscal Year Ending April 13, 1885. N.p.

Annual Report of the Health Department of the City of St. Louis. 1879. St. Louis, Mo.: The Printing House, 1879.

Beck, Theodoric Romeyn Beck, and John B. Beck. *Elements of Medical Jurisprudence*, 12th ed., with notes by an association of the friends of Drs. Beck; the whole revised by C. R. Gilman. Philadelphia: J. B. Lippincott & Co., 1863.

Dacus, Joseph A., and James W. Buel. *A Tour of St. Louis: or, The Inside Life of a Great City.* St. Louis, Mo.: Western Publishing, 1878.

Directory of Physicians, Dentists and Druggists of Missouri, 1889. St. Louis, Mo.: G. Gonser & Co., 1889.

Durkheim, Emile. *Suicide: A Study in Sociology.* 1897. Reprint. Translated by John A. Spaulding and George Simpson. New York: The Free Press, 1951.

Fifth Annual Report of the St. Louis Health Commissioner for the Fiscal Year Ending April 10, 1882. N.p.

First Annual Report of the Health Department of the City of St. Louis. 1877. Under the Provisions of the New Charter for Fiscal Year Ending April 10, 1878. St. Louis, Mo.: The Printing House, 1878.

Fourth Annual Report of the Health Commissioner of the City of St. Louis. For the Fiscal Year Ending May 31, 1881. N.p.

Goldstein, Max Aaron, ed., *One Hundred Years of Medicine and Surgery in Missouri: Historical and Biographical Review of the Physicians and Surgeons of the State of Missouri and Sketches of Some of Its Notable Medical Institutions.* St. Louis, Mo.: St. Louis Star, 1900.

Gould & Aldrich's Annual Directory of the City of St. Louis, for 1872. St. Louis, Mo.: Review Steam Press, 1872.

Gould's St. Louis Directory. St. Louis, Mo.: Gould Directory Co., 1874, 1880, 1881, 1889, 1892, 1897, 1898.

Guernsey, R. S. *Suicide: History of the Penal Laws Relating to It in Their Legal, Social, Moral, and Religious Aspects, in Ancient and Modern Times.* New York: L. K. Strouse & Co., 1883.

Gunn, John C. *Gunn's Domestic Medicine.* 1830. Reprint. Edited by Charles E. Rosenberg. Knoxville: University of Tennessee Press, 1986.

Hard, William. *Injured in the Course of Duty: Industrial Accidents, How They Happen, How They Are Paid for, and How They Ought to Be Paid For.* New York: The Ridgway Company, 1910.

Journal of the Missouri State Medical Association. St. Louis: Missouri State Medical Association, 1904–1952.

McCandless, Carl A. *Government, Politics and Administration in Missouri.* St. Louis, Mo.: Educational Publishers, 1949.

Morselli, Henry. *Suicide: An Essay on Comparative Moral Statistics*. 1882. Reprint.
New York: Arno Press, 1975.

Scharf, J. Thomas. *History of St. Louis and County, from the Earliest Periods to the
Present Day: Including Biographical Sketches of Representative Men, Volume II*.
Philadelphia: Louis H. Everts & Co., 1883.

*Seventh Annual Report of the Health Commissioner for the Fiscal Year Ending
April 7, 1884*. N.p.

Simpson, Keith, ed. *Taylor's Principles and Practice of Medical Jurisprudence*. 1865.
Reprint, 12th ed. Boston: Little, Brown and Company, 1965.

Winslow, Forbes. *The Anatomy of Suicide*. London: Henry Renshaw, 1840.

Newspapers

The Cleveland Herald
Daily Evening Bulletin (San Francisco,
    California)
Daily Rocky Mountain News
The Galveston Daily News
Inter Ocean
Milwaukee Sentinel

New York Times
New York Tribune
Potosi Journal
St. Louis Globe-Democrat
St. Louis Post-Dispatch (formerly
    St. Louis Post and Dispatch)

Pamphlets

Allen, B. J. *Physician's Report of the St. Vincent's Institution for the Insane, for the
Years 1862 and 1863*. St. Louis, Mo.: 1864.

Primary Sources—Unpublished

Leisure Jr., Baxter W. Executive Assistant of the Office of the Medical Examiner
of St. Louis. Interview by Author, St. Louis, Missouri, August 13, 2015.

Papers, Johnson, Charles P. (1836–1920), (Collection CA6380). The State
Historical Society of Missouri, University of Missouri, Columbia, Missouri.

Government Documents and Official Records

Ancestry.com. *Missouri Death Records, 1834–1910*. Accessed online: ancestry.com.

Ancestry.com. *Missouri Marriage Records, 1805–2002*. Accessed online: ancestry.com.

Ancestry.com. *St. Louis City Death Records.* Accessed online: ancestry.com.

Ancestry.com. *St. Louis City Wills.* Accessed online: ancestry.com.

Ancestry.com. U.S. Civil War Pension Index: General Index to Pension Files, 1861–1934. Accessed online: ancestry.com.

Francis, David R., Stephen H. Claycomb, and Joseph J. Russell, eds., *Revised Statutes of the State of Missouri, Volume I.* Jefferson City, Mo.: Tribune Printing Company, State Printers and Binders, 1889.

General Statutes of the State of Missouri. Jefferson City, Mo.: Emory S. Foster, 1866.

Hockaday, John A., Thomas H. Parrish, Benjamin F. McDaniel, and Daniel H. McIntyre, committee, eds. *Revised Statutes of the State of Missouri, Volume I.* Jefferson City, Mo.: Carter and Regan, State Printers and Binders, 1879.

"Historical Census Browser." University of Virginia Library. Accessed online: http://mapserver.lib.virginia.edu/php/county.php.

Journal of the Missouri House, Fourteenth General Assembly, First Session, 1846, p. 416, General Assembly, Record Group 550, Missouri State Archives, Jefferson City.

Laws of Missouri, General Assembly Twenty-Eight, Regular Session, 1875, p. 99, State Documents Collections, Missouri State Archives, Jefferson City.

Laws of the State of Missouri. St. Louis, Mo.: E. Charless, 1825.

Missouri Death Certificates. Missouri State Archives, Jefferson City, Missouri. Accessed online: http://www.sos.mo.gov/archives/resources/deathcertificates/default.asp.

Missouri Secretary of State. Coroner's Inquest Database. Accessed online: http://www.sos.mo.gov/archives/resources/coroners/.

Missouri Secretary of State. Missouri State Penitentiary Database. Accessed online: http://s1.sos.mo.gov/records/archives/archivesdb/msp/Detail.aspx?id=35156.

Missouri Secretary of State. Naturalization Records, 1816–1955 Database. Accessed online: https://s1.sos.mo.gov/records/archives/archivesdb/naturalization/default.aspx.

Revised Statutes of the State of Missouri. St. Louis, Mo.: Argus Office, 1835.

Revised Statutes of the State of Missouri. St. Louis, Mo.: J. W. Dougherty, 1845.

The Statutes of the State of Missouri. Compiled by David Wagner. St. Louis, Mo.: W. J. Gilbert, Law Book Publisher, 1872.

St. Louis City Office of the Coroner—Inquests, 1845–1900. St. Louis, Missouri, Missouri State Archives, Jefferson City, Missouri. Missouri.

St. Louis, City of. Circuit Court Case Files. Missouri State Archives, St. Louis, Missouri. *Criminal Court Record Book.* Volumes 19 and 20.

St. Louis City Wills. St. Louis, Missouri, Vol. K2, p. 539, SLCL film CIWI-15, FHL film 1405582.

St. Louis Department of Public Welfare, Division of Health. *Annual Report of the Health Commissioner, St. Louis Department of Public Welfare*, Volume 28. St. Louis, Mo.: Nixon-Jones Printing Company, 1896.

St. Louis, Missouri, Health Department. *Laws, Ordinances, Rules and Regulations for the Government of the Health Department of the City of St. Louis, 1878.* St. Louis, Mo.: Max Olshuasen, Printer, 1878.

Statutes of the State of Missouri, 3rd ed. St. Louis, Mo.: W. J. Gilbert, 1872.

United States Bureau of the Census. Records for Missouri, 1850, 1860, 1870, 1880, 1900, 1910, 1920.

United States Bureau of the Census. Records for Illinois, 1870, 1880.

United States Bureau of the Census. Records for Kentucky, 1850, 1870, 1880.

United States Bureau of the Census. Veterans Schedules, 1890.

Secondary Sources—Published

Articles

Adler, Jeffrey S. "'I Loved Joe, but I Had to Shoot Him': Homicide by Women in Turn-of-the-Century Chicago." *Journal of Criminal Law and Criminology* 92, no. 3/4 (2002): 867–898.

———. "'If We Can't Live in Peace, We Might as Well Die': Homicide-Suicide in Chicago, 1875–1910." *Journal of Urban History* 26, no. 3 (1999): 3–21.

———. "'We've Got a Right to Fight; We're Married': Domestic Homicide in Chicago, 1875–1920." *Journal of Interdisciplinary History* 34, no. 1 (2003): 27–48.

Atkinson, J. Maxwell. "Societal Reactions to Suicide: The Role of Coroners' Definitions." In *Images of Deviance*, ed. Stanley Cohen. Middlesex, England: Penguin Books, 1971.

Berry, Stephen. "The Historian as Death Investigator." In *Weirding the War: Stories from the Civil War's Ragged Edges*, ed. Stephen Berry, 176–188. Athens: University of Georgia, 2011.

Brancaccio, Maria Teresa, Eric J. Engstrom, and David Lederer. "The Politics of Suicide: Historical Perspectives on Suicidology before Durkheim. An Introduction." *Journal of Social History* 46, no. 3 (2013): 607–619.

Breyfogle, Herbert S. "The Laws of Missouri Relating to Inquests and Coroners." *Missouri Law Review* 10 (1945): 34–63.

Gearing, Robin E., and Dana Lizardi. "Religion and Suicide." *Journal of Religion and Health* 48, no. 3 (2009): 332–341.

———. "Religion and Suicide: New Findings." *Journal of Religion and Health* 57 (2018): 2478–2499. https://doi.org/10.1007/s10943-018-0629-8.

Haag, Pamela. "The 'Ill-Use of a Wife': Patterns of Working-Class Violence in Domestic and Public New York City, 1860–1880." *Journal of Social History* 25, no. 3 (1992): 447–477.

Hanzlick, Randy, and Debra Combs. "Medical Examiner and Coroner Systems: History and Trends." *Journal of the American Medical Association* 279, no. 11 (1998): 870–874.

Higginbotham, Evelyn Brooks. "The Politics of Respectability." In *Righteous Discontent: The Women's Movement in the Black Baptist Church, 1880–1920.* Cambridge, Mass.: Harvard University Press, 1993.

Johnstone, Gerry. "From Vice to Disease? The Concepts of Dipsomania and Inebriety, 1860–1908." *Social and Legal Studies* 5 (1996): 37–56.

Kudlick, Catherine J. "Disability History: Why We Need Another 'Other.'" *American Historical Review,* 108, no. 3 (2003): 763–793.

Kushner, Howard I. "Biochemistry, Suicide, and History: Possibilities and Problems." *Journal of Interdisciplinary History* 16, no. 1 (Summer, 1985): 69–85.

———. "Immigrant Suicide in the United States: Toward a Psycho-Social History." *Journal of Social History* 18, no. 1 (1984): 3–24.

———. "Suicide, Gender, and the Fear of Modernity in Nineteenth-Century Medical and Social Thought." *Journal of Social History* 26, no. 3 (1993): 461–490.

———. "Taking Biology Seriously: The Next Task for Historians of Addiction?" *Bulletin of the History of Medicine* 80, no. 1 (2006): 115–143.

———. "Women and Suicide in Historical Perspective." *Signs* 10, no. 3 (1985): 537–552.

Langer, Susanne, Jonathan Scourfield, and Ben Fincham. "Documenting the Quick and the Dead: A Study of Suicide Case Files in a Coroner's Office." *Sociological Review* 56, no. 2 (2008): 293–308.

Laragy, Georgina. "'A Peculiar Species of Felony': Suicide, Medicine, and the Law in Victorian Britain and Ireland." *Journal of Social History* 46, no. 3 (2013): 732–743.

Laurin, Jennifer E. "Remapping the Path Forward: Toward a Systemic View of Forensic Science Reform and Oversight." *Texas Law Review* 91, no. 246 (2013): 1051–1118.

Lehmann, Jennifer M. "Durkheim's Response to Feminism: Prescriptions for Women." *Sociological Theory* 8, no. 2 (1990): 163–187.

———. "Durkheim's Theories of Deviance and Suicide: A Feminist Reconsideration." *American Journal of Sociology* 100, no. 4 (1995): 904–930.

Lender, Mark. "A Special Stigma: Women and Alcoholism in the Late 19th and Early 20th Centuries." In *Alcohol Interventions: Historical and Sociocultural*

Approaches, ed. David L. Strug, S. Priyadarsini, and Merton M. Hyman, 41–57. New York: The Haworth Press, 1986.

Levine, Harry Gene, "The Discovery of Addiction: Changing Conceptions of Habitual Drunkenness in America." *Journal of Studies on Alcohol* 39, no. 1 (1978): 143–174.

Jansson, Asa. "From Statistics to Diagnostics: Medical Certificates, Melancholia, and 'Suicidal Propensities' in Victorian Psychiatry." *Journal of Social History* 46, no. 3 (2013): 716–731.

Marsh, Ian. "The Uses of History in the Unmaking of Modern Suicide." *Journal of Social History* 46, no. 3 (2013): 744–756.

McIlroy, John M., Jr. "The Coroner v. The Medical Examiner in Missouri." *Missouri Law Review* 34, no. 2 (1969): 219–235.

Miller, Laura J. "Postpartum Depression." *Journal of the American Medical Association* 287, no. 6 (2002): 762–764.

Prestwich, Patricia E. "Female Alcoholism in Paris, 1870–1920: The Response of Psychiatrists and of Families." *History of Psychiatry* 14, no. 3 (2003): 321–336.

Reagan, Leslie J. "'About to Meet Her Maker': Women, Doctors, Dying Declarations, and the State's Investigation of Abortion, Chicago, 1867–1940." *Journal of American History* 77, no. 4 (1991): 1240–1264.

Snyder, Terri L. "Suicide, Slavery, and Memory in North America." *Journal of American History* 97, no. 1 (2010): 39–62.

———. "What Historians Talk about When They Talk about Suicide: The View from Early Modern British North America." *History Compass* 5, no. 2 (2007): 658–674.

Sommerville, Diane Miller. "'A Burden Too Heavy to Bear': War Trauma, Suicide, and Confederate Soldiers." *Civil War History* 59, no. 4 (2013): 453–491.

———. "Will They Ever Be Able to Forget?" In *Weirding the War: Stories from the Civil War's Ragged Edges*, ed. Stephen Berry, 321–339. Athens: University of Georgia, 2011.

Swingle, H. Morley. "Coroner's Inquests in Missouri: Modern Usage of the Hue and Cry." *Journal of the Missouri Bar* 63, no. 2 (2007). http://www.mobar.org /284a1e15-4298-418a-8a06-97cdfa2e39e7.aspx.

Books

Adler, Jeffrey. *First in Violence, Deepest in Dirt: Homicide in Chicago, 1875–1920*. Cambridge, Mass.: Harvard University Press, 2002.

Atkinson, J. Maxwell. *Discovering Suicide: Studies in the Social Organization of Sudden Death*. Pittsburgh: University of Pittsburgh Press, 1978.

Baggett, Ashley. *Intimate Partner Violence in New Orleans: Gender, Race, and Reform, 1840–1900*. Jackson: University Press of Mississippi, 2017.

Baldasty, Gerald J. *The Commercialization of News in the Nineteenth Century.* Madison: University of Wisconsin Press, 1992.

Berry, Stephen. *Count the Dead: Coroners, Quants, and the Birth of Death as We Know It.* Chapel Hill: University of North Carolina Press, 2022.

Brodie, Janet Farrell. *Contraception and Abortion in Nineteenth-Century America.* Ithaca, N.Y.: Cornell University Press, 1994.

Burnham, John C. *Health Care in America: a History.* Baltimore: Johns Hopkins University Press, 2015.

Cooter, Roger, and Bill Luckin, eds. *Accidents in History: Injuries Fatalities and Social Relations.* Amsterdam: Editions Rodopi B.V., 1997.

Corbett, Katharine T. *In Her Place: A Guide to St. Louis Women's History.* St. Louis: Missouri Historical Press, 1999.

Dubow, Sara. *Ourselves Unborn: A History of the Fetus in Modern America.* New York: Oxford University Press, 2011.

Edwards, Rebecca. *New Spirits: Americans in the Gilded Age, 1865–1905.* New York: Oxford University Press, 2006.

Friend, Craig Thompson, and Lorri Glover. *Death and the American South.* New York: Cambridge University Press, 2014.

Gamber, Wendy. *The Boardinghouse in Nineteenth-Century America.* Baltimore: Johns Hopkins University Press, 2007.

Gersuny, Carl. *Work Hazards and Industrial Conflict.* Hanover, N.H.: University Press of New England, 1981.

Gilfoyle, Timothy J. *City of Eros: New York City, Prostitution, and the Commercialization of Sex, 1790–1920.* New York: W. W. Norton & Company, 1992.

Gordon, Linda. *Heroes of Their Own Lives: The Politics and History of Family Violence: Boston, 1880–1960.* New York: Viking, 1988.

Grob, Gerald. *Mental Illness and American Society, 1875–1940.* Princeton, N.J.: Princeton University Press, 1983.

Hecht, Jennifer Michael. *Stay: A History of Suicide and the Philosophies Against It.* New Haven, Conn.: Yale University Press, 2013.

Holdren, Nate. *Injury Impoverished: Workplace Accidents, Capitalism, and Law in the Progressive Era.* Cambridge: Cambridge University Press, 2020.

Holmes, Ronald M., and Stephen T. Holmes. *Suicide: Theory, Practice, and Investigation.* Thousand Oaks, Calif.: SAGE, 2005.

Jamison, Kay Redfield. *Night Falls Fast: Understanding Suicide.* New York: Alfred A. Knopf, 1999.

Jentzen, Jeffrey M. *Death Investigation in America: Coroners, Medical Examiners, and the Pursuit of Medical Certainty.* Cambridge, Mass.: Harvard University Press, 2009.

Johnson, Walter. *The Broken Heart of America: St. Louis and the Violent History of the United States.* New York: Basic Books, 2020.

Kushner, Howard I. *American Suicide: A Psychocultural Exploration.* New Brunswick, N.J.: Rutgers University Press, 1991.

Lane, Roger. *Violent Death in the City: Suicide, Accident, and Murder in Nineteenth Century Philadelphia.* Cambridge, Mass.: Harvard University Press, 1979.

Laqueur, Thomas W. *The Work of the Dead: A Cultural History of Mortal Remains.* Princeton, N.J.: Princeton University Press, 2015.

Longmore, Paul K., and Lauri Umansky. *The New Disability History: American Perspectives.* New York: New York University Press, 2001.

Luker, Kristin. *Abortion and the Politics of Motherhood.* Berkeley: University of California Press, 1984.

Lunbeck, Elizabeth. *The Psychiatric Persuasion: Knowledge, Gender, and Power in Modern America.* Princeton, N.J.: Princeton University Press, 1994.

Martin, Scott C. *Devil of the Domestic Sphere: Temperance, Gender, and Middle-class Ideology, 1800–1860.* DeKalb: Northern Illinois University Press, 2008.

McClellan, Michelle L. *Lady Lushes: Gender, Alcoholism, and Medicine in Modern America.* New Brunswick, N.J.: Rutgers University Press, 2017.

McGoff-McCann, Michelle. *Melancholy Madness: A Coroner's Casebook.* Douglas Village, Cork: Mercier Press, 2003.

Minois, Georges. *History of Suicide: Voluntary Death in Western Culture.* Translated by Lydia G. Cochrane. Baltimore: Johns Hopkins University Press, 1999.

Mintz, Steven, and Susan Kellogg. *Domestic Revolutions: A Social History of American Family Life.* New York: The Free Press, 1988.

Mohr, James C. *Abortion in America: The Origins and Evolution of National Policy, 1800–1900.* New York: Oxford University Press, 1978.

———. *Doctors and the Law: Medical Jurisprudence in Nineteenth-Century America.* New York: Oxford University Press, 1993.

Mumford, Kevin. *InterZones: Black/White Sex Districts in Chicago and New York in the Early Twentieth Century.* New York: Columbia University Press, 1997.

Murdock, Catherine Gilbert. *Domesticating Drink: Women, Men, and Alcohol in America: 1870–1940.* Baltimore: Johns Hopkins University Press, 1998.

Neff, John R. *Honoring the Civil War Dead: Commemoration and the Problem of Reconciliation.* Lawrence: University Press of Kansas, 2005.

Nielsen, Kim E. *Beyond The Miracle Worker: The Remarkable Life of Annie Sullivan Macie and Her Extraordinary Friendship with Helen Keller.* Boston: Beacon Press, 2009.

———. *A Disability History of the United States: Revisioning American History.* Boston: Beacon Press, 2012.

Petchesky, Rosalind Pollack. *Abortion and Woman's Choice: The State, Sexuality, and Reproductive Freedom.* New York: Longman, 1984.

Pickering, W. S. F., and Geoffrey Walford, eds. *Durkheim's Suicide: A Century of Research and Debate.* London: Routledge, 2000.

Pleck, Elizabeth. *Domestic Tyranny: The Making of Social Policy against Family Violence from Colonial Times to the Present.* New York: Oxford University Press, 1987.

Rambo, Kirsten S. *"Trivial Complaints": The Role of Privacy in Domestic Violence Law and Activism in the U.S.* New York: Columbia University Press, 2009.

Reagan, Leslie J. *When Abortion Was a Crime: Women, Medicine, and Law in the United States, 1867–1973.* Berkeley: University of California Press, 1997.

Rogers, Donald W. *Making Capitalism Safe: Work Safety and Health Regulation in America, 1880–1940.* Urbana: University of Illinois Press, 2009.

Rorabaugh, William J. *The Alcoholic Republic: An American Tradition.* New York: Oxford University Press, 1979.

Rosen, Ruth. *The Lost Sisterhood: Prostitution in America, 1900–1918.* Baltimore: Johns Hopkins University Press, 1982.

Rosenberg, Charles E. *The Trial of the Assassin Guiteau: Psychiatry and Law in the Gilded Age.* Chicago: University of Chicago Press, 1968.

Roth, Randolph. *American Homicide.* Cambridge, Mass.: Belknap Press of Harvard University Press, 2009.

Rothman, David J. *Conscience and Convenience: The Asylum and Its Alternatives in Progressive America.* Rev. ed. New York: Aldine de Gruyter, 1980.

Schudson, Michael. *Discovering the News: A Social History of American Newspapers.* New York: Basic Books, 1978.

Shapiro, Barbara J. *"Beyond Reasonable Doubt and Probable Cause": Historical Perspectives on the Anglo-American Law of Evidence.* Berkeley: University of California Press, 1991.

Silkenat, David. *Moments of Despair: Suicide, Divorce, and Debt in Civil War Era North Carolina.* Chapel Hill: University of North Carolina Press, 2011.

Snyder, Terri. *The Power to Die: Slavery and Suicide in British North America.* Chicago: University of Chicago Press, 2015.

Solinger, Rickie. *Pregnancy and Power: A Short History of Reproductive Politics in America.* New York: New York University Press, 2005.

Sommerville, Diane Miller. *Aberration of Mind: Suicide and Suffering in the Civil War-Era South*. Chapel Hill: University of North Carolina Press, 2018.

Srebnick, Amy Gilman. *The Mysterious Death of Mary Rogers: Sex and Culture in Nineteenth-Century New York*. New York: Oxford University Press, 1995.

Srole, Carole. *Transcribing Class and Gender: Masculinity and Femininity in Nineteenth-Century Courts and Offices*. Ann Arbor: University of Michigan Press, 2010.

Stanley, Amy Dru. *From Bondage to Contract: Wage Labor, Marriage, and the Market in the Age of Slave Emancipation*. Cambridge: Cambridge University Press, 1998.

Stansell, Christine. *City of Women: Sex and Class in New York, 1789–1860*. New York: Alfred A. Knopf, 1986.

Starr, Paul. *The Social Transformation of American Medicine: The Rise of a Sovereign Profession & the Making of a Vast Industry*, updated ed. New York: Basic Books, 2017.

Stormer, Nathan. *Articulating Life's Memory: US Medical Rhetoric about Abortion in the Nineteenth Century*. Lanham, Md.: Lexington Books, 2002.

———. *Sign of Pathology: U.S. Medical Rhetoric on Abortion, 1800s–1960s*. University Park: Pennsylvania State University Press, 2015.

Suzuki, Akihito. *Madness at Home: The Psychiatrist, the Patient, and the Family in England, 1820–1860*. Berkeley: University of California Press, 2006.

Thompson, F. M. L. *The Rise of Respectable Society: A Social History of Victorian Britain, 1830–1900*. Cambridge, Mass.: Harvard University Press, 1988.

Timmermans, Stefan. *Postmortem: How Medical Examiners Explain Suspicious Deaths*. Chicago: University of Chicago Press, 2006.

Tomes, Nancy. *A Generous Confidence: Thomas Kirkbride and the Art of Asylum-Keeping, 1840–1883*. Cambridge: Cambridge University Press, 1984.

Tracy, Sarah W. *Alcoholism in America: From Reconstruction to Prohibition*. Baltimore: Johns Hopkins University Press, 2005.

Tracy, Sarah W., and Caroline Jean Acker, eds. *Altering American Consciousness: The History of Alcohol and Drug Use in the United States, 1800–2000*. Amherst: University of Massachusetts Press, 2004.

Ussher, Jane M. *Women's Madness: Misogyny or Mental Illness?* Amherst: University of Massachusetts Press, 1991.

Wagner, Allen E. *Good Order and Safety: A History of the Metropolitan Police Department, 1861–1906*. St. Louis: Missouri History Museum, 2008.

Walkowitz, Judith R. *Prostitution and Victorian Society: Women, Class, and the State*. Cambridge: Cambridge University Press, 1980.

Weaver, John C. *A Sadly Troubled History: The Meanings of Suicide in the Modern Age*. Montreal: McGill-Queen's University Press, 2009.

Weaver, John C., and David Wright, eds. *Histories of Suicide: International Perspectives on Self-Destruction in the Modern World*. Toronto: University of Toronto Press, 2008.

Werth, James L. *Rational Suicide? Implications for Mental Health Professionals*. Washington, D.C.: Taylor and Francis, 1996.

Whites, LeeAnn. *Gender Matters: Civil War, Reconstruction, and the Making of the New South*. New York: Palgrave Macmillan, 2005.

Whites, LeeAnn, Mary C. Neth, and Gary R. Kremer, eds. *Women in Missouri History: In Search of Power and Influence*. Columbia: University of Missouri Press, 2004.

Witt, John Fabian. *The Accidental Republic: Crippled Workingmen, Destitute Widows, and the Remaking of American Law*. Cambridge, Mass.: Harvard University Press, 2004.

Wood, Sharon E. *The Freedom of the Streets: Work, Citizenship, and Sexuality in a Gilded Age City*. Chapel Hill: University of North Carolina Press, 2005.

Ziegler, Mary. *Dollars for Life: The Anti-Abortion Movement and the Fall of the Republican Establishment*. New Haven, Conn.: Yale University Press, 2022.

Zittel, Kimberley. *Postpartum Mood Disorders: A Guide for Medical, Mental Health, and Other Support Providers*. Washington, D.C.: National Association of Social Work Press, 2010.

Secondary Sources—Unpublished

Atkins, Chloe. "What U.S. Abortion Access Looks Like, in Graphics." NBC News.com. https://www.nbcnews.com/news/us-news/what-u-s-abortion-access-looks-graphics-n1274859.

The Biographical Directory of the United States Congress: 1774–Present, http://bioguide.congress.gov/scripts/biodisplay.pl?index=B000719.

Centers for Disease Control and Prevention. "Death Investigation Systems." https://www.cdc.gov/phlp/publications/coroner/death.html.

———. "Missouri Coroner/Medical Examiner Laws." https://www.cdc.gov/phlp/publications/coroner/missouri.html.

Everett, Avery. "Target 8 Update: Howard County Coroner Faces Opposition This Election." KOMU.com. https://www.komu.com/news/target-8-update

-howard-county-coroner-faces-opposition-this-election/article_22d6d90d
-b00d-5d9e-8147-372930f8e8b0.html.

Fabrizio, Maria. "'Off the Charts' Rise in Alcoholic Liver Disease in Young Women." https://www.npr.org/2021/05/21/999071685/off-the-charts-rise-in -alcoholic-liver-disease-among-young-women.

FindAGrave. www.findagrave.com.

Gawande, Atul. "Why Americans Are Dying from Despair." The New Yorker .com. https://www.newyorker.com/magazine/2020/03/23/why-americans-are -dying-from-despair.

"Happy Anniversary to Us." St. Louis Today.com. https://www.stltoday.com /news/archives/happy-anniversary-to-us-take-a-journey-through-history-with -the-post-dispatch/collection_ca197e6f-b80a-552c-bd89-564d42efe172.html.

Jeong, Andrew. "Missouri County Coroner Removed Covid from Death Certifi- cates to 'Please' Grieving Families." The Washington Post.com. https://www .washingtonpost.com/nation/2021/08/04/covid-missouri-macon-deaths/.

Kluger, Jeffrey. "Domestic Violence Is a Pandemic within the Covid-19 Pan- demic." Time.com. https://time.com/5928539/domestic-violence-covid-19.

Leonhardt, David. "Nine Mass Shootings." *The New York Times.com.* https:// www.nytimes.com/2022/03/23/briefing/crime-shootings-anomie-america .html.

"Derek Chauvin Guilty in Death of George Floyd." CNN.com. https://www.cnn .com/us/live-news/derek-chauvin-trial-04-20-21/index.html.

"Medical Examiner Who Ruled George Floyd's Death a Homicide Blames Police Pressure for His Death." NBC News. https://www.nbcnews.com/news/us -news/medical-examiner-who-ruled-george-floyd-s-death-homicide-blames -n1263670.

"Medicine: Crime Doctor." Time.com. https://content.time.com/time/subscriber /article/0,33009,805849,00.html.

Menon, Rajan. "Suicide Is Becoming America's Latest Epidemic." *The Nation .com.* https://www.thenation.com/article/archive/suicide-rate-americas-latest -epidemic/.

Missouri Coroners' and Medical Examiners' Association. http://www.mcmea.org /index.html.

National Coalition Against Domestic Violence. "Statistics." https://www.stlouis -mo.gov/government/departments/mayor/initiatives/domestic-violence-2015 -2021.cfm.

———. "Why Do Victims Stay?" https://ncadv.org/why-do-victims-stay.

National Institute on Drug Abuse. "Opioid Overdose Crisis." https://www .drugabuse.gov/drug-topics/opioids/opioid-overdose-crisis.

National Public Radio. "Fatal Police Shootings of Unarmed Black People Reveal Troubling Patterns." https://www.npr.org/2021/01/25/956177021/fatal-police-shootings-of-unarmed-black-people-reveal-troubling-patterns.

———. "Medical Examiner's Autopsy Reveals George Floyd Had Positive Test for Coronavirus." https://www.npr.org/sections/live-updates-protests-for-racial-justice/2020/06/04/869278494/medical-examiners-autopsy-reveals-george-floyd-had-positive-test-for-coronavirus.

———. "Understanding 2021's Rise in Gun Violence." https://www.npr.org/2021/06/19/1008304493/understanding-2021s-rise-in-gun-violence.

Nissen, Nicholas. "Despite Increase in Depression During Pandemic, Suicides May Have Decreased: Studies." ABCNews.com. https://abcnews.go.com/Health/increase-depression-pandemic-suicides-decreased-studies/story?id=77039876.

Office of the Medical Examiner. http://www.stlouisco.com/HealthandWellness/MedicalExaminer.

Pizarro, Jesenia, William Werner, Millan AbiNader, Jill Messing, and Jacquelyn Campbell. "Domestic Violence Assaults in St. Louis City, Missouri: A Trend Analysis of 2015–2021." https://www.stlouis-mo.gov/government/departments/mayor/initiatives/domestic-violence-2015-2021.cfm.

Saunt, Claudio, and Stephen Berry. "CSI: Dixie." https://csidixie.org/.

St. Louis City Office of the Medical Examiner. "Information for Family and Friends." March 22, 2021. https://www.stlouis-mo.gov/government/departments/medical-examiner/documents/information-family-friends.cfm.

St. Louis University School of Medicine. "Medicolegal Death Investigators Training." https://www.slu.edu/medicine/pathology/medicolegal-death-investigators-training/index.php.

Williams, Paige. "The Wrong Way to Fight the Opioid Crisis." The New Yorker.com, February 3, 2020. https://www.newyorker.com/magazine/2020/02/10/the-wrong-way-to-fight-the-opioid-crisis.

Italicized page numbers indicate figures.

SARAH E. LIRLEY specializes in nineteenth-century U.S. history, the history of women and gender, and the history of death and death investigations. She earned her PhD in U.S. History from the University of Missouri in 2018, where she also earned a Graduate Minor in Women's and Gender Studies. She is an Assistant Professor of History at Columbia College in Columbia, Missouri.